School-Based Evaluation

Evaluation in Education and Human Services

Editors:

George F. Madaus, Boston College, Chestnut
  Hill, Massachusetts, U.S.A.
Daniel L. Stufflebeam, Western Michigan
  University, Kalamazoo, Michigan, U.S.A.

Previously published books in the series:

Kellaghan, T., Madaus, G., and Airasian, P.:
  The Effects of Standardized Testing
Madaus, G. (editor):
  *The Courts, Validity, and Minimum
  Competency Testing*
Brinkerhoff, R., Brethower, D., Hluchyj, T., and
Nowakowski, J.:
  Program Evaluation, Sourcebook/Casebook
Brinkerhoff, R., Brethower, D., Hluchyj, T., and
Nowakowski, J.:
  Program Evaluation, Sourcebook
Brinkerhoff, R., Brethower, D., Hluchyj, T., and
Nowakowski, J.:
  Program Evaluation, Design Manual
Madaus, G., Scriven, M., Stufflebeam, D.:
  *Evaluation Models: Viewpoints on
  Educational and Human Services
  Evaluation*
Hambleton, R., Swaminathan, H.:
  Item Response Theory
Stufflebeam, D., Shinkfield, A.:
  Systematic Evaluation
Nowakowski, J.:
  *Handbook of Educational Variables: A
  Guide to Evaluation*
Stufflebeam, D., McCormick, C., Brinkerhoff,
  R.O., and Nelson, C.
  *Conducting Educational Needs
  Assessments*
Abrahamson, S.:
  *Evaluation of Continuing Education in the
  Health Professions*
Cooley, W., Bickel, W.:
  Decision-Oriented Educational Research
Gable, R.K.:
  *Instrument Development in the Affective
  Domain*
Sirotnik, K.A., Oakes, J.:
  *Critical Perspectives on the organization
  and Improvement of Schooling*

School-Based Evaluation

A Guide for Board Members, Superintendents, Principals, Department Heads, and Teachers

John W. Wick

Kluwer-Nijhoff Publishing
a member of the Kluwer Academic Publishers Group
Boston   Dordrecht   Lancaster

Distributors for the United States and Canada:

Kluwer Academic Publishers
101 Philip Drive, Norwell, MA 02061, U.S.A.

Distributors for UK and Ireland:

Kluwer Academic Publishers, MTP Press Limited
Falcon House
Queen Square
Lancaster LA1 1RN, UK

Distributors for all other countries:

Kluwer Academic Publishers Group
Distribution Centre
P.O. Box 322
3300 AH Dordrecht
THE NETHERLANDS

Library of Congress Cataloging in Publication Data

Wick, John W., 1935–
  School-based evaluation.

  (Evaluation in education and human services)
  Bibliography: p.
  Includes index.
  1. Curriculum evaluation. 2. Teachers — Self-rating of.
3. Language arts — United States — Evaluation — Case
studies. 4. Mathematics — Study and teaching (Secondary) — United States — Evaluation — Case studies.
5. Interdisciplinary approach in education — United
States — Evaluation — Case studies. I. Title. II. Series.
LB1570.W55734   375'.006   86-10390
ISBN 0-89838-178-9

Printed in the United States of America

To my dad, who epitomized tough independence. From him I learned to compete, and I learned to avoid the mob. I miss him.

To my mom, whom I know is the source of the compassion I feel for children.

And to Marti, from whom I learned, finally, that love can endure and grow with time.

Contents

Preface

During the 1962–63 academic year, as a graduate student at the University of Iowa, I enrolled in a beginning tests and measurements course from Professor Leonard Feldt, who was even then a nationally respected scholar in this field. That year was also my inaugural year as a high school teacher; I was employed full-time at nearby Lone Tree High School to teach all the math and most of the science.

The two coinciding experiences planted a question in my mind: "How come the teachers and administrators I deal with in the school each day pay almost no attention to the things I'm learning in this excellent course?" The question eventually evolved into a quest for ways that the measurement aspects of evaluation might be seen as a unifying theme in student performance improvement programs. That quest has been the theme of my professional work.

In 1971, collaborating with Don Beggs, now the Dean of the School of Education at Southern Illinois University, I wrote *Evaluation for Decision-Making in the Schools*. In the preface we wrote of our desire to ". . . function as a bridge between . . ." the practitioner and the quantitative specialists. In 1973 I wrote *Educational Measurement: Where Are We Going and How Will We Know When We Get There*, the title of which conveys its theme. Neither book made anyone's best-seller list. In 1974, finally realizing that if I wanted to write about school practices I should really experience them, I went on leave from Northwestern University to found and then direct the Department of Research and Evaluation for the Chicago public schools. The leave was extended twice, and I stayed in that position until late 1979. Many of my strong feelings about local control were solidified at that time.

Toward the end of that tenure I undertook the leadership of a team of about 30 authors who developed a nationally standardized testing program, including achievement, aptitude, and interest tests for students from pre-school through high school. The series, the *Comprehensive Assessment Program*, was published in 1980. The experience provided some first-hand insights into this industry; you will find, sprinkled through this book, some fairly critical comments about what I consider the overselling of standardized tests.

Finally, after returning to Northwestern from Chicago I began teaching more general courses — courses in curriculum, instruction, and the evaluation of instruction. I became convinced that the theorists, the practitioners, and the outcomes people were not talking to each other because they lacked a common language.

The evaluate-your-instruction process is designed to provide the common language.

This book is aimed at the people who make decisions about schooling in a building. I am an unswerving believer in the local control of education — with just enough external monitoring to avoid situations where idiosyncratic foolishness would do damage to students. The book is designed to help board members, superintendents, principals, other administrators, department heads, and teachers build student improvement programs at the local level.

It is impossible to acknowledge all of those who have helped shape my thinking over these years. The evaluate-your-instruction process went through many iterations with graduate students, each of whom contributed ideas. Dr. Roy Turnbaugh, Superintendent of the Geneva Public Schools, has contributed substantially to the way I view instruction. Conversations with my colleague Ben Bloom have been most helpful, and my colleague Jim Hall can be counted on to debunk my wilder ideas. The late John Vaughn, then Executive Director of the North Central Association, provided good feedback on both chapters 2 and 3, and Associate Dean Roxie Smith of the School of Education at Northwestern gave good comments on chapter 7.

I hope the book is useful to people who care enough about education to want to improve it from within. Even a good school can get better. Better districts become the sum of better schools — and the process builds upward.

School-Based Evaluation

1 An Overview and Some Foundations

1.1. Evaluation and the Interrelated Nature of Philosophy-Beliefs, Process-Program, and Outcomes

One step in the evaluate-your-instruction process asks, "Which person, or explicitly definable group of people, is in charge of the learning event about to be evaluated?" The question addresses issues like content (who can decide what to present?), classroom organization (who decides if it will be individualized, small groups, whole group, lecture, or whatever?), teacher behavior, and expected student behavior. It seems like a reasonable question; to some, a question whose answer is so obvious it does not need asking.

This trivial-sounding question is very frequently difficult to answer in practice. Learning events do occur, events like reading comprehension, math concepts, programs for the gifted and talented, and even character development. Are these presented because someone said, "I believe in these areas; that's why we include them as learning events," or does it work the other way around, "Since these are part of our program, I must believe in them."

Each educational program presented to students was, at least at some

1

time, a function of a philosophy or a belief system. These programs cause outcomes. Einstein's creed, "Subtle is the Lord, but malicious He is not," reflected his commitment to the role of reason in the interpretation of complex data. Outcomes don't just happen; they happen because of the events (hopefully planned learning events) that preceded.

The three — beliefs or philosophy, process or presentation, and outcomes — are inextricably entwined. Is one person, or one explicitly definable group of people, in charge of all three elements in the program called "reading"in the typical school? How about programs for the gifted and talented, or programs designed to develop character?

Educators at all levels specialize. At the university level, the third element — outcomes — is the domain of professors who teach courses like tests and measurements, measurement theory, evaluation methods and models, and, to a certain extent, statistics and research methods. Evaluators communicate through journals such as *Educational Evaluation and Policy Analysis*, and the *Review of Educational Research* and give papers at annual meetings like those of the American Educational Research Association or the National Council for Measurement in Education. Evaluators tell one another about evaluation models (discrepancy model, goal-free model, utilization-focused model, decision-oriented model, pathway-comparison model, the CIPP model). The models proliferate; occasionally, an article appears to summarize the models (see Nevo, 1983).

Issues about process, at the university level, are left to specialist areas. Methods in social studies, or mathematics, or reading, possibly differentiating among preschool-primary, the elementary school, and the high school, are defined areas of instruction regarding process. In the schools themselves, the process area is where teachers, teachers-turned-principals, directors of instruction, superintendents, and even school boards feel most comfortable.

Issues about philosophy or purpose draw the attention of educational sociologists, professors of curriculum, governmental agencies (elected and appointed), and special interest groups. The most visible of these special interest groups has specific religious goals, but other groups exist around themes of education and the law, educational and economics, and global education. The question, "Who should make these philosophy of curriculum decisions?" is obviously still unanswered when the most visible organization in the curriculum field reports that one outcome of a conference addressed to core curriculum questions asks, as a result of the conference, "What agencies should determine curriculum, and how much authority to impose it should they have?" (*ASCD Update*, 1986).

Philosophy/belief is causally related to process/practice. When, in the late 1950s and early 1960s, academics and educators became convinced that science programs must be improved, the philosophy adopted was the students should study content about the very structure of the discipline. This philosophy changed the focus to structure and process away from specific content and methods ("kitchen physics"); and the philosophy had an impact on course content, classroom organization, and expected student and teacher behavior. The method was to involve inquiry. Rather than be the expert, the teacher was to establish an environment where the student could redevelop basic scientific or mathematics concepts. The underlying logic of our number system, for example, would be learned by working with number systems in base-4 or base-5 or the more difficult base-12.

But the philosophy/belief-process/practice link is not a one-way street. Back in 1962 when Mager (1962) published a short and persuasive book on teaching according to specific behavioral objectives, many school administrators quickly adopted this philosophy as their own. But the process turned out to be quite tedious, teachers were not generally enthusiastic, and there was the fear that broader, more difficult-to-define goals might get lost. The process itself caused a change in philosophy.

Outcomes are due to process. This obvious statement has been abundantly confirmed by the time-on-task research. But it is not just the time; it is what is done with the time that impacts outcomes. What are the mechanisms linking process and outcomes? What mechanism is thought to cause a student to improve in reading comprehension, create an original product, punctuate a theme properly, make an ethical decision, or conform to acceptable social norms? Is the mechanism always inquiry, mastery learning, lecture, telling, individualized instruction, computer-assisted instruction, peer tutoring, multilevel grouping, team teaching, addressing each student's learning style, or whatever else is this year's acknowledged educational salvation? Is each of these mechanisms appropriate in at least one learning event? Is one of them always the best?

It works the other way, too; outcomes also make an impact on process. When, for example, many perceived that basic skills in math computation declined under the inquiry approach, philosophies and processes were altered. The national report, *A Nation at Risk* (National Commission on Excellence in Education, 1983) resulted from a generally-held perception that outcomes were substantially below expectations. The report addressed the need for educators to change in both philosophy and process.

So beliefs lead to process; and observations seen during the process can also alter beliefs. A mechanism — more properly, many mechanisms — connect outcomes to process. The outcomes themselves cause educators to rethink beliefs/philosophy and process/practice.

And while these clear relationships among philosophy or beliefs, process or presentation, and outcomes exist, the key players in each element tend to stay within their own boundaries. The process people include teachers, principals, other administrators, and university specialists. Teachers belong to organizations based on content (science teachers, English teachers), level (elementary school, preschool), or specialty (learning disabilities, gifted and talented). Principals have their organization; school administrators have theirs. The American Educational Research Association lists specialist groups in classroom management, communication and instruction, instructional supervision, and instructional technology. The outcomes people have their organizations and journals, mentioned earlier. The philosophy and beliefs people have theirs.

No wonder the evaluation of instruction is so often treated as though the three components operated independently of one another. Each group has its own journals, organizations, constituency, and terminology.

The point in all of the above is that one person, or one explicitly defined group of people, is probably not responsible for all of the elements that go into a learning event. Any learning event contains elements of philosophy or beliefs, translated into process or presentation, and represented by outcomes. An evaluation cannot focus only on the outcomes; the evaluation must take into consideration each element as well as the way they are linked.

That is why the first two questions in the evaluate-your-instruction model, presented in detail in chapter 2, are "What is the learning event?" and "Who is the person or group of people, closest to classsroom, who can make decisions about content, organization, and teacher and student behavior for this learning event?" The evaluate-your-instruction process is designed to function as a communication system among these three issues.

The third question in the evaluate-your-instruction process addresses both philosophy and outcomes. "Why are you staging this learning event in the first place? What changes do you expect student to manifest because they have participated?" Take an obvious learning event: Why does an elementary school have a reading program? Is it to maximize reading comprehension level? To provide happy reading experiences? To learn study skills? To develop a complete compendium of word analysis skills? To appreciate and interpret great literature? All of the above? Some combination thereof? These are not all complementary approaches. Why do schools have programs for the gifted and talented? Is it so some preselected percentage can be taught how to develop their creative potential? Is it to focus on those who have, on their own initiative, demonstrated the capability to develop a creative product? Is it to expand to a maximum the number of students capable of carrying to completion a project in a self-chosen area? These are not complementary either.

The way the person in charge answers the questions is related to the expected outcomes. If the goal of reading is to maximize reading comprehension levels, then the expected outcome for students is maximum reading level. Each of the other listed reasons implies a somewhat different expected outcome. The question includes both philosophy and outcomes in one because the two are so related. Additionally, people frequently find it helpful to state philosophies in terms of expected outcomes.

The fourth question provides the link between outcomes and process. It asks, "Given the expectations for students (stated in response to the last question), what do you think is the best way to go about changing students in the desired direction? What is the *mechanism*, in your (the person in charge's) professional opinion, for desirable change?" The mechanism, it is argued herein, is not always the same. The mechanism decision foretells how the process variables (content, classroom organization, teacher and student behavior) will be interrelated. The decision should not be made by default ("We always used mastery learning here," or "We always individualize here.") The decision indicates how the professional-in-charge believes growth is best facilitated under the conditions that exist at that school. In the chapters that follow, it will be argued that the mechanism whereby reading comprehension is maximized differs from the mechanism to develop character; that these differ from the mechanism to develop competence in language arts skills areas; and so forth.

When the person-in-charge has defined the learning event, stated the reason for having it (including expected behaviors of those who participate), and the mechanism whereby change is believed to occur, then specific process variables can be delineated. What combination of content (printed, lecture, experiences), teacher behavior (catalyst? facilitator? expert?), classroom organization (whole group? small groups? mastery learning? individualized?), and expected student behavior (Is student to work independently? Are students to work cooperatively? Do students speak only when asked?) is consistent with the mechanism proposed?

The three reasons are linked by the person-in-charge. The reason for having the learning event is tied to the expected outcomes; these two are linked to a statement of mechanism — a statement by the person-in-charge of "What I think works here." And the program in the classroom is designed to conform.

1.2 Measurement Should Drive, Not Pull, Instruction

The final step involves measurement issues. The measurement step is not final at all; measurement is implied throughout the process. Measurement precedes, or occurs concurrently, with instruction. Before any learning event can begin, teachers make some presumptions about necessary entry-level skills. What skills, knowledge, and prior experience — things not usually considered a part of the learning event in question — must the student have to successfully begin this learning event? This issue is addressed frequently in the chapters that follow, for a distinction is drawn between prior experiences (so often used in tracking and screening) and entry-level skills.

Measurement is therefore involved right away, in the definition and measurement of entry-level skills. A second measurement need is the determination of the extent to which the students know what is expected of them; know what the goals of this learning event are. The third measurement need involves information-gathering which goes on while the instructional program is underway, commonly known as formative measurement. The final measurement focus, all too often the only measurement focus, is on the learning event's outcomes.

When the belief/philosophy, process/practice, and outcomes of a learning event are viewed as an interrelated whole in the evaluation process, then measurement can be the binding element that "drives"instruction. Measurement-terminology is used to define the learning event; to define entry-level skills, measure them; define outcome expectations, make sure students know what they are, and measure them; and to gather formative information during the instructional process to better focus the instruction itself

When the measurement element in an evaluation concentrates primarily on outcomes, the opposite effect can occur. Now measurement does not drive instruction; it pulls instruction. The measurement plays a coercive role — an adjective not usually synonymous with "helping." A recent article, improperly using the term "measurement-driven instruction," is an example of the dangers in using measurement in this coercive manner (Popham, Cruse, Rankin, Sandifer, and Williams, 1985). The authors conclude (p. 628) that "A carefully conceived testing program can yield improvements in students' basic skills." The article reports on a process whereby four legislative bodies (three state legislatures and one large-city school board) mandated performance monitoring at specific grade levels on specific performance skills. In each of the four cases, the article reports that student performance gains have occurred since the time the legislative bodies imposed their standards. The inference is clear: Legislative bodies are encouraged to establish monitoring programs since these monitoring programs cause higher performance. Indeed, the authors argue (p. 628), "The common conclusion of these reports is that measurement-driven instruction works."

Before these external monitoring mandates could actually drive instruction, they would have to address issues of information timing and breadth of mandated monitoring. Information that appears years later can hardly be driving instruction; a narrowly-focused set of objectives is certain to refocus instruction such that those objectives get more attention. That's not necessarily an improvement.

Almost by definition the timing is wrong. The mandate occurs; the schools scramble to respond. Testing occurs later, after the appropriate agency has had time to develop the test. Even after the tests are developed, the testing can be formative only for a small proportion of schools where instruction happens to conform to the testing schedule. Even for these few districts, the results will not be immediately returned. If "driving instruction" is defined as "having the information available during the instructional program to improve instruction" then these external programs are not driving instruction. The timing is wrong. The mandated monitoring systems are, instead, coercing schools to concentrate on certain specific and defined objectives. Is that so bad?

One of the reports from the article concerns a state monitoring program. The article reports (p. 629), that ". . . improvement of fifth-graders between 1980 and 1984 on 28 of 29 objectives ranged from 3% to 36%, with an average increase of 13%." At fifth grade, 29 objectives were assessed. None were assessed at grades 1, 2, 4, 6, 7, or 8. Think of the major objectives still in the instructional system at grade 5, and the new ones that are just entering. In math alone, there must be 60; and then language, study skills, science, reading, and social studies need to be added. It is not so surprising that schools were able to show growth on this narrowly defined group of 28 objectives in a four-year period. The schools simply reallocated instructional time so that these objectives were addressed and measurable growth occurred.

But what of the objectives not on the list? The test mentioned above focused on math, reading, and the mechanics of writing. Did anyone monitor, during the time growth was observed on the 28 of 29 objectives tested, what happened to science instruction, the study of the country's history, knowledge of the Bill of Rights, or in areas of self-expression, such as art, music, and dance? Suppose the few math items did not include testing in the theory of numbers, or measurement concepts, or place value. If public release of results (with the potential for embarrassment) is one part of such a monitoring program, would one not predict that time will be found to make sure the monitored ones are addressed — and over-addressed? Since overall time was not increased, it is reasonable to argue the time was taken at the cost of nonmonitored areas.

For measurement to drive instruction, the information must be available at the time a decision needs to be made. Time allocations should be based on students' needs. The information determines the needs. To improve instruction, information (frequently from measurement devices like tests) is most useful when gathered *before* instruction (the entry-level skills) or *during* instruction (making sure students know what is expected, and from gathering formative progress data). Outcomes information is important too; but, standing alone, can hardly have much of an impact on the instruction that preceded.

1.3. The Local School Is Education's Profit Center

Those who legislate monitoring mandates have the proper motivation. And increases in student performance results are worth writing about. Even schools currently doing an excellent job probably have some area of the instructional program that could use improvement. But the improvement should start at what is currently the local school's weakest area. The issue raises still another problem with legislated mandates.

The usual administrator in a district is not averse to student improvement programs. Generally speaking, the momentum for performance improvement, which exists as a response to *A Nation at Risk* and other national reports critical of student performance levels, is viewed as an opportunity to get some things moving which, for a variety of reasons, have been difficult through the 1970s. However, experienced educators know the importance of getting started in the right direction. A district cannot mount a response to every critical article, book, legislative statement, or current research report. The critics are not marching in step. Should the local school have more programs for the gifted and talented? More computer literacy? Writing skills? Communications? Literature? Math and science? School climate? Back-to-basics?

One approach at the local level is to wait for mandates and respond as necessary. In their 1985 session, the Illinois legislature passed a series of acts which will lead to more state monitoring of student performance in schools. Illinois educators could simply bide their time. First the guidelines have to be drawn up; then the districts need to report; then these data need to be accumulated and reported back to the public. Only after this step will there be a potential for criticism for those districts whose results are in some way not up to expectations.

But this reactive approach has some problems. In the first place, valuable time is lost; so is a golden opportunity to mount an improvement program. In the second place, the externally mandated areas may not be the most needy areas at the local level. Finally, and most seriously, this reactive approach implicitly relinquishes to the legislative body decision-making authority which could be most usefully exercised at the local school level.

Meaningful improvements don't happen in a month; an improvement program may need to be in place for a number of years before the desired student performance gains occur. This type of improvement program requires a commitment that can inspire staff support over this extended time period. Competing improvement programs, sometimes contradictory in purpose, dilute the district's response capability. The identification of the most needy area or areas at the local level should be done by those who know local conditions best; namely, a broad cross-section of the staff at a school. By first agreeing that an improvement program is going to be undertaken, then deciding the areas in that building where improvement is most needed, the necessary broad-based, long-term commitment to improvement can be generated.

The evaluate-your-instruction process is designed for this purpose. The questions are nontechnical. Any teacher or administrator in a school should be able to respond to questions like "What is the program?", "Who is in charge of it closest to the classroom?", "Why are you teaching it at all?", "What are your expectations for the students?", "How do you think growth occurs?", "How is your organization to teach consistent with this belief?", and "What evidence do you have about all of these questions?" The expectation is that the leadership role in evaluating a learning event will be exercised by a principal, other instructional leader, or teacher. Outside technical help might be sought, but ownership and control remain in the school.

Please note that only one answer is required per question. It is not necessary to list all possible reasons for having a learning event, or all possible expectations, or all possible mechanisms whereby improvement occurs, or all possible combinations of content, organization, and student/teacher behaviors. The answer to each question that best conforms to local conditions is the one that should be given.

A basic premise of this book is that the local school is the educational profit center. Broad-based improvement will most likely accrue when the process starts with a representative committee at the local level. Schools differ in their needs. Each school can mount an improvement program but, instead of responding to a mandated area where no need (or at least a lesser need) exists, the locally initiated program responds to its weakest link or links. Of course, each local school should not be asked to reinvent the wheel. As necessary, external resources and external validations should be drawn in.

1.4. Evaluate-Your-Instruction and Staff Development

Measurement is a theme woven through the evaluate-your-instruction process, but so is communication. When asked who was in charge of the reading program at a local school, the principal replied, "A committee of primary teachers chooses their materials, a second committee of intermediate teachers chooses theirs, and the junior high teachers select theirs." To this principal, "who is in charge" translates to "who selects the materials." Additionally, it sounds like "the reading program" is defined as three separate learning events. That doesn't seem reasonable; at a minimum, the learning event should be "the school's reading program."

Chapter 5 applies the evaluate-your-instruction process to a hypothetical elementary school. The learning event is defined as the reading program for the school. Responses to the evaluate-your-instruction questions are made. The reader might not agree with the decision made by the person in charge (the principal of the school) that the purpose of a reading program is to maximize reading comprehension levels for the students. Some may feel her focus was too narrow. The principal also decided to use a particular approach to initial reading acquisition. Some might not agree with that decision either.

But that's the point. Every one of the six questions in the evaluate-your-instruction process is likely to trigger some areas where reasonable, caring people do not agree. Some schools will have "turf" problems just defining the learning event as the entire K–8 reading program. Some high schools' social studies departments won't want to define the learning event as "the social studies taught at this high school." Instead, the more simple, "There are many learning events in this department. One is American History (Regular), a second is American History (Superior), a third is World Geography . . . ," and on and on until all courses are listed.

Many will not want to list the person or group in charge. "That's done informally here." Some look quizzical when asked, "Why are you having this learning event?" But the four example chapters that follow addressing reading, language arts, character development, and high school math will show that there exists a substantial amount of disagreement about why these things are done. Each step of the way, even for those questions which at first seem obvious, will bring out areas where experienced staff do not agree. "Why are you using a measure of reading proficiency when our primary goal in French is oral proficiency?" "Why are you using a reading comprehension test when we are most interested in instilling an appreciation for reading into our students?" Each question is worth discussion. Bring them out in the open and have the discussion.

The issue is not finding out who is the most clever; the issue is embarking on some interactions among the educators in the building about important issues. It is not terribly important that everyone eventually be brought to identical viewpoints; but it does seem important that everyone is aware of the diversity of viewpoints that exist, and adopt approaches that are at least not contradictory.

Of course, ambiguity is better than clarity if short-term harmony among staff is particularly important. Consider this interchange recently observed:

> The members of the art department were meeting with me to discuss why certain learning events were offered. The head of the department routinely said the primary rationale was to provide vocational training. Half of the staff was aghast! They thought the purpose was for self expression; for the student to obtain a better understanding of self. The one hour meeting extended much longer, and finally had to be continued on another date.

Was it a bad thing that this fundamental difference in philosophy was brought out into the open? The viewpoint taken in this book is that clarity of communication is a central ingredient in the process of improving the consistency and effectiveness of learning events in schools. Reasonable people can disagree and still maintain satisfactory human relations. Sergiovani and Carver (1980, p. 20) put it this way:

> Tension should be considered as a stimulus to creativity but with calculated caution. An excess of tension in the school as an organizational system, like an excess of penicillin in the human system, can have damaging effects. Yet the absence of tension produces stagnation which is equally damaging in the long run.

The task here is evaluating your instruction. Questions directed toward defining learning events, determining who is in charge, asking why the event is being staged and what changes in students are expected, asking for an expression of the mechanism which is expected to cause the desired growth, linking the mechanism to things like content, organization, teacher behavior, and expected student behavior, and finally asking how this interrelated process is to be measured — these questions have the makings of instituting some tensions. The learning events described in chapters 4 to 7 are good examples of this. In each case, some hard decisions have been made. Some readers might not agree with the answers.

Good. But it is not fair to say simply, "I don't agree." Where does the reader's viewpoint differ? Why?

Tension is only negative when no effort is made to open a dialogue to dissipate it. Disagreements on the questions posed represent professional differences of opinion. Sergiovani and Carter continue:

> The focus should not be on winning or losing in a personal sense but on the viability of one alternative over another — with the commitment of all participants to the improvement of education assumed. A healthy web of tension is one which is task- and problem-centered, rather than people and feeling centered.

The evaluate-your-instruction process is consistent with this viewpoint. Clarity of communication is necessary because it will, ultimately, lead to improvements in instruction and higher level of student performance.

1.5. A Quick Overview of Chapters 2 to 10.

The next chapter presents in greater detail the steps in the evaluate-your-instruction process. Following this, in chapter 3, the frequently confused issues of measuring educational productivity, quality, and quality-with-equity are addressed, along with cost effectiveness and instructional efficiency.

Chapters 4 through 7 are the example chapters. The examples have been selected to cut a wide path across the educational scene. They deal with high schools and elementary schools; with cognitive and affective areas; and with defined content areas as well as cross-cutting areas.

Chapter 4 concerns a high school. Here the learning event is the mathematics program developed for the college bound. Chapter 5, mentioned earlier, concentrates on evaluating a reading program at a K–8 elementary school. Chapter 6 goes back to the elementary school for another important area: the language arts program. This chapter is not repetitive of chapter 4, for the skills addressed in chapter 6 are seen as objectives-driven, as contrasted with reading comprehension, which is described as difficulty-driven. Chapter 6 is presented as a prototype for other objectives-driven areas, such as math computation, math concepts, reference skills, and parts of the science and social studies programs. The learning event in chapter 7 is an affective one; the program for character development in a school system. Many will question the manner used to define and evaluate this much-honored, unevenly understood school goal, but such criticisms open up communications, and, as was stated earlier, such communication is part of the justification of this process.

The last three chapters cover measurement issues frequently needed in evaluating learning events. They are designed to provide some background for people implementing an evaluate-your-instruction program at the local level. Chapter 8 contrasts measures of maximum versus typical performance and norm-referenced versus criterion-referenced tests. The chapter also reviews the use of aptitude tests, providing a definition based on the use made of the results rather than based on the test's title. This is followed by a discussion of the changing environments for testing at three levels of schooling: the primary levels, the rest of elementary school, and the high school. The chapter ends with a discussion of three pairs of terms that are interrelated in important ways: issues of reliability and validity, standard error of measure and standard error the mean, and tests designed for individual evaluations versus tests designed for group evaluations.

Chapter 9 addresses issues in the maximum performance measurement. The theme is information: how achievement information is gathered at the elementary school and high school with norm-referenced and criterion-refereneced tests. The last section of chapter 9 covers a timely issue: using microcomputers to administer and score tests and maintain building and district performance records.

The final chapter covers affective measures. Only those measures expected to be part of evaluation projects at the local level are included. Although maximum-performance and typical-performance are covered in separate chapters, chapter 10 notes that cognitive learning events certainly have affective elements, and that affective learning events have content also.

These last three chapters are the types one usually associates with a book with the word Evaluation in its title. Measurement and evaluation certainly are key elements in the other seven chapters as well, but these first seven chapters are also extensively concerned with beliefs and philosophies about instruction and with the instructional process itself. The evaluate-your-instruction process links philosophy or beliefs to process to outcomes, and includes the mechanisms that link these three as well. Measurement is a theme throughout; but so is communication, particularly emphasizing communication across the boundaries of beliefs, practice, and outcomes. An assumption is made that improvement is possible in all schools, even those now deemed excellent; that overall improvement in schooling is accomplished best by starting at the school, seen as the educational equivalent of business's profit center; and that improvement initiatives should start at the local school level under the direction of a representative group from that school, focusing on the elements in that program found to be most in need by this representative group.

References

ASCD Update (1986). "Who should say what all should know?" 28(1):1,6.

Mager, R.F. (1962). *Preparing Instructional Objectives*. Palo Alto, CA: Fearon.

National Commission on Excellence in Education (1983). *A Nation at Risk: The Imperative For Educational Reform*. Washington, D.C.: U.S. Government Printing Office.

Nevo, D. (1983). "The conceptualization of educational evaluation." *Review of Educational Research* 53(1):117–28.

Popham, W.J., Cruse, K.L., Rankin, S.C., Sandifer, P.D., and Williams, P.L. (1985). "Measurement-driven instruction: It's on the road." *Phi Delta Kappan* 66(9):628–634.

Sergiovani, T.J. and Carver, F.D. (1980). *The New School Executive*. New York: Harper and Row.

2 The Evaluate-Your-Instruction Process

The evaluate-your-instruction process includes five sequential steps. The measurement needs (prior to, during, and after instruction) are treated as a sixth step, although they are actually defined at different points in the process and interwoven throughout.

As background, it is important to remember that how one proceeds on an evaluation depends on the breadth of potential options studied. Most school district comparisons are essentially internal. Generally, a district evaluates a program in place or just being put in place in one building, or all the buildings in a district. The goal is to get information about that program's effectiveness as contrasted with prior or other approaches.

On the other hand, evaluations can be external. In this case, programs designed to achieve the same goals are compared across schools or districts. The comparisons might address the same approach to the learning event, or different approaches. One district, a group of districts, a funding agency working with many schools, might undertake such a comparative study. A state legislature might mandate such a comparative study for all districts in that state.

For purposes of this book, an internal evaluation means it is locally referenced. An external evaluation means it will involve comparisons among schools or districts.

2.1. Step 1

The first step is to define the learning event in question. "Learning event" is used instead of "instructional event" because not all expected learning involves direct instruction. In some learning events, the role of the instructor is to simply get the students talking to each other about a particular topic. The students are to learn from each other, not the teacher.

A learning event to be evaluated should be a substantial activity. At least at the outset, it need not be stated in the form of specific objectives. The learning event should be a substantial activity stated in a manner such that most reasonable people would agree on what was meant. Some examples of learning events which would be appropriate for evaluation are:

> The math computation objectives for fourth grade.
> The math computation objectives for grades 1 to 8.
> The math computation and concepts objectives for fourth grade.
> The math computation and concepts objectives for grades 1 to 8.
> Reading comprehension at grade 4; reading comprehension in grades 1 to 8.
> The five-course French sequence in a high school.
> The seven-course electronics concentration in the vocational education department of a high school.
> The word analysis program for beginning readers.
> Punctuation basic skills in a K–12 district.

A learning event could have a broader focus:

> The communication skills program in an elementary school.
> The writing program in a high school.
> Programs to develop an understanding of the interdependence of all people and societies.
> Programs designed to develop good study habits.
> The character development program in a district.

A learning event should not be a single small objective or unit of instruction. To be avoided are learning events like:

> The medial diphthongs of the word analysis program.
> Multiplication of a whole number by a one-digit whole number.
> Addition and subtration of fractions.

Each of these is more directly called a unit of instruction; each is part of a broader learning event. The first is part of a word analysis program; the last two part of the computation program. The whole program should be viewed at once; each objective standing alone is too isolated. Programs that focus individually on hundreds of isolated objectives soon become incoherent.

The learning event should not be so vague its interpretation would vary widely across observers. A vaguely stated learning event is:

Programs to help children respond to change in a changing world.

Programs to help students become good citizens. (Chapter 7, however, addresses a character development learning event, which is no less vague.)

Programs to develop a life-long love for learning.

To assist students in developing problem-solving attitudes and skills through the process of discovering and organizing knowledge and critically evaluating information.

Each of these is a laudable goal. However, people differ widely on the meaning of each of these; each is pretty much impermeable to measurement, especially while the students are still in school.

The way the learning event is defined represents an important decision; it gives a message to the educators involved. A too-narrow definition inappropriately causes people to view measures as outcomes which are really formative.

For example, a K–6 school might choose to evaluate its reading program. There is a temptation to split the event into three: prereading and initial reading in grades K and 1, first reading in grades 2–4, and more advanced reading in 5 and 6; or just between primary and elementary; or separate word analysis skills from reading. Or the split might be between reading comprehension and study skills.

Pursue the most common of these, the split between the primary and elementary grades, further. The problem is that the split itself implies that the measures of student performance at the end of the primary grades are outcomes; final assessments. In fact, the split is arbitrary; the measures are formative since, in the children's eyes and in reality, the move from grade 2 to 3 is the same as from grade 3 to 4. The program should be defined as a coherent reading program without arbitrary end points.

The concept of defining learning events so measures which are, or should be, formative appear to be formative is even more apparent at the high school. Chapter 4 addresses a learning event called "the math program for the college bound students." Defining the event this way helps the educators remember that each course, and each instructional level, is part of a whole program. End-of-course tests, under this broader definition, are viewed as formative; under a course-by-course definition, they are improperly viewed as summative or final.

A learning event definition which is too broad can remove the learning event from the accountability sphere of the school. The school, through its teachers and principal, cannot be held accountable for what they cannot control. A K–6 school feeds its students to some junior high, and the coordination between the two schools might be excellent. But the K–6 school should still define the learning event in terms of the grades and programs offered there. Diluting responsibility across school lines removes some of the incentive to improve. Each building should be responsible for its own; district improvements accumulate out of those attained at each site.

2.2. Step 2

What person (or group of persons, or office), closest to the classroom, can independently make decisions about the content, classroom organization, teacher behavior, and expected student behavior for this learning event? Under conditions of local control, the school board has ultimate responsibility for these, except in areas where the state legislature has jurisdiction. Moving toward the classroom, potential decision-makers include the state legislature, the school board, a central office department (e.g., curriculum department), the principal, a department head, a teacher committee, or the teacher, or, ultimately, a committee of students. The question is not who *could* make the decisions, but rather who, closest to the teacher, can and *does* exercise this option.

The answer to the question is empirical, not theoretical; it should be determined not from reading the district policy or curriculum guides but rather by observing actual practices. For example, in one district, two eighth grade science teachers in the same building introduced units quite differently. One always had a hands-on experiment; the other never used experiments. Obviously, content and organization decisions are made at the classroom level, at least in the science program, in this district. The author once surveyed coverage in American History courses in a major urban school system. Some teachers spent 80% of the time on the Civil War; other teachers gave this topic 10% of the time. Many never covered events after 1900; some never covered events prior to 1900. In some classes, students were asked to write a research paper; in others, they were asked to develop a history of their family; in others, no writing was required. Clearly the decision-making about content, organization, and teacher behavior was left to the teacher at the classroom level.

In another school visited, the language arts program is individualized using a variety of self-instructional materials. Each fourth grade classroom visited had the same materials, being used in the same way, with the same teacher behavior, and the same expected student behavior. Clearly the decision-making for this learning event was at a level different from the classroom (I hate to say "higher." The classroom is where the action is, not in the state legislature.) Perhaps a teacher committee, the principal, or the language arts director had made this decision and monitored it in such a way that it actually is happening.

That comment on monitoring is important because the decision making for learning events which are not monitored go by default to the classroom. In the example above about American History courses, a curriculum guide did exist. It specified quite clearly which topics should be covered, how they should be approached, and time allotments. This may be a bit of an overgeneralization, but it does seem that without monitoring, teachers will do what is most comfortable for them. If leaving the decision-making authority to the classroom teacher is by design, that's one thing; if it just happens that way because no one ever gave it much thought, that's another.

For a given learning event, comparisons about the location of decision-making authority can be instructive; it can become a variable, to see what works best. If all other elements are held constant, one could determine the impact that "location of decision-making authority over content, class-room organization, teacher behavior and expected student behavior" has on outcomes.

2.3. Step 3

Why is this learning event being staged in the first place? That is, what changes are expected in students because of the presence of this learning event? The question explicitly links philosophy to outcomes.

In many cases, this is the time to talk about specific objectives. Chapter 9 addresses the issues of specification and measurement of specific learning objectives, and the appendices provide illustrative lists of specific objectives for math and language arts. But the objectives do not always need to be defined with this level of specificity. In reading, the answer to the questions in step 3 might be, "Because reading comprehension is a crit-ically important area of learning for our students, and the objective is to maximize growth in reading comprehension performance to the extent possible."

If the learning event has to do with a basic skills area like punctuation or reading comprehension, the answers to the questions of step 3 will be fairly common across schools. Even with reading, as chapter 5 will illustrate, people differ about what the primary focus should be. The learning event in a high school could be "the four-course sequence in Spanish." One high school could set as its reason, "So students can learn to read the Spanish-language literature." Another might declare, "So students can develop a level of speaking proficiency to allow them to interact fully in the cultures of Spanish-speaking nations." Does a school offer a jewelry-making class for vocational reasons or to provide a vehicle for self-expression? Does the Pep Band exist so its members can obtain the experience needed to get jobs in other bands, so the members can have a vehicle for musical expression, or so the athletic teams have some organization to rouse student enthusiasm — or some combination thereof? Suppose the high school learning event included four one-semester courses about working with wood (the machines, types of wood, fixing wood objects, making cabinets, building things). Is the reason for staging this event to provide vocational training, to prepare students to be the "handyman or handywoman" of the house, or what?

Generally, it is just assumed that everyone agrees about the reason for having each learning event, and, since the reason is presumed to be both obvious and commonly accepted, the issue is not discussed. This is unfortunate, because even at the basic skills level an open discussion frequently unearths substantial philosophical differences among well-meaning people. Is the purpose of the reading comprehension time in grade four to provide a wide variety of new reading materials, written at a level which is currently comfortable for each child? Or is the purpose to provide materials which are constantly at a challenging level to each child? In other words, is the program designed for coverage and enjoyment or growth? The answer may be neither; the reading program may staged to the student can learn specific reading study skills.

Of course, a given learning event may have multiple purposes. In a sense, "to help socialize the students" or "to help the students become good citizens" might be partial motivation for every learning event. This is the time, however, to identify the major purpose. If two or more purposes for staging the learning event are stated at this point, a statement of relative importance should be made.

Asking the question in step 3 is important because the *reason a school has a learning event* should have an impact on *how the learning event is implemented*. If the woodworking series is for vocational placement, the courses should be structured to approximate the conditions and tasks of those in actual woodworking vocations. If the purpose is for the household handy-person, the structure would be substantially different.

So much for the internal responses to the question of step 3. The comparative responses could be extremely enlightening. Now schools or districts would find out that motivations for staging precisely the same learning event vary across different locations. Such variation might be just fine. Local conditions might dictate that two districts stage the same learning event for very different reasons. Too often, though, the differences exist because no one ever asked the question ("Why is this learning event being staged in the first place?") so that the possibility of alternative motivations was never discussed.

2.4. Step 4

What is the *mechanism* whereby the person (or persons, or office) who can determine the content, classroom organization, teacher behavior, and expected student behavior believes growth (movement toward the desired objectives) occurs for this learning event? How is the time-on-task maximally translated into opportunity-to-learn time?

Again, there is the tendency to declare that the answer to the question is obvious and common to all learning situations — a given. But that just isn't true; different learning events have different mechanisms for growth. In the chapters that follow, many examples of this will be given; for illustrative purposes, consider these two different learning events from an undergraduate nursing program:

> Develop mastery of the names and points of interaction of all of the body's bones.
> Develop an acceptable sense of nursing ethics.

The first learning event involves learning a long list of new terms and interrelating them. The mechanism has to do with direct learning. Time-on-task should be structured such that each minute the student spends is directed toward learning those terms s/he doesn't already know until all of the content is mastered. The students don't need to talk to one another; in fact, individualized instruction would be just fine. The teacher should be in charge.

The second learning event is very different. One experienced teacher felt that the mechanism was to present realistic situations in which decisions regarding nursing ethics had to be made, and then have the students themselves work out the most appropriate response, with minimal intervention from the teacher. Her rationale was that outlyers (students whose ethics were outside commonly accepted bounds) were more easily changed through interactions with peers than by printed materials or a lecture by her. The mechanism is to use the time-on-task in such a way that students learn from one another. The two mechanisms are different; they would require different combinations of content, organization, teacher behavior, and expected student behavior.

The mechanism addresses the issue of how the teacher structures time-on-task so that it becomes opportunity-to-learn time. The nursing instructor felt that lecturing or providing written material on ethics would have used time-on-task time, but would not effectively provide opportunity-to-learn time. She felt the students would only change (move in the desired direction) through a process of observing the normative standards expressed by peers. The mechanism expresses the way the educator-in-charge believes the percentage of opportunity-to-learn time during time-on-task can be maximized.

Here is where among-school comparisons would be useful. Do schools which have precisely the same learning event *and* reason for staging it also assume the same mechanisms? If not, these differences become the basis for productivity studies (see chapter 3). They also, and obviously, become the basis for outcome studies. Which mechanism seems to deliver the most desirable outcomes?

One final comment: The person (or group or office) in charge is not expected to list all possible mechanisms and defend the one deemed most appropriate in this learning situation. That would be an unfair expectation. It is not unfair, however, to ask the person in charge to provide his/her answer to this question for a given and specific learning event. People do make decisions; learning events do exist; and courses are structured because someone felt that was the best way to structure them. Just because the decision-maker was never asked to explicate the rationale behind the decisions made does not mean such a rationale did not exist. If the decision-maker's answer is, "Because we've always done it that way," or "Because nearby schools do it that way," then it is particularly important to get that person to give his/her answer to the mechanism questions. Decisions of this level of importance shouldn't be left to chance or be made by default. The reason one stages a learning event should be consistent with the statement of the mechanism whereby it is believed growth occurs; and these two should be consistent with the combination of course materials, classroom organization, and student/teacher behaviors designed for the learning event.

2.5. Step 5

Which combination of content, classroom organization, teacher behavior, and expected student behavior, consistent with the proposed mechanism for growth, will be used? The statement is written to suggest that a variety of different combinations could conform to the proposed mechanism. The question explicitly links the classroom process variables to the reason for having the learning event and the expected outcomes.

Content includes the books, extra materials, and information presented by the teacher in lectures. In chapter 7, the content was seen as the responses to ethical situations made by the students in the classroom. The content can include a radial arm saw in shop, or the microcomputers in a keyboarding class.

The classroom can be organized to facilitate a lecture-discussion format, dominated by the teacher. On the other hand, the chairs might made into a circle, facilitating student-to-student discussion, or put in little groups, facilitating small group cooperative efforts. Whole-group mastery learning is a form of classroom organization. The presumption is whole-group instruction until a formative test is administered. At that point, correctives are done with small groups. The organization of the classroom is intimately related to the presumed mechanism whereby growth is believed to occur.

There is also no single best teacher behavior for all mechanisms. Sometimes the teacher should be the expert: be dominant and authoritative if the percentage of opportunity-to-learn time is to be maximized. Sometimes the teacher needs to be the authority but classroom interactions are critical. Sometimes the teacher needs to be a catalyst; the classroom interactions are the entire focus. In a similar way, the expected student behavior is a variable. Sometimes the students should work independently, quietly; other times they will need to express themselves about something they have read, so the teacher can determine if understanding has occurred. Sometimes the students should work cooperatively; other times that is not an efficient approach.

The content, classroom organization, teacher behavior, and expected student behavior decisions should be consistent with the statement of mechanism of student growth which comes in response to the question of step 4. The mechanism whereby growth is presumed to occur was to have been consistent with the reason for having the learning event in the first place, which explicitly suggests expected outcomes. By asking the person in charge to respond explicitly to the three questions, rather than just assuming that the answers are so obvious that "everyone already knows and agrees" about them, the evaluate-your-instruction process helps the school develop an internally consistent presentation of this learning event.

Some will argue that students and teachers cannot "change gears" that quickly. Of course they can! Most children already have a whole variety of different behavior modes, depending on where they are. One mode is for free play with peers; another when in the home environment; another when (if the family is religious) they are participating in a religious activity; another when they are with a group of strange children; another when they are afraid; another when they are alone. In the same manner, teachers do not have just one way of behaving; they too can change.

Neither will change in the school setting if they don't know there exists good reasons to do so. The communication must be direct and explicit; it must reach every student in the room. These three steps (steps 3 to 5) of the evaluate-your-instruction process will make it clear to the teacher how s/he is supposed to behave, and it is the teacher's responsibility to communicate to the students how they are suppose to behave. Of course, students don't always behave in the manner the teacher wants; but to get them to do so falls under the heading of the "art of teaching."

In the author's experience, when educators (teachers, principals, department heads, curriculum-instruction leaders) talk about the "evaluation of instruction" they attend almost entirely to the issues addressed in this step 5. Step 5 is the process/practice issue. It deals with what actually is happening in the classroom. The quality of instruction is determined by the way these process variables are addressed.

Differences unearthed in among-schools comparisons of this issue would be fertile ground for studies of comparative outcomes, productivity, and quality. Internally, the evaluate-your-instruction process should result in internal consistency. But just because the responses are internally consistent does not mean they will represent the most appropriate responses to presenting the given learning event. Sometimes a school or department, working in isolation, will, by consensus agreement, head off in an inappropriate direction.

This is where the external comparisons (sometimes actually representing an attempt to find some external validation of the internal system) are valuable. For the same learning event and an agreed-upon mechanism whereby growth occurs, how do different schools approach the process question?

Environments differ. A combination of content, organization, and student/teacher behaviors which is appropriate for one place may not be appropriate for another. But these are empirical questions. Are the two process approaches to the same learning event equally productive? All other things being equal (time alloted, for example) that depends on the outcomes, and that leads to step 6, dealing with measurement issues.

2.6. Step 6

What are the measurement needs for this learning event? Measurement provides information. A central theme of this book is that information, not tradition or perceptions, should "drive" instruction.

In general, the measurement needs fall under these four categories:

1. Measures to determine the extent to which the student can demonstrate the necessary entry-level behaviors which are necessary if the student is to benefit from participating in this learning event.
2. As the learning event begins and continues, measures to determine the extent to which each student enrolled knows why this learning event is being presented and what s/he is suppose to be doing and producing at checkpoints along the way.
3. As the learning event continues, at intervals determined by the idiosyncratic nature of each learning event, formative measures should be taken such that the students can be reinforced for what they have learned and corrected when the measures indicate problems exist. Through these formative measures, instructional efficiency is enhanced. (More about instructional efficiency in chapter 3.)
4. When the learning event is completed, measures of outcomes should be gathered to determine the extent to which student growth has approximated expectations.

The last category, the measurement of outcomes, tends to get the most attention. Ralph Tyler (1974) noted, "Schools . . . (are) likely to be preoccupied with grading, classifying, and other sorting functions. Testing was adopted and developed as a tool for these functions." Too often people equate measurement to testing and testing to outcomes.

This is a shame. It seems paradoxical that in learning events designed to improve outcomes, the measurement of outcomes is the *least* important of the four categories listed above if current outcome levels are to be maximized. The other three types of measurement occur while the event is actually being staged; thus the information obtained from these three types can be used for mid-course corrections designed to improve the outcomes. After all, it is for the improvement of instructional efficiency that the first three types of measures are gathered at all. The outcomes, on the other hand, are measured only after the learning event is complete. While information could be used to make changes the *next* time the learning event is offered, its impact on the current event is questionable. (In fact, the value of outcomes-only information is questionable. Knowing only that the outcomes were not up to expectations is not very diagnostic. The diagnostic feedback is provided by the other three measurement categories.)

Table 2.1 relates the steps 1 through 5 of the evaluate-your-instruction process to the measurement needs. Information about the second category (what is expected of the student) and the last category (outcomes) is provided at step 3 (when the person in charge of the learning event explains why it is being staged and what changes are expected in participants). Information about prerequisite entry-level behaviors and formative measures (the middle two measurement categories) is provided in steps 4 and 5, when the person in charge of the learning event proposes a growth mechanism and a way of implementing it.

Some further comments on the four measurement categories:

Table 2.1.   How the Evaluate-Your-Instruction Process and Measurement Needs Are Related (step 6)

Evaluate-Your-Instruction	*Measurement Needs*
1. Define the learning event.	1. Entry-level prerequisite behaviors.
2. Who is in charge?	2. Do students know why event is being staged, and what is expected of them?
3. Why have this learning event being staged? What are expectations for students?	3. Formative measures taken while learning event is going on.
4. What is the proposed mechananism whereby growth occurs?	4. What are the outcomes?
5. What combination of content, classroom organization, teacher behavior and expected student behavior is to be used?	

"Entry-level prerequisite behaviors" are *not* the same as "required prior experiences"; and this is an important distinction. Here are examples of "required prior experiences" which the author has seen used to determine if a student can or cannot be enrolled in some learning event:

A grade of "B"or better in algebra.
Recommendation of the sixth grade teacher.
A percentile rank of 85 or above on the reading comprehension subtest of a standardized test.
A current grade point average of 2.5 or above.

Any one of these events may have contributed to providing the student with the necessary entry-level behaviors. Each, however, is a general measure, much broader than the specific entry-level behaviors needed for success in a learning event. These four prior experiences are more appropriately labeled "screening measures" or the less-flattering "sorting devices."

At this stage, the emphasis should be on the skills necessary if the student is to embark on this learning experience without immediately being overwhelmed because of inadequate entry-level performance capabilities. The needs should be specific to the learning event at hand, and not be based on generalized prior experiences. It is expected that learning these entry-level prerequisite behaviors will *not* be part of the planned learning event. The student is expected to carry them in to the first day of class.

The label "entry-level prerequisite behaviors" is purposely broad. Sometimes, but certainly not always, these would be defined in terms of specific knowledge or skills. A beginning algebra class might include in its list of expected entry-level skills "interpreting exponents," "using rational numbers," "combining like terms," or "finding a common denominator for fractions expressed in variable form." A second-year French class might look to the outcome expectations from first-year French for its list. However, even here caution is needed. If, for example, the main purpose of first-year is the development of reading vocabulary and grammar, while the primary focus of second-year French is oral communication, then the first course is not a complete source for entry-level behavior needs.

The prerequisite behaviors might be expressed as performance capabilities. Some examples:

Be able to carry out an independent ERIC search.
Be able to program using COBOL language.
Be able to use the APPLEWRITER 2.0 word processor package.
Be able to use the tools, chemicals, and lab equipment necessary to dissect small animals.
Be able to sight-read an unfamiliar vocal score.
(For a preschool) be toilet trained.

Sometimes the prerequisite behaviors would have to do with attitudes. In a child-development course, an expressed willingness to work with a child-care center might be a prerequisite; for a work-study program, an expressed positive attitude toward promptness.

How are these prerequisite entry-level behaviors determined? Primarily by doing a content analysis of all the techniques of instruction. This would include the actual content (textbook, other material) plus lecture material; it would include a review of the behaviors expected of the student. As these techniques of instruction are reviewed, the question is asked, "As this learning event is presented, what knowledge, skills, and behaviors are expected of the student *which are not going to be taught in this learning event?*" The task is tedious, but not difficult; an experienced teacher, looking at each instructional element, can delineate presumed background for each new element. At first, the list may be too long and too detailed. With experience, much distillation will occur.

Defining these necessary entry-level behaviors is somewhat tedious and will take some in-the-classroom iterations before the list reaches its final form. But there are some good reasons to persevere.

One fairly obvious benefit: If necessary entry-level behaviors are made explicit, and if this information is then communicated to potential enrollees, then it is quite likely that these enrollees will concentrate some energy on attaining the prerequisite behaviors before they begin the learning event. The list would also allow potential enrollees to do some self-screening.

At the elementary school level, these lists of entry-level expectations for the next school year could be given to the student as the summer recess begins. Providing this information to the student does not ensure that the student will invest any effort in them over the summer. However, providing a specific list of necessary skills offers more promise for summer effort than just saying to the student, "Do some reading this summer."

At the high school level, a list of specific and necessary entry-level behaviors for each course sequence can have a salutary impact on feeder schools. The elementary school can then concentrate on those behaviors deemed necessary by the high school department. After some time, it seems reasonable to suspect that students would appear on the first day of these high school sequences at a higher state of readiness than before such a list was developed.

Equity is introduced in the next chapter as part of the discussion of evaluating educational quality. Screening on the basis of a list of necessary entry-level behaviors seems more fair than screening on the basis of prior experiences. Prior experience prerequisites have a very real potential for locking students into fairly rigid tracks. While it frequently makes sense to group students to better serve wide variations in current performance capabilities, it is not appropriate to lock the students into a group. If the prerequisite for the advanced level of seventh-grade Life Science is ". . . a grade of C or better in sixth-grade Earth Science, plus teacher's recommendation," it is unlikely that anyone *but* the advanced sixth-grade class can be enrolled in the advanced seventh grade program. But Earth Science is actually quite different from Life Science. It is entirely possible, if enrollment in the seventh-grade program were based on prerequisite entry-level skills, that some new students, not in the advanced sixth grade program, could prepare themselves for the seventh grade program; or that some D-students in sixth grade could prepare themselves. It is also possible that some of the higher performers in grade six have not yet developed entry-level requirements for the grade seven advanced program.

A very similar argument can be made for high schools having different entry level courses (e.g., in math, science, and English) at the freshman level. The enrollment decision should not be based on prior experiences or generalized test performance or recommendations; they should be made on performance capabilities on tasks specifically related to each level. Too often leveling decisions are made by a quota system (upper 5% in the honors program, next 20% in the advance program, next 50% in the regular program, . . .). By defining necessary entry-level behaviors, each level can be opened up to any student who can demonstrate the incoming capability to handle the course. More about that in chapter 3.

But there is another compelling reason to list and measure necessary entry-level behaviors: Student who have the necessary entry-level behaviors have higher outcomes than students who don't. This very-sensible conclusion was reported by Bloom (1984) (he used the term "enhanced prerequisite mastery"), who reported an effect size of 0.6 standard deviation improvement in favor of those who had mastered prerequisites.

Bloom, however, adds another dimension to this issue. He assumes the necessary entry-level behaviors will be defined and measured and, in addition, that the necessary remediation (correctives) will be done before the regular part of the learning event begins. This type of investment of time at the beginning of the learning event makes a lot of sense at the elementary school level, where grade-level enrollment is not optional. Some programs which are optional, even at the elementary school level, might use these necessary entry-level behaviors as a screening device prior to enrollment; or an assessment of them might be done as the learning event opens, followed by excluding those incapable of demonstrating the behaviors. This last approach goes contrary to the helping tendency for most teachers; yet even this exclusion approach seems more fair than allowing the student to persist knowing s/he does not have the prerequisite behaviors.

The second category of measurement task is to determine if each learner knows why this learning event is being staged, what types of participation are expected of him/her, and what the expected outcomes are. Much has been previously written about "expected student behavior" and how it, like teacher behavior, should be in harmony with one another and with the mechanism whereby learning is presumed to occur for each learning event. There is no sense assuming that the student will be able to guess how s/he is supposed to behave. [footnote: Maybe the capability of intuitively understanding expectations is what separates high performers from low performers.] Why not just tell the student, straight out? There is something inherently sinister about a learning event whose purpose has to be hidden from students. Imagining a situation where the student would be better off *not* knowing why the learning event is being staged is difficult; imagining benefits which can accrue from clear communication and feedback are easy. Ausubel and colleagues (1978, p. 424), comment, ". . . many experiments show that deliberate learning in response to explicit instructions is both more effective and more precise and specific."

Efficiency, discussed further in chapter 3, has to do with the proportion of effort that is directed toward the desired goals. If the learner knows what the desired goals are, and what behaviors are expected on the way to attaining them, then energy will tend to be directed into these behaviors and toward the desired goals. Research shows quite clearly that people attain goals more effectively when the goals and expected degree of attainment are specifically stated.

The measurement needs at this stage could be accomplished by a checklist of expected outcomes and behaviors. Feedback would go to each student throughout the time that the learning event is happening. This feedback at intervals can build up a sense of momentum as the student progresses past each checkpoint. The point must be emphasized that communication must be maintained with *every* student — not just the higher performing ones — so each knows where the checkpoints are and which s/he has passed.

The third measurement category has to do with the formative stages — measurements that occur during the time of instruction. This measurement has three purposes: to reinforce the student for learning accomplished, identify for the teacher areas of trouble so they can be corrected, and generally improve the efficiency of the instructional process. The purpose of formative measures is primarily to improve instruction and learning and *not* for use in assigning grades. Bloom (1974) addresses this point: ". . . we found the development of brief diagnostic-progress tests to be most useful.

In general, these formative tests were not used to grade or judge the student, but were of value in providing feedback to both teacher and student on what aspects or elements of the learning unit still needed to be mastered."

However, although formative measures frequently are short, criterion-referenced achievement tests, they can take other forms to conform to the nature of the learning event at hand. The formative measure might be simply the production of some product (a drawing, a science project, a bird house, a book report). The processes of the learning event in question will define the form of the formative measure; it is not mandatory that formative measures take the form of paper-and-pencil tests.

The final category deals with the measurement of the expected outcomes of the learning event. Outcomes are generally measured when all activities of the learning event are completed; any measurement during the presentation of the learning event is considered formative. The measurement of outcomes, then, is not meant to be particularly diagnostic; outcome measurement determines the extent to which the stated purposes of the learning event have been accomplished. Outcomes can be measured by paper-and-pencil achievement tests, by performance (a recital, oral report, lab report), by product (a bird house, sonata, poem, research report), or by later behavior (going to college, getting a job in a specific vocational area, participating in certain leisure activities).

The list above demonstrates that outcome measures can either occur as soon as the learning event is complete, or sometime later. This sets outcome measures apart from another common term with a similar meaning — summative evaluation. Formative and summative are terms usually used in tandem; formative used to depict measures taken during instruction, summative to depict measures taken when the learning event has ended. Outcomes, as used here, goes a little further than the usual meaning of summative. An outcomes measure might be gathered long after the learning event has ended.

Summative measurement, as the word implies, is a totalling up. The interpretation is usually, "That's the end. The slate is clean. In the next course we start fresh." Hopefully, by defining learning events more realistically, the interrelated nature of "courses" will receive closer attention. If courses exist in sequences, as most courses do, then end-of-course measures are formative, not summative.

At the elementary school, a school year ends but a program does not. The fourth grade teacher might assign a final grade in grammar usage, based on some measurement of what has been part of the program that year. In this sense, it would usually be viewed as a summative measure.

But it really isn't summative at all; it should be viewed as formative, since language arts, and the grammar usage part of it, will continue in grade five. If the elementary school is organized as a Kindergarten to sixth grade building, the learning event in that school should be the K–6 language arts program, emphasizing that year-end evaluations are not summative, but formative.

At the high school, the final exam in freshmen algebra is usually viewed as a summative measure; but it is not. The freshmen algebra course is part of a course concentration (actually, in this case, a common course sequence, since these courses are presented in order). The end-of-year outcomes in algebra should provide instructional information for the geometry teacher as that course begins the next year; thus the algebra test is formative, not summative.

The outcome measures, as shown in table 2.1, are determined from the response at step 3 in the evaluate-your-instruction process. In responding as to why a learning event is being staged in the first place, the person (persons, office) in charge also addresses expectations for change in students because of participating in this learning event. How the school proposes to attain these outcomes becomes the topic of steps 4 (the proposed mechanism) and 5 (the content, organization, and student-teacher behaviors). However, the measurement of outcomes is independent of these implementation procedures. As long as the learning event and the purpose for having the learning event are the same, the measurement of outcomes should be approached the same way, irrespective of the implementation philosophy or strategy.

For example, three elementary school districts might agree that "writing (reports, stories, personal communications)" is an important learning event, staged because "good writing is fundamental to good citizenship, most vocations, further learning, and personal satisfaction." The expecations for students are commonly stated as, "To increase the quantity and quality of written materials as the students move through the grades above current production levels."

Using equal amounts of money and student time, the three districts approach steps 4 and 5 differently, even though their goals were the same. One installs word processor labs, based on the belief that this will free students from the mechanics of writing and will facilitate rewriting, corrections, printing, and cooperation. The second school sends all their teachers to a three-week inservice training course designed to improve their skills in teaching writing. The third hires consultants who are professional writers to work with the students during the year on a pull-out basis.

The outcomes would be measured in the same way for all three districts;

do the quantity and quality of writing increase across the grades and above input levels? The other three measures (prerequisite skills, student knowledge of expectations, and formative measures) could at times be the same, and at times different across the three approaches. They are, in a certain sense, a function of the method. Obviously, with the word processors, competency with the machine itself is an ingredient — an ingredient not present in the other two approaches. The common three-week inservice program used in the second school probably would have unique elements not present in the other two. These uniqueness elements would make the prerequistite, expectation, and formative measures somewhat different from the other two programs.

This chapter has summarized the evaluate-your-instruction process. The process links philosophy of instruction ("Why are you having this learning event?") to implementation ("What combination of content, classroom organization, teacher behavior, and expected student behavior will be used?") to expected outcomes ("What are your expectations for the students?"). The process demands more, though; it asks for the mechanisms whereby those in charge believe growth toward desired outcomes is best attained. And it uses measurement as the "glue" which uniquely links this combination of purpose, implementation, and outcomes.

Additionally, the process differentiates between an internal evaluation, which is locally referenced, and an external one, which involves comparisons among different districts. Comparisons can be done in a variety of ways. Earlier, an example was given of three districts, all of which had the same learning event and student expectations. Each, however, implemented the program differently. This is one comparison basis.

Many districts have not only the same learning event and expectations but essentially the same implementation strategies. For example, many districts have an advanced placement program which ends with the calculus course (AB or BC). The presentation of this common learning event, which has a common outcome expectation (a passing grade on the advanced placement exam), is probably quite similar across schools. Comparisons of outcomes across different schools might be enlightening, particularly if they went past the measure "number of passing grades" and onto passing grades as a proportion of senior class size, or size of entry group at the first course, and/or size of entry group at the senior level.

The evaluate-your-instruction process deals with learning events, broadly defined. A learning event is more than an objective and more than a unit. Taking a hard look at each of these learning events — internally, to make sure it is internally consistent among the various elements, externally to make sure it isn't internally consistent but foolish and to see how the outcomes compare to approaches used elsewhere — certainly represents a worthwhile school activity, standing alone. But the totality of a school's educational program is only partially explained by a summary of the individual learning events. These broader looks might cover much of the same ground but from a somewhat different direction.

Some thoughts on these issues are the topic of the next chapter. In this chapter, the issue of evaluating productivity, quality, and quality-with-equity in education, will be addressed.

References

Ausubel, D.P., Novak, J.D., and Hanesian, H. (1978). *Educational Psychology*. New York: Holt, Rinehart and Winston.

Bloom, B.S. (1974). "An introduction to mastery learning." In *Schools, Society and Mastery Learning*. New York: Holt, Rinehart, and Winston.

Bloom, B.S. (1984). "The search for methods of group instruction as effective as one-to-one tutoring." *Educational Leadership* 41(8):4–18.

Tyler, R.W. (1974). "Introduction: A perspective on the issues." In R.W. Tyler, and R.M. Wolf, (eds.), *Crucial Issues in Testing*. Berkeley, CA: McCutchan Publishing Co.

3 The Evaluation of Productivity, Quality, and Quality-with-Equity in Education

3.1. The Evaluation of Productivity in Education

Productivity is "a measure of the relationship between quantity of resources used and quantity of output" (Greenberg, 1973). Greenberg adopts one form of productivity measurement for his guide, the unit of output per man-hour. (In a more updated version, he would probably have used output per person-hour.) In an industrial setting, measures like 0.23 sweaters/man-hour or 14.7 hair brushes per man-hour are productivity measures.

Productivity information can be useful standing alone or through comparisons. Greenberg (1973, p.1) primarily has comparisons in mind as he comments on the need for "a system of information by means of which firms can compare themselves with each other, with the industry and with other industries." The sweater-manufacturer, knowing the productivity is 0.23 sweater/man-hour, could have a basis for estimating maximum weekly production capability. The principal who knows that the school's current reading comprehension productivity measure is 0.9 grade equivalent years per class year (which could, to conform more closely to Greenberg's definition, be restated in terms of "per student class hour") has a way of estimating where the current second graders will be by the end of grade

6. In a comparative sense, if the sweater-maker's competition is turning out 0.31 sweaters/man hour some internal investigating would be called for (maybe the competition's sweaters are not as good; maybe their employees are paid more; maybe his/her employees are not being as efficient as they might). For the school example, if a nearby school, enrolling from the same basic population, has a productivity of 1.0 grade equivalent years per class year, that principal should do some investigating, too.

Although Greenberg prefers "per man-hour" as the comparison unit, he does note the presence of other input units in productivity measures. Some of these (p. 46) include output per dollar of labor costs, output for dollar of total capital invested, output per unit of material (e.g., sweaters per roll of yarn). Some other productivity indices include "weighted student credit hour taught per full-time-equivalent faculty member" in a study comparing the productivity of the faculty across many colleges (Bloom, 1983), "street-light lamps relighted per year" and "service calls made within the first hour after the call per year" in a discussion of a productivity increase program for municipal employees (Paul and Gross, 1983), and "dollars per learning point gain" in a study of two different ways to prepare teachers (Denton and Smith, 1985). Walberg (1982) speaks of cure rates in medicine (presumably cures per population unit), yield rates in farming (bushels per acre), and finished output per unit of raw input as measures of productivity. The production equation he provides, which relates learning to age, ability, motivation, quality and quantity of schooling, and the home and school environments, is not a productivity measurement at all, at least not in Greenberg's sense; it is a statement of production or a production function. To this issue, Greenberg (p. 1) cautions that productivity "is not a measure of production although many students of economics and many businessmen have failed to comprehend the difference between productivity and production." Production measures have no denominator; "10,214 sweaters" or "4.7 years of reading comprehension growth" mean little unless the amount of input is known. Walberg's relationships could be turned into productivity measures, singly or in combination:

> Learning (e.g., in grade equivalent units of growth) per year,
> learning per IQ point,
> learning per IQ point per year,
> learning for eight-year-olds per IQ point per hour of instruction, or
> learning per IQ point per motivation unit per socioeconomic status indicator
> per hour of instruction per quality of instruction indicator.

Productivity is a ratio of the dependent measure to the independent measure. Output is presumed to depend on input. "Sweaters produced" depends on "man-hours"; the ratio of dependent to independent measures is "sweaters per man-hour." Learning, it has been fairly well established, depends on time spent. Levin, (1984, p. 152), however, cautions, "The consequences of increasing the time allocated to schooling and making its use more effective are hardly as straightforward or as effective in improving achievements as they have been advertised.") Therefore, "grade-equivalent years per year of instruction" is an appropriate productivity measure.

A common measure in education is the student-teacher ratio. As a productivity measure, "22.4 students per full-time-equivalent teacher" is backwards. The number of teachers depends on the number of students (districts don't first hire the teachers and then go out and recruit students); the number of teachers is the dependent measure, and the number of students is the independent measure. As a productivity measure, it should more properly be called "teachers per student" — a very important productivity measure. Here are some fairly common ratios used in education, stated as productivity measures:

> Teachers per student
> Guidance counselors per student
> Microscopes per student
> Grade-equivalent growth per hour of instruction
> Word-analysis units mastered per hour of instruction
> Graduation units completed per year in high school
> Graduation units completed per full time teaching equivalent
> Students per dollar expenditure
> Teachers per dollar expenditure.

Stated in this format, many of the numbers would be small. The student-teacher ratio of 22.4:1 students per teacher, restated in a productivity ratio, is 0.0446 teachers per student. Most people aren't terribly excited about using small decimals, so this could be restated in terms of each 100 students; 4.46 teachers per 100 students is a productivity ratio which is a little easier to interpret.

Consider a combination of two of these examples: graduation units completed per dollar expenditure. Dollars are almost always an independent variable. Educators argue for more dollars, translated into more teachers, higher pay for teachers, more material, more equipment, and/or more days of schooling (presumably accompanied by more pay for the teachers), at least partly on the presumption that these will lead to higher levels of learning outputs. Using cost as the independent variable is a type of productivity measure. Remember that the dependent variable is some sort of output or measure of effectiveness, like grade-equivalents years of growth. The productivity ratio of output to input becomes a ratio of effectiveness to cost — an "effectiveness-cost" ratio. Barnett (1985) uses the term "benefit-cost" in his analysis of a preschool program.

If one puts the independent variable in the numerator and the dependent variable in the denominator (i.e., takes the reciprocal of the effectiveness-cost ratio), a "cost-effectiveness" ratio emerges. Greenberg (p. 5) calls these the "unit resource requirements." Here 0.31 sweaters per man-hour translates to 3.22 man-hours per sweater. As it turns out, little is written about effectiveness-cost ratios, but much is written about cost-effectiveness ratios. Since the latter is just the reciprocal of the former, it is appropriate to bring cost-effectiveness measures into this discussion of productivity. Although cost-effectiveness is the term used in this literature, Greenberg's term (unit resource requirements) seems more directly descriptive. Indeed, Barnett (1985, p. 339) uses "benefits per child" as his final index. This might be termed a "unit resource benefit" (since the benefits were reported as positive); otherwise it would have been a "unit resource cost."

Looking at effectiveness (outputs) and costs (inputs) makes the most sense when used to make comparisons. The comparisons could come in three ways.

First, for a defined set of goals and an accepted way of measuring the goals, productivity comparisons could be made across different approaches to the same learning event. For example, if the goal is to increase reading comprehension above current levels and the accepted measurement is with reading comprehension tests, then productivity comparisons could be made among a computer-aided instruction approach, a mastery learning approach, or some new, highly touted set of instructional materials. The comparisons would be in terms of "number of dollars needed to cause a 1-year gain in reading comprehension performance" (a cost effectiveness statement or more descriptively a unit resource requirement). The reciprocal, "growth in reading comprehension per dollar (or thousand dollars)," is a productivity measure. The comparisons could be made equally well using either index.

Second, the productivity of the same program could be compared across various implementations. Many high schools have advanced placement programs. The goals are known. For each advanced placement area, there is an advanced placement test having fairly explicit coverage. The goal is to get the students to pass the test. If "number of students scoring a passing grade (3 or better)" is the commonly accepted measure of effectiveness, then productivity comparisons ("number of passing grades per dollar," or more sensibly "number passing grades per thousand dollars," or, to balance for the impact of different salary schedules, "number of passing grades per full time faculty equivalents assigned to the program") could be made across different high schools. The presumption here would be that advanced placement programs are all implemented in the same format. If they were not (say one was handled in a self-instructional, individualized approach and not in the usual class-with-teacher format), then the comparisons fall under the heading mentioned first (different program implementations with the same goals and measures of effectiveness).

A third comparative approach would be longitudinal. Within one district (or more), the productivity of certain programs could be monitored each year. These would be most sensible if some effort had been expended to attempt to improve productivity.

The measure of outputs (effectiveness) has been the topic of this book. Some measures of input are trivially easy (number of students, number of years of schooling) and some would require measures which are more difficult, such as number of hours of instruction. When costs are the input, however, the situation gets a little more tricky. Fortunately, some advice for developing cost estimates is available (Levin, 1975; Rossi, Freeman, and Wright, 1979; Levin, 1981). What at first seems straightforward (i.e., go to the budget and find the costs associated with a program) is not quite so obvious. Levin (1981, p. 31) calls for first identifying all of the "ingredients" that are required to produce a program. Then a financial value or cost must be assigned to each ingredient. Difficult decisions involve ingredients like volunteers (they aren't in the budget but their contributions have value) or space which is already paid for (it is no longer in the budget but could have been used for something else to produce income; therefore it is to be treated as a cost). Issues like this are discussed in more detail in the citations above. As an example of the problem, Barnett (1985) had to estimate costs and benefits for things like reduced schooling costs since the preschool program made the children easier to educate, estimated cost reduction to society since the programs outputs indicated a lowering of criminal acts by participants, and estimated decrease in welfare costs.

A productivity measure is a ratio of outputs to inputs. In making decisions among alternatives, not just the ratio but the actual values of both input and output should be viewed. Suppose the effectiveness measure is reading comprehension performance and the inputs are two different approaches to accomplishing this task. The potential comparative outcomes can be seen in table 3.1.

Unless there exist some insurmountable logistical implementation problems, a program that delivers greater results for less costs or greater results for the same cost would probably be put in place. The same result from less cost is good, but most educators get more pleasure from raising performance than from lowering costs. This leads to (A), a situation with higher results at higher expense. Obviously, adopting a higher cost program means either more money needs to come in or expenditures on something

Table 3.1.   Interpreting Costs and Effectiveness Interactions

| | | *Measures of Costs* | | |
		Less $	*Equal $*	*More $*
Measures of Effectiveness	Higher Results	Great	Great	See A
	Equal Results	Good	See B	Why?
	Lower Results	See C	No	No

else need to be curtailed. In (B), equal results and equal costs, the decision would have to be made on the basis of other information: teacher attitudes, parent attitudes, logistics of implementation and maintenance, or whatever. Situation (C), lower costs and lower results, might become important for a district which is involved in budget deficits leading to program reductions. Productivity analysis here might be viewed in terms of "damage control."

Two cautions regarding productivity comparisons need to be raised. These are not raised in attempt to discourage productivity comparisons; they are made to alert the user to potential misinterpretations.

In the first place, many of the decisions about what are and are not ingredients (the complete listing of personnel, facilities, and materials), and decisions about assigning costs to listed ingredients, are subjective. Use facilities as an example. Many school buildings have been paid for many years ago. A devious administrator could attempt to make a program look "good" by using square-foot estimates of value based on construction costs which occurred 40 years earlier; to make productivity look bad, estimates of square-foot costs could be based on current values of premium office space. Denton and Smith (1985) speak of a "shadow cost" approach to this. They comment (p. 199), "Facilities costs were determined by the 'shadow cost' technique, that is, the expense of renting space from a local government or private facility to hold class." To make a program look productive, key ingredients could be overlooked (ignoring significant efforts made by personnel holding other responsibilities in the district, or ignoring or underpricing volunteer efforts). To make a program look nonproductive, these ingredients could be overstated.

The second caution has to do with a tendency to treat a generic program label as if it adequately described all of the programs included under it. Suppose the goal were to compare the productivity of four approaches to increasing performance in mathematics; and that the four approaches are peer-tutoring, increasing the time alloted, decreasing class size, and a computer-assisted instruction program. Irrespective of how the comparative productivities come out, it must be remembered that programs, as actually implemented, vary widely within each of these generic headings.

Computer-assisted instruction conjures up an image of a student seated in front of a keyboard and monitor being taught by a software program stored in the computer. That is just the common element; from that starting point on, much variation is possible. Student learning growth will occur only to the degree the computer is able to present information that the student does not already know. If the program spends 10 minutes drilling something the student already knows, no learning can occur (opportunity-to-learn time is zero); if the program teaches the student a concept in 60 seconds, then spends 19 minutes more drilling on this now-mastered concept, most of the interaction was wasted. The adequacy of the diagnostic system, be it embedded in the software or simply left to the teacher's discretion, is pivotal. This is not the place to discuss what makes systems to teach by computer good or bad; the point is that implementations under the generic heading "computer-assisted instruction" can range from very effective to useless.

So can increasing instructional time or decreasing class size. If 10 minutes per day were added to mathematics instruction and this time used to diagnose and correct current specific shortcomings in the students' knowledge of mathematics, then the extra 10 minutes will pay dividends in terms of higher performance. If, however, the same amount of material usually presented in 30 minutes is now presented in 40 minutes, or if the teacher uses the extra 10 minutes for a housekeeping chore, then it is unlikely that additional time will increase opportunity-to-learn time or raise outputs. A teacher whose primary teaching approach is teacher-dominated group instruction might as well have 30 students as 15. Only if the smaller class size is used to implement some sort of more precise teaching strategy (more diagnoses of students followed by effective correctives) will smaller class size lead to higher results.

If a productivity analysis studies four specific implementations, and reports that one (for example, peer tutoring) has the best productivity ratio *among these specific implementations*, this does not allow the generalization that peer tutoring is always the most productive approach. This particular comparison might involve a good implementation of peer tutoring compared to horrendous implementations of the other three (see Wick, 1985).

This second caution leads back to the fourth step in the evaluate-your-instruction process. In this step, the person in charge was asked to delineate what s/he believed was the mechanism whereby the desired type of student growth occurs. It is known that results of programs implemented under the same generic heading vary widely. The variation in outcomes is due to a reason; it is more than randomness. In the past few years a whole series of meta-analysis studies (statistical accumulations of all available research studies under a single generic heading, like "bilingual education," "reduced class size," or "computer-assisted instruction") have been carried out. Such studies document variation of effects within a generic heading; then they report on the average effect across all of these different implementations. Rather than do these sterile statistical compilations, it would seem more sensible to contrast the least effective and the most effective implementations in an effort to find out why some implementations get higher results. That is, concentrate the research effort on a search for the *mechanism* within implementation strategies that *causes* the variation. (Of course, this suggestion would be disruptive to these researchers since it would require that they leave the university and go into schools and classrooms as different implementations are studied. A comfortable element of meta-analysis studies for the researcher is that s/he need only analyze published results of studies done by others who did interact with superintendents, principals, teachers, and students in schools. The meta-analysis researcher needs only a library and a computer center, both of which are situated on the university campus.)

And this discussion of mechanism leads to the issue of efficiency. Efficiency ratios look like productivity ratios. Paul and Gross (1983), cited earlier for their productivity study of workers in a municipality, use the ratio "productive work hours per available work hours" as an efficiency ratio. In this book, the ratio "opportunity-to-learn minutes per minutes of class" is an efficiency measure. The efficiency ratio has been viewed as *the mechanism* of interest in programs directed toward improvement of performance in objectives-driven areas, as well as in programs designed to improve performance in reading comprehension.

Productivity is the ratio of outputs to inputs. Comparisons of productivity can be made across approaches (programs), all of which have the same output goals; but they can also be made across different implementations under the same generic heading or longitudinally in one program. For implementations found to be the most productive, further study is needed to establish the mechanism in these more successful implementations which seems to trigger more productivity. These mechanisms, in the instances cited above, have to do with efficiency — a ratio which sounds like a productivity measure but is not.

And this leads to a discussion of the evaluation of quality in education. As will be developed, efficiency across programs is an important part of the evaluation of quality-with-equity in educational systems.

3.2. The Evaluation of Quality in Education

Quality is an attribute or a characteristic of something. One quality of a banana is that it doesn't keep well; one quality of a school is that it has teachers and students. Usually the definition is narrowed to refer to that something's perceived excellence or superiority. "Northwestern University has a quality Management School" implies that the speaker thinks Northwestern's Management School is an excellent one. It is the latter meaning that people usually think of in the context of educational quality. To say that a school has a "quality program" is a compliment — high praise.

Quality is not measured by rate, as in the case of productivity; quality is measured by outcomes. Some potential measures of quality for a high school include:

. . . proportion of the senior class scoring 3 or better (generally considered to be a passing grade) on at least one test in the Advanced Placement Testing Program of the College Entrance Examinations Board. (In my estimation, this is the single best comparative measure of the quality of a high school at the *upper end* of the student performance distribution. It is certainly much preferable to "number of Merit Scholars" or "average College Board or American College Testing Program (ACT) score.")

. . . proportion of the senior class scoring above the national average on the Composite Score of the ACT. (Please take note of the distinction here between "proportion of the senior class" and "average score on the ACT." The average score is, of course, sensitive to the number taking the test. Taking a college entrance test is not an event randomly assigned to students. Generally, the test-taking group includes those who also routinely are part of the upper end of the performance distribution and high enough in this distribution so that the thought of going to college is a real one. The focus should be on increasing the size of the pool capable of doing well on the test; it should not be limited to maximizing the performance of those who enter the school at the upper end of the distribution.)

. . . proportion of students with four or more years of one foreign language who score a passing grade on an accepted measure of oral proficiency in that language.

. . . proportion of each senior class cohort who complete a four-year college education in four years.

. . . proportion of those completing a specific vocational program who sought, and found, full time employment in that skill area.

For an elementary school (kindergarten through grade 8), some measures of quality might include:

. . . proportion of graduating eighth graders with a measured reading comprehension beyond 8.0; or with a measured reading comprehension two or more years beyond national averages.

. . . percent of the eighth grade class who go directly into advanced math courses in ninth grade.

. . . proportion of junior high students who choose to participate in at least one co-curricular activity.

The lists above are meant to be illustrative, not exhaustive. Each represents a fairly direct and specific measure of quality. Some will argue that measures of quality are more impressionistic than specific.

Those with such a viewpoint would contend that educational quality is a matter of perception. A school is a quality school, such people would argue, if it is perceived to be a quality school by its constituency (most directly, the students, their parents, and the community that pays the bills.) Some might go so far as to argue that the presence of a positive school climate represents quality; if the instructional staff believes (or can be brought to believe) that the school is a quality school, then it is.

The notion that a school *is* a quality school if it is *perceived to be* a quality school appears to be very pervasive. Schools perceived to be quality schools are able to maintain that perception even in the absence of any hard evidence from the types of measures listed earlier. A cynic might argue that a school perceived to be a quality school should avoid gathering any evidence which might be contradictory for fear of disclosure to its constituency. Such a school would rather know the answer to the question, "What proportion of the citizens in this community *think* the high school provides adequate preparation such that students will experience success in college?" than to the question, "What proportion of the senior class scores over the mean on college entrance tests?," or even better, "What proportion of the senior class has scored 3 or better on at least one test of the Advanced Placement Testing series?"

The example is a little strained, but there is an important point to be made: By focusing attention on the perception of quality, instead of on more direct indicators of quality, the central administration has moved its attention away from the students and onto the external constituency. If the goal is to improve the educational system which is in place, the perceptions of adults cannot be construed to be a precision diagnostic tool. Measures of quality that focus on student performance are diagnostic. Such measures can be used to maintain good programs and improve those which do not meet expectations. Measures of perception of quality, admittedly pervasive and obviously comforting to those with the luxury of a widespread positive image, are less appropriate in a climate concentrating on school improvement than are direct measures of quality which concentrate on the students themselves.

On the other hand, it's just as silly to ignore completely the perceptions that the school's constituency has developed. The third step in the evaluate-your-instruction process asks, "Why are you staging this learning event in the first place?" The constituency might be brought in to comment as this question is answered.

Actually, there are a number of different elements in the school's constituency. There are those organizations who are the next step in the life of a school's graduate: a high school, for an eighth grade graduate, or an employer or college for the high school graduate. Then there is the constituency group who actually provides the education: the teachers and administrators in the school. Finally, there is the community surrounding the school, and that special subpopulation of the community, the parents of the students in the schools.

Chapter 10 has some suggestions on how these different constituency groups might be surveyed. Their perceptions of the school's quality are important.

The constituency's perceptions of quality are important, but the more direct measure of quality is through the measurement of outcomes. In particular, quality should be measured by the extent to which actual outcomes approximate legitimate expectations across the school's diverse programs. This measurement results of this outcomes interpretation of quality can lead directly to improvement of the school's programs, where outcomes do not reach expectations. A school which has quality programs but whose constituency does not perceive them as such should not change the programs. Rather, it should communicate better with its public. And even a school perceived as quality by its constituency should assess quality via outcomes. If the school is declining, eventually the indicators will become known to the now-satisfied constituency. The school is better off if its administration finds out, and implements, corrections first.

Quality, then, is an attribute or characteristic of a school. Generally, people use the term "quality school" to indicate praise — not just an attribute but a good, exemplary attribute. The viewpoint taken here is that quality should be measured by actual outcomes and not by only by a perception of outcomes. The two viewpoints, however, are not contradictory; the measurement of the perception of quality on the part of important constituencies is indeed the measurement of one outcome.

The preceding discussion of the quality issue has tended to concentrate on the upper end of the performance distribution. There is a hint of some sort of an absolute quality scale; a school has quality or it has not. From this perspective, the implication is that the quality decision is independent of the conditions surrounding the school and the entry-level preparation of the students in a given building. Where do these two issues — concentration only on the high performers and ignoring entering characteristics of the student body — fit into the assessment of educational quality? To pay attention only to the upper end of the distribution is universally unfair to those not at the upper level. Their programs also need quality outcomes. To ignore, in the evaluation of quality, incoming performance characteristics of the students is unfair to those schools, elementary or secondary, who enroll students with lower entering performance levels.

What is needed, it seems, is a measure of quality which is fair to all. A pilot approach to this concept has been developed by one of the six regional school accreditation associations. The North Central Association, whose accreditation program puts it in touch with schools representing a full spectrum of input characteristics, faced this issue by developing the term "quality-with-equity." The plan calls for the use of both input and output measures in the assessment of quality. As the term "quality-with-equity" suggests, these measures would be done across the full range of programs in the to-be-accredited school and would contrast actual outcomes to reasonable expectations, and not be based only on the comparison of actual outcomes. The approach also is fully consistent with the philophy expressed in section 1.2, that measurement should drive, not pull, instruction, and 1.3, that the local school is the equivalent of business's profit center. (For a complete description of this pilot plan, which involves the use of a broad range of measures similar to those described in chapter 2, see the Commission on Schools, 1985.)

Talking about the assessment of quality-with-equity has a nice ring; it appeals to the egalitarian sense in most teachers. It seems only fair. But obtaining meaningful measures of quality-with-equity is not so easily done. Even more difficult, it would seem, would be to get the constituency to begin perceiving a school as a "quality school" according to the degree to which programs are successful in improving the lot of students across the entire performance range, and not simply on the basis of output measures which focus only on the high performers and ignore input characteristics. The Commission on Schools has apparently foreseen this difficulty, for in the Preface to their *Handbook*, they write (p. ii), "The chief product of Outcomes Accreditation should be increased learning for the students being served. To recognize the school as one succeeding in achieving the objective of quality-with-equity education for all students, the Commission has undertaken development of an accreditation program which will provide public commendation for the school as well." Here they link *increased learning* (not absolute level of learning) to *public commendation.*

3.3. Quality-with-equity

Quality *without* equity, whether it be based on the real measurement of outcomes or just through the perceptions of the consitutuency, has two problems. First, the focus on the upper end of the performance range diverts attention from what is happening elsewhere — at the middle or at the other end of the distribution. Second, it ignores the issue of causality. Is the school a "quality" school, based on outputs, because the incoming students were so well prepared at the outset? Or was it that the school's programs caused the students to exit at a high level? (Of course, both could be true.)

One cannot move the discussion from quality to quality-with-equity without addressing the relationship between inputs and outputs. Equity requires a discussion of outcomes *relative to inputs* and *across the full range of input characteristics.* Think of this two-way table relating quality (real, perceived, or both) to productivity for four schools, labelled A, B, C, and D.

Table 3.2. Relating Quality to Equity in Four Hypothetical Schools

| | | Quality? | |
		Yes	No
Productivity	Yes	A	B
	No	C	D

School A is getting high levels of output per unit of input, and is (or at least is perceived to be) a quality school. One can conjecture that this school is receiving students who are well prepared at the outset and is building on this preparation to produce high performers in output areas considered to be important by the constituency. School B, on the other hand, is also productive, bringing about a high rate of output per unit of input (e.g., grade equivalent growth in reading comprehension per student year, or passing scores on the advanced placement exams per full-time equivalent teachers in these programs). One can conjecture that this is a school with a less prepared incoming student body; the growth is occurring, but not to an absolute level high enough to attract attention.

School C represents complacency — maybe arrogance. Here is a school whose student output characteristics allow for a "quality" label which also has, in its productivity measures, low output per unit input. One can conjecture that such a school receives students with input characteristics so high that they are still exemplary even after participating in a nonproductive environment. School D (no growth and no cigar) looks burned out. Clearly its staff has not figured out how to bring growth (productivity) to the students they enroll.

In chapter 2, a distinction was made between internal evaluations, which were defined as locally referenced, and external evaluations, which involve comparisons among schools. The distinction is useful in discussing the issues of quality and quality-with-equity as well.

The first issue that distinguishes quality from quality-with-equity is the breadth of the review. Quality alone is usually interpreted in terms of a degree of excellence or superiority. Quality-with-equity implies a look at the full range of outputs. This distinction is meaningful in both internally and externally focused evaluations. The rationale for looking at the full range applies equally in both.

The second distinguishing issue, the use of entry characteristics as an input in quality-with-equity evaluations, is generally more of an issue with external than with internal reviews. Generally speaking, the range of significant input characteristics (such as socioeconomic status of the neighborhood) is smaller than is the range of those same characteristics across all schools. Although there are notable exceptions to this rule (magnet schools or schools involving long-distance busing), generally within-school variation is substantially less than among-school variation. The task of finding acceptable common measures of quality-with-equity becomes more difficult in an external evaluation, given the wide variations in the incoming characteristics of students across the schools. These problems could be somewhat ameliorated by limiting the external evaluation to schools which have the same input characteristics. This approach seems to be contrary to the spirit of quality-with-equity, within which a way is sought to compare the quality of all schools on some sort of common metric.

The road to finding ways to assess quality-with-equity has some traps. One has to do with defining equity in terms of minimum competencies;

the second, with using variables over which the school has little control.

A minimum competency approach to quality-with-equity would derive from a conviction that equity is served if the school brings all students to some baseline level. This baseline level is defined such that students who attain this level, and no higher, are deemed functionally competent. Obviously, the expectation is that others will attain this level and much more. Minimum competency measures have some problems (see Linn and associates, 1982). An obvious one is a lack of a defensible means for defining competency coupled with a lack of confidence in the measure's validity with respect to the decision being made. Added to these are the measurement errors associated with these measures (see chapter 8 on the discussion of the accuracy of tests used for group versus individual decisions) and the adverse impact the minimum competency measures have on minority and handicapped students.

So minimum competency measures have a lot of problems having nothing to do with the evaluation of quality-with-equity. In one sense, minimum competency and quality-with-equity represent a fundamental contradiction in terms. Quality-with-equity means quality will be a function of program success across the full range of students; minimum competency measures deal primarily with the lower end of the distribution. The error of ignoring the middle and upper ends of the distribution is just as bad as ignoring the middle and lower ends.

There is a second trap in the quest for quality-with-equity measures; this trap is a little less obvious. It involves selecting comparison variables which are outside the control of the school. The school can hardly ameliorate what it cannot control.

The task is to make quality-with-equity comparisons across programs based on the same variables even though the programs themselves may be quite different. These variables would serve as a sort of "common denominator" across programs which are designed to serve students with sharply different entering characteristics. One's thoughts turn quite quickly to variables which are beyond the reach of the school. At the high school level, boys generally score higher on math tests than do girls. This is fairly pervasive; one school or school district will have some trouble overcoming whatever factors it is in our society that cause these differences. Some will turn to socioeconomic status of the surrounding community; the percent of students who live in single-parent homes; the amount of transience of the student body; or the support for homework one finds in the home. Private schools can control some of these by refusing enrollment to students on the basis of rules, but public schools cannot choose their location or student body. If quality-with-equity comparisons are going to be fair to all, as the name suggests, then the comparisons need to be made on the basis of what the school can control and influence.

Four approaches to addressing the quality-with-equity issue come to mind. They are hardly independent of one another; neither are they exhaustive. They more appropriately signify points of view in addressing this issue. The four are:

1. Face the "we can't control it" trap directly. That is, adjust output expectations to make them a function of input variables known to be related to level of learning.
2. Evaluate the range of programs offered by the school to determine (a) if they are consistent with the needs of the students enrolled there, (b) if the right students are in the right programs and if each program has capacity for all those who need it, (c) if realistic outcome expectations have been established for each such program, and (d) if, across the full range of programs, outcomes are consistent with expectations and, where they are not, a system is in place to correct this problem.
3. Address the issue in terms of quality of instruction across all programs.
4. Address the issue in terms of efficiency of instruction across all programs.

Consider each of these in more depth:

1. The relationship between certain input characteristics and level of school learning has been documented elsewhere. Wolfe (1979) reports correlations near 0.80 between reading comprehension, literature, and science scores and background variables. Walberg (1971) reports (p. 17) that ". . . precise measures of the home environment" can account for more than 60% of the variance in school learning. The Coleman Report (1966) found similar strong relationships. The social class of the home was the best predictor of school success found in this study.

One approach to quality-with-equity would simply be to temper expectations as a function of the key input characteristics. A hypothetical relationship between socioeconomic status (SES) and learning level is depicted in figure 3.1.

School A is seen as one where the average home environment is on the low end of the SES scale; school B's average home environment is between "Medium" and "High." The curved (and purely hypothetical) line depicts the functional relationship between SES and learning level. (The line is conceptually consistent with the research studies cited earlier; view it as a schematic and not a precise mathematical relationship.) The prediction of

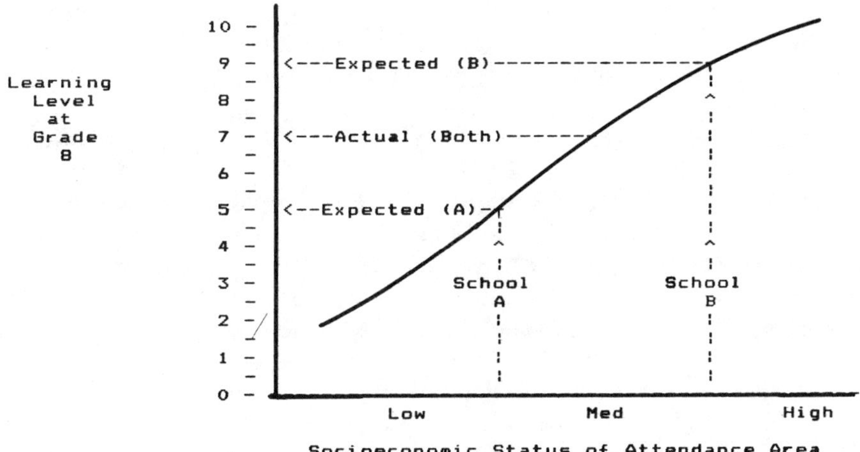

Figure 3.1.   A Hypothetical Relationship Between Performance and a Key Input Variable

actual learning level of students would be based the average SES of the student body. Thus the prediction of average student learning level for school A will be less than that for school B. The predictions are made by plotting the average SES of each school on the horizontal axis; extending a vertical line to the curved relationship line; and running a horizontal line from that intersection over to the vertical axis. (This could be done much more eloquently if an actual mathematical relationship were developed.)

In any event, what if later measurements indicated that the average performance level of students were precisely the same at both schools? School A surpassed expectations; school B did not even attain expectations. Using SES as a controlling variable, the conclusion would be that school A is more of a quality school than B, even though the outcomes were the same.

This approach has some appeal. Undoubtedly it is most appealing to those districts where the average SES of the home is at the lower end of the horizontal scale. But it has some dangers.

In the first place, measuring these input characteristics is an inexact science. "Socioeconomic status" is one of those generally understood but imprecisely defined terms. Family income is one obvious indicator. But family income is difficult if there is no income tax return, or if the family operates on a cash or barter system, or if the "family" is hard to define. The measure can get more specific, including highest educational level of the parents, number of books in the house, or availability of newspapers or dictionaries. The more precise the definition gets, the more intrusive and difficult the measures get. But to remove the difficulty and intrusiveness is to settle for measures which are probably too inexact to be of much use.

Additionally, the impact of these conditions varies by locations. The cost of living is much higher in some parts of the country than in others. The definition of "low SES" would have to be adjusted to conform.

Finally, there is the expectations issue. By defining quality-with-equity as "expected performance levels adjusted for input characteristics," there is the fear that a school might strive to only attain the average performance level of schools like itself. A statistical legitimization of unacceptably low performance levels doesn't seem like a very noble exercise — "Your students can't read but that's ok — neither can the average student from schools like yours."

On the other hand, this approach might put some pressure on the upper end of the distribution. The education journals and popular press like to report on schools where the students do very well despite input characteristics which would suggest much lower performance rates, or on schools which seem to make dramatic gains. It is indeed unfortunate that the other side of this issue is ignored; schools from high SES areas whose students do not do nearly as well as one might expect. An analysis of school practices which differentiate these two categories of schools (high SES, low performance; low SES, high performance) might move toward unearthing some of the causal factors associated with school learning.

This first approach to evaluating quality-with-equity involves tempering performance expectations according to germane input characteristics. The approach has some problems but, with some serious effort directed toward the measurement issues, could provide some useful information. The measurement issues include carefully defining the input measures, expending the energy necessary to obtain these with precision, and developing relationships between these inputs and school learning outputs which are sensitive to the differing conditions around the schools. These tasks are a long way from trivial.

For a lot of reasons, then, this approach is quite questionable. It could provide information to researchers about school practices; it could provide succor to the educators in those unnoticed schools where students have succeeded despite very difficult circumstances. But it is hard to imagine that the level of effort necessary to obtain the necessary measures will be forthcoming. And the bottom line is that the taxpaying public would probably view the whole thing as a "cop out" — an attempt to justify unacceptably low performance levels.

2. A second approach to quality-with-equity would involve looking at

the school's range of programmatic responses to student needs. If the input characteristics of incoming students vary across schools (for whatever reasons) then the schools need to vary their responses.

To begin with, has the school developed a range of programs consistent with the range of input needs of the student body? A public school cannot develop programs and then seek students to fit the programs; the student is the independent variable here, and it is the programs that must conform. At a very general level, all schools have programs to address the occupational, citizenship, and self-fulfillment needs of the student. And elementary schools all have reading and math; and high schools have biology and algebra; but the way the programs are structured and distributed must match the needs of the incoming students who are specific to each facility. Given the needs and traditions of the community, expectations of the students, and entry-level performance characteristics of the students, is there an appropriate program for all students? The measurement task of responding to this question is cumbersome but not insurmountable.

Second, are there satisfactory methods available for matching students with programs? The issue here is matching, not screening or sorting. Once again, the distinction must be drawn between enrolling students in programs based on prior experiences, or enrolling them based on whether or not they have the necessary entry-level skills needed in the program. The decision should depend on what is best for the student (where the student's views and expectations are inputs), and on the match between the performance capability of the student and the needs of the program. Screening and sorting techniques make these decisions on the basis of prior experience, such as completing a prior course, or completing the course with a certain grade, or obtaining a teacher's recommendation, or scoring above a required percentile rank on a general achievement test, or attending a summer school class.

However, even the approach of matching entry-level needs of program to entry-level performance capability of student needs some flexibility. Sometimes it would be in the student's best interests to enroll in a particular program even though s/he cannot demonstrate acceptable performance on entry-level skills prior to enrollment. In this kind of setting, it would be necessary for the school to build a remediation activity into the very beginning of this instructional program, to enhance the level of prerequisite mastery. To enroll such a student, without such a specifically developed remediation package, would indeed be a cruel hoax.

Capacity in programs is closely related to this measurement issue. The capacity of a program should be determined by students' needs, and not by tradition, teacher needs, or organizational ease. In a nearby district which enrolls about 300 students per grade, one honors math class for 25 students is annually scheduled for grade 8. The 25 are selected on the basis of teacher recommendations, standardized test scores, and prior grades. This is screening at its worst. Capacity is predetermined to conform to the needs and expectations of the faculty. Enrollment is based on prior experiences instead of on the absence or presence of the entry-level skills which would make participating in this program profitable. By changing selection techniques, and making capacity a function of student needs, two or three times as many students could be entered into the advanced math level at the eighth grade.

Third, for each program, are performance expectations clearly delineated? If so, are they realistic and are they consistent with the student's needs? As the student enters the program, is s/he aware of what these performance expectations are?

Finally, are the outcomes continually monitored and compared with expectations? When outcomes do not come up to expectations, is there a routine mechanism within the district which is brought to bear to address this situation?

By this time, this programmatic approach to quality-with-equity should have a familiar ring to it; it is a partial restatement of many of the steps in the evaluate-your-instruction process. The equity is obtained by applying the process across all of the school's programs; but this only occurs after the evaluation determines if programs exist to match the needs of all entering students, if the right students are in the right programs, and if there is capacity in a given program to handle the needs of those who should be enrolled.

This second approach to evaluating quality-with-equity is cumbersome but still appealing. It avoids the negative, defeatist tone of the first approach. Instead, this second approach concentrates on those variables over which the school has control; namely, its instructional programs. It addresses coverage, capacity, expectations, outcomes, and remediation. In a very real sense, this approach provides a common denominator for all schools — those serving students from high, middle, or low SES communities. Do they have the right programs? Are the students matched to programs on the basis of needs and entry characteristics? Do the programs have enough capacity? Are expectations realistic? Are outcomes consistent with expectations? And, most importantly, is there a system developed such that all these elements are routinely monitored and which initiates improvements as necessary?

3. A third approach to quality-with-equity is to concentrate attention on the classroom. Herein, quality-with-equity is defined in terms of quality of instruction. In the previous chapter, this topic was addressed in step 5 of the evaluate-your-instruction process. Quality of instruction is basically

an input measure, although (obviously) the presumption is that higher quality of instruction is linked to higher outputs. Quality-of-instruction comparisons would require program-by-program analyses since, as was discussed in step 5 of chapter 2, the specific combination of content, classroom organization, teacher behavior, and expected student behavior should be consistent with the purposes for having a learning event, student expectations, and the mechanism whereby performance growth is presumed to occur.

This approach to quality-with-equity is appealing because it approximates what a substantial proportion of school people consider the equivalent of evaluating instruction; that is, they focus their attention almost entirely on what happens in the classroom. But it is a limited perspective. This approach takes programmatic coverage and student assignment to programs as a given, to be accepted without question. Not only is this exclusion limited but so also is the presumption that quality instruction (defined in some manner) lead to higher levels of learning. The outputs should be stated as expectations and they should be monitored. There is no reason to just assume the outcomes will occur, and therefore not measure them.

4. A fourth approach to quality-with-equity is to look at the instructional efficiency. This issue was raised briefly toward the end of section 3.1 (the evaluation of productivity.) Efficiency ratios look like productivity ratios, but they differ. Productivity ratios have units (work attack objectives mastered per $1,000 expenditure, grade equivalent growth per hour on instruction, scores of 3 or better on advanced placement tests per full-time equivalent faculty assigned to the program). Efficiency ratios are unitless (opportunity-to-learn minutes per class minutes, number of correctly spelled words per words attempted; minutes spent at the wheel per minutes in a driver-education class).

Efficiency measures are related to mechanism issue described in step 4 of the evaluate-your-instruction process. In this step, the person in charge of the learning event was asked to describe the mechanism s/he believed caused student growth (in the desired direction) for the learning event at hand. Some examples of mechanisms were given in chapter 2, and others will be developed in the applications shown in chapters 4 to 7. For illustrative purposes, some will be repeated here and linked to efficiency measures:

> . . . For math computation, one proposed mechanism was to "maximize the proportion of time the student is dealing with concepts s/he is ready for but have not yet mastered." The efficiency ratio here is "opportunity-to-learn minutes per minutes of instruction."
>
> . . . In a program designed to lead to growth in reading comprehension, one mechanism mentioned was "have the student read and interpret material con-

ceptually and syntactically at a challenging level, with reinforcing interpretive feedback from the teacher." One part of the efficiency measure would be "number of minutes student is faced with conceptually and syntactically challenging material per minutes of instruction."

. . . If the stated mechanism requires hands-on experience (running a lathe, driving a car in traffic, rolling out a pie crust, drawing a blood sample from a patient, or using a word processor) then the efficiency ratio is simply "number of minutes of hands-on experience per minutes of class time."

. . . Other mechanisms mentioned (or which will be mentioned) include self-directed learning, peer-group interactions, experiencing new environments, and repeated replication of the same activity to develop speed and endurance. The efficiency ratios for each of these are pretty obvious.

The efficiency ratio, then, follows from the statement of expected mechanism. However, they have a commonality which might be called instructional efficiency; the proportion of time available used to directly address the proposed mechanism whereby growth is presumed to occur.

Evaluating quality-with-equity through measures of instructional efficiency across diverse programs is also appealing. It addresses the relationship between inputs and outputs. The issues involved are within the purview of the school. Even though the learning events in a school vary widely, as do the expected growth mechanisms, the efficiency measures put them all on a fairly common metric. Of course, there are some problems. Much depends on the school identifying an appropriate growth mechanism. The denominators in the ratios are easy to measure; the numerators will provide some serious practical difficulty.

Four approaches to evaluating quality-with-equity have been outlined. They are obviously interrelated. The first suggested tempering expectations to make them consistent with predictive input characteristics. "High quality" would then be attributed to schools whose outputs exceeded expectations by significant amounts. A program-by-program evaluation, similar in many ways to the evaluate-your-instruction process of chapter 2, constituted the second approach. The third approach looked at quality of instruction, and the last at instructional efficiency.

The use of one of these methods does not preclude the use of any others. Combining the second (a program approach) with the third (quality of instruction) makes sense; so does combining the second with the fourth (instructional efficiency); or combining the second, third, and fourth.

Equity cannot be forgotten. Andrig (1985, p. 623) cautions, "It is too early to tell whether this drive for excellence will protect and enhance the hard-won gains in equity of the last 30 years. . . . Excellence must not be a new code word for a retreat from equity." Arlin (1984, p. 83) argues that the approximation of equal outcomes can only be accomplished by providing disproportionately more instructional time to those who enter the learning event less prepared. Strike (1985, p. 415) states quite directly that the simultaneous realization of excellence and equity is logically impossible. Neither author, however, has defined quality-with-equity in the manner described here.

The evaluation of quality-with-equity is not easy. Those looking for an easy way will need to use quality-by-perception, or quality-by-testimonial, or quality-by-anecdote. An hour in the teachers' lounge, 30 minutes with the principal, or interviews with two students at random each represents a pretty hollow surrogate for the evaluation of quality-with-equity.

In many districts, the tasks required by one or a combination of the quality-with-equity approaches do not appear in the job description of any current staff member. Instructional programs are, or have been, developed; students are assigned; instruction does occur. Some system assigns the students; someone is in charge of teacher evaluations. But systematically checking to see if programs match students, determining entry-level skills for programs and ensuring that students are assigned that way, making sure expectations are established and students are aware of them, monitoring outcomes, and, most importantly, initiating changes where the programs are not responding appropriately are not commonly part of school districts' routine operating procedures. Some efforts may be directed toward monitoring quality of instruction, but monitoring instructional efficiency is unlikely.

Thus to institute quality-with-equity procedures, for most districts, would require additional expenditures or reallocations within the existing budget. Clearly this is a detriment.

Yet quality-with-equity seems to go at the heart of that for which schools exist in a free society. Without monitoring, things drift. That which was satisfactory at its inception may no longer be appropriate. To not have these tasks as part of someone's job description is shortsighted.

In the preface to its description of an outcomes accreditation program based on quality-with-equity, the North Central Association document states that one purpose is to ". . . (develop) an accreditation program which will provide public commendation for the school as well." This is a very important issue. The goal is to link students to programs to outputs; and to open to the public those programatic efforts underway to improve the relationship among student characteristics, programs available, and outputs. By addressing these issues directly and openly, the rules for assignment of the commendation "this is a quality school" might be changed. The assignment would move from general perceptions, which so often favor schools which are either in very wealthy areas or extremely selective, to a method whereby it is based on the extent to which the school meets the needs of the students it serves.

This move from quality-by-perception to quality-with-equity, where these latter evaluations are based on firm measurements, might not be viewed with favor by districts where low productivity has gone undetected simply because no one has yet asked the right questions. Yet all schools, even the ones which are now quite excellent, would benefit from a systematic quality-with-equity review; and so would the education profession.

References

Andrig, G.R. (1985). "Educational standards, testing, and equity." *Kappan* 66(9):623–625.

Arlin, A. (1984). "Time, equality, and mastery learning." *Review of Educational Research* 54(1):65–86.

Barnett, W.S. (1985). "Benefit-cost analysis of the Perry preschool program and its policy implications." *Educational Evaluation and Policy Analysis* 7(4):333–342.

Bloom, A.M. (1983). "Differential instructional productivity indices." *Research in High Education* 18(2):179–183.

Coleman, J. (1966). *Equality of Educational Opportunity*. Washington, D.C.: U.S. Government Printing Office.

Commission on Schools (1985). *An Introduction to Outcomes Accreditation* and *A Handbook for the Outcomes Accreditation of Schools*. Boulder, CO: North Central Association of Schools and Colleges, the Commission on Schools.

Denton, J.J. and Smith, N.L. (1985). "Alternative teacher preparation programs: A cost-effectiveness comparison." *Educational Evaluation and Policy Analysis* 7(3):197–205.

Greenberg, L. (1973). *A Practical Guide to Produuctivity Measurement*. Washington, D.C.: Bureau of National Affairs, Inc.

Levin, H.M. (1975). "Cost-effectiveness analysis in evaluation research." In E. Struening and M. Guttentag (eds.), *Handbook of Evaluation Research* (vol. 2). Beverly Hills, CA: Sage.

Levin, H.M. (1981). "Cost analysis." In N.L. Smith, (ed.) *New Techniques for Evaluation*. Beverly Hills, CA: Sage.

Levin, H.M. (1984). "About time for educational reform." *Educational Evaluation and Policy Analysis* 6(2):151–163.

Linn, R.L., Madaus, G.F., and Pedulla, J.J. (1982). "Minimum competency testing: Cautions on the state of the art." *American Journal of Education* 97(1):1–35.

Paul, C.F. and Gross, A.C. (1983). "Increasing productivity and morale in a municipality." *Journal of Applied Behavioral Psychology* 17:59–78.

Rossi, P.H., Freeman, H.E., and Wright, S.R. (1979). *Evaluation: A systematic Approach*. Beverly Hills, CA: Sage.

Strike, K.A. (1985). "Is there a conflict between equity and excellence?" *Educational Evaluation and Policy Analysis* 7(4):409–416.

Walberg, H.J. (1971). "Models for optimizing and individualizing school learning." *Interchange* 2(3):15–27.

Walberg, H.J. (1982). "Educational productivity: Theory, evidence, and prospects." *Australian Journal of Education* 26,115–122.

Wick, J.W. (1985). "Including assessment of student outcomes in the school accreditation and evaluation process." *The North Central Association Quarterly* 20:363–369.

Wolf, R.M. (1979). *"Achievement in the United States." In H.J. Walberg (ed.), Educational Environments and Effects.* Berkeley, CA: McCutchan Publishing Co.

4 The Learning Event: A High School's Math Program for the College Bound

4.1. Applying the Model

In this section, the evaluate-your-instruction process will be applied to a learning event defined as (for step 1), "a high school's math program for its college-bound students." The data in this chapter are neither totally hypothetical nor come from any one district. The data represent a composite of information collected by the author over a five year period from quite a number of different high schools.

This section will primarily describe what the math department head did in the evaluation, and the results obtained. A more complete discussion of the process and results can be found in section 4.2.

Step 1

Just about every high school presumes that at least some of its graduates will continue on to college. And just about every college has some entry-level requirements for the successful completion of some minimal number of high school units. For example, the university which employs the author

61

requires three high school math credits for admission. This requirement is for all potential students, not just those requesting admission to the math, science, or engineering schools. Thus, even though the high school itself may require only one math unit for graduation, the college-bound students will take three or even four units.

High schools vary in the way they present a math program. If the school is large enough, some sort of course-leveling will be established. The school involved in this learning event has five levels of course sequences. Available enrollment and college entrance data for the five levels are shown in table 4.1.

Overall, just under three-fourths of the seniors in this high school indicated on an exit questionnaire that they intended to begin college the next fall. The table shows that even at the fourth level from the top (the Modified level), slightly more than half of the students intend to at least begin a college experience.

Step 2

What person (or group of persons) closest to the classroom, can independently make decisions about content, classroom organization, teacher behavior, and expected student behavior?

The district has more than one high school. The principals report directly to the superintendent of schools. The superintendent has a central office staff which includes a director of curriculum and instruction. Each separate building has a math department director. Each of these directors teaches one course per year.

Although the official organizational chart indicates that the department

Table 4.1. Enrollment and College-Entrance Percentages by Level of Math Program

Level	Percent of Class Whose Primary Enrollment Was at This Level	Percent of These Who Begin College
Adv. plmt.	7%	100%
Superior	23%	100%
Regular	45%	72%
Modified	19%	53%
Basic	6%	3%

heads report to the principal, with the principals reporting to the superintendent, unofficially the superintendent and principals have left contact with the department heads almost entirely up to the curriculum director. Broad general guidelines for department head behavior have been drawn (e.g., frequency of required supervision visits for tenured and nontenured teacher), but the more specific curriculum-instruction coordination issues are left to the curriculum director and the department heads. The director of curriculum and instruction, who does not have line-authority over the department heads, views this department's role as one of facilitator and coordinator. The curriculum director serves the department heads and not the other way around.

Ergo, the real control is delegated to the department level. (Although this is a hypothetical, composite high school, this is a realistic portrayal of large high schools with which I have worked. There are some good reasons for this situation. In the first place, a curriculum director can hardly be a content expert across all departments. In the second place, the curriculum director is spread pretty thin; most high schools have between 8 and 12 departments. Finally, lacking line authority, a coordinator-facilitator stance is easiest to maintain over the long term.) Generally speaking, department heads are selected from within. The department head in math is no exception; in fact, many of the teachers in the department were teachers in this school at the time the current department head was appointed. The relationship is colleagial. The department head has more kinship with the teachers than with the administration. Decision-making about courses and course content reflects this.

Texts are chosen by the teachers currently teaching the course in question. The department head has always taken these committees' recommendations without question. Except in certain very specific elective offerings (like computer courses), whole-group, teacher-dominated instruction is used, paced so that agreed-upon chapters in the chosen text can be completed.

Step 3

Why is this learning event being held in the first place? That is, what changes are expected in students because of their participation in this learning event?

Much of the first question was answered at the outset: A large proportion of students go to college and colleges generally perceive that a high school graduate should have substantial math background irrespective of the chosen field of study. Additionally, experience has shown that certain high school experiences can earn advanced standing or even the award of college credit when the student matriculates. After discussions with the department's teachers, this general statement about student performance expectations was made:

> The expectation is that each student will be placed in the highest possible math course sequence, consistent with his/her capabilities, such that an acceptable performance level can be maintained.

Step 4

What is the mechanism whereby the person in charge believes growth occurs for this learning event?

The department head's primary response to this question is embedded in the statement above: highest possible course sequence placement within which acceptable performance can be maintained. Challenge is the key for this department head. Overall math performance in the school is maximized, he believes, by having the students in the highest possible level consistent with their capabilities. The department head addresses time-on-task considerations by actively fighting any school activity which will take instructional time from a math course. This includes frequent admonitions to begin class on time and "teach until the bell rings." Highest possible placement and maximum teaching time are, in this department head's eyes, the mechanism that maximizes overall math performance.

Step 5

What combination of content, classroom organization, teacher behavior, and expected student behavior is to be used?

The content in all courses is almost entirely textbook-driven. The textbooks, as mentioned earlier, are chosen by the teachers involved in teaching each course. Except for some computer courses offered by the department, organization is always whole-group instruction, with the teacher first going over the previous day's work, then presenting new material. The teacher behavior is that of the content expert and performance judge. The students are expected to attend class, complete their work, ask questions when they need to, and conform to the school's overall rules for behavior.

Step 6

What are the measurement needs? After some discussions among curriculum director, department head, teachers, and an outside consultant, these questions, each of which would require some measures, were posed:

1. To what extent are the procedures for entry-level course placement making accurate placements?
2. Do the students know what the performance expectations are for each course and sequence?
3a. To what extent is their coordination and continuity evident in the sequences of courses the students experience?
3b. Do students maintain "acceptable performance levels" in the sequence to which they are assigned?
3c. To what extent are formative measures used to inform and adjust instruction in the sequence?
4. To what extent is the overall performance level consistent with expected levels at the time the students graduate?

Consider each of these in more detail:

1. Initial placement is done by a committee of high school math teachers. This group, which meets in the February which precedes the current cohort's first enrollment in high school, uses these data for placement:

> . . . Scores on the math subtest of the standardized achievement test administered to the students in the first semester of grade 8.
> . . . An IQ test administered as part of the standardized test battery.
> . . . A reading test administered at the same time.
> . . . Grades in math for grade 7 and the first semester of grade 8.
> . . . Recommendations of the junior high school teachers.

One approach to evaluating the stability of these placements is to look at the high school records of the last graduating class. Once placed, to what extent do the students tend to stay in that course sequence? Table 4.2 shows the results.

The data suggest a substantial amount of level-shifting at the three times shown. The general trend is to move students upward. The percentages in the top two levels increase at the expense of the third and fourth levels. This, however, reflects overall final placements. A substantial percentage of students move in each direction.

The department head knows that much of this shifting is triggered by grades received. A student who has a grade of "A" at the semester or end-

Table 4.2.   Level Change Percentages for Those Students Who Enrolled in Two or More Math Courses

Level	% Assigned by Tcher. Committee	Of Those Assigned, % Changing Level						Totals Up, Down	Final Plmt. %'s
		1st 3 Wks.		*End 1st Sem.*		*End 1st Yr.*			
		Up	*Down*	*Up*	*Down*	*Up*	*Down*		
Adv. Pl.	5%	–	4%	–	3%	–	7%	–,14	7%
Superior	12%	8	7	6	4	14	10	28,21	23%
Regular	54%	13	1	5	2	10	4	28,7	45%
Modified	25%	8	0	7	4	9	8	24,12	19%
Basic	4%	0	–	4	–	7	0	11,–	6%

of-year marking period is an automatic candidate for upward placement. A student manifesting low performance (grade lower than "C") is automatically reviewed for a lower placement.

2. To what extent are the students informed of performance expectations? The department head was required to make a certain number of classroom observations of tenured and untenured staff. As part of these visitations, records were kept on this question. The department head determined that only short-term expectations were articulated to the students. When a new unit was introduced, for example, the date of the chapter test, and frequently the topics which would be covered on this test, were given to the student. Long-term expectations, such as how each unit fit into the structure of that course, or how each course fit into the course sequence, were not articulated in any classroom visited.

3a. Coordination and continuity in the programs experienced by the students were addressed in two manners. First, a second transcript analysis was carried out to determine the extent to which students followed prescribed sequences. Then the content of courses which made up the more heavily used sequences was studied.

The student's registration guide lists the prescribed math sequences. Within the five course-sequence levels, there is some flexibility in the junior and senior level. Actually seven, not just five, sequences are recommended in the registration guide. A review of the transcripts for the last graduating class indicated that:

> . . . of the students with just 2.0 math credits, 74% had conformed to one of the prescribed two-course sequences.
> . . . of the students with 3.0 math credits, 57% had conformed to one of the prescribed three-course sequences.
> . . . of the students with 4.0 math credits, 51% had conformed to one of the prescribed four-course sequences.

Since the textbooks represented the primary instructional content for each course, the continuity of these for prescribed sequences was reviewed. It was determined that the first three to five weeks of each course covered content that had appeared at least once in a previous book.

3b. Do students maintain "acceptable performance levels" in the sequences to which they are assigned? The department head obtained a distribution of grades by level as shown in table 4.3.

Grades for the regular track are assigned a value of 4 for an "A," 3 for a "B," 2 for a "C," 1 for a "D," and 0 for an "F." Weighting by level is done as shown in the column above.

3c. To what extent are formative measures used to inform and adjust

Table 4.3. Percentage of Letter Grades by Course Sequence Level for One Graduating Class

Level	Grade Weight	\% at Each Letter Grade					Avg. Grade
		A	B	C	D	F	
Adv. Pl.	+1.0	62%	30%	7%	1%	0%	A −
Superior	+0.5	51%	28%	17%	4%	0%	B +
Regular	−	37%	34%	18%	9%	2%	B
Modified	−0.5	18%	42%	21%	15%	4%	B −
Basic	−0.5	12%	64%	18%	0%	6%	B −

instruction in each sequence? The department head, during visits to classrooms for teacher observation sessions, watched for two general instances of the use of formative measures. The first was in the use of chapter and unit tests; the second was between courses in a sequence.

Much testing was observed in each course. These tests were invariably written and scored by the teacher of the course. The department head observed that the tests were scored and returned to the student promptly — usually at the next class session. Only on rare occasions, however, was the next unit or chapter delayed to address information found in the last test given.

No evidence of using end-of-course tests as information for the next course in the sequence could be found by the department head. Indeed, only three of the department's courses had departmental exams. Even on these three, the results were used for grading and, in some instances, level changes; but the results were not passed onto the next teacher in the course sequence.

4. To what extent are the overall performance levels consistent with expected performance levels at the time the students graduate? This is clearly an outcome measure. The department head sought for the highest possible sequence placement and minimum time disruptions. These were based on the belief that, overall, these represent the mechanisms that would lead to maximizing the performance level of the group.

The learning event has to do with math programs designed for the college bound students. The department head uses the following generally available college entrance measures in the analysis of outcomes:the Preliminary Scholastic Aptitude Test (PSAT); the American College Testing Program (ACT); the Scholastic Aptitude Test (SAT) (usually called the College Boards); and the Advanced Placement Program (AP) of the College Board.

Just reporting mean scores would be inadequate to address the goal of *maximizing performance levels*. At issue was neither the mean scores nor the proportion taking the test; at issue was the proportion of the class scoring at a high level on these measures.

The publishers of these testing programs provide annual summaries of scores earned by the students in each building and in the district. These summaries provide frequency distributions showing the number of students at each performance level. Using these readily available summaries, these performance levels were defined as "satisfactorily high" by the department head:

For the PSAT (where the national mean is about 50):proportion of senior class scoring over 50 on the Math section, and proportion of senior class scoring over 60 on the Math section.

For the ACT (where the national mean is about 24): proportion of the senior class scoring over 20 on the math subtest, and proportion of the senior class scoring over 25 on the math subtest.

For the SAT (where the math mean is about 460): proportion of the senior class scoring over 500 on the math subtest, and proportion of the senior class scoring over 600 on the math subtest.

For the AP (where a score of 3 on a 5-point scale is considered passing): proportion of senior class taking at least one of the two math subtests on the AP, and proportion of the senior class scoring 3 or better on at least one subtest of the AP.

More consistent measures could have been defined. Since the means and standard deviations are known for the first three measures, standardized cutoffs (such as "proportion scoring above the mean" or "proportion scoring one or more standard deviations above the mean") might have been used. These would require some fairly substantial recoding, however. The categories chosen could be read directly from the publisher's summary sheets. Since the department head was more interested in trends than absolute values, the more easily used cutoffs were considered preferable.

To overcome idiosyncratic differences in graduating classes, the department head gathered the information for the most recent five classes. Three levels of comparisons were made.

First was a five-year longitudinal comparison for the percents above the predetermined cutoffs for the students in this building.

Second was a comparative study, for students in this building, of AP results above the cutoffs as compared to the percentage of comparable English scores above the cutoffs.

Finally, with the cooperation of other high schools around this one, comparisons were made of the proportion of students performing at designated high levels at this school compared to other schools.

Table 4.4 shows the results only for this department over a five-year period.

The lines headed by "% taking" are based on the number of tests reported on each publisher's summary report divided by the number of seniors in the graduating class. Even though some of the students taking the test are juniors, and even though some students take the test more than once, this figure is a satisfactory approximation in this instance. After all, it is the *trend* which is of interest, and not the absolute values. For comparisons, across years or across schools, it is reasonable to assume that the proportion of juniors and repeat-takers will stay fairly constant. The time cost necessary to separate out the juniors and repeat-takers would be substantial, for not only would these students need to be identified from the lists, but the frequency distributions and means would need to be recalculated. Additionally, by using the data summaries as they come from the publisher, there is no need to even know the names of the students tested. This is a great benefit, for it avoids having to obtain permission-to-use statements from each student.

For this school, the proportion taking the ACT is consistently high. In the Midwest, this is fairly commonplace. In fact, in Illinois, state scholarships are based on ACT scores, which leads to test-taking percentages beyond 90% in many schools.

In this school, the English department's programs for the college bound had a generally high reputation. With this in mind, the math department

Table 4.4. Test-Taking and High Performance Percentages in Tests for the College Bound over a Five-Year Period

Test	Category	Year of the 5-year Cycle				
		1	2	3	4	5
PSAT	% taking	51%	54%	53%	53%	54%
	%>49	10%	9%	11%	11%	12%
	%>59	2%	2%	2%	3%	3%
ACT	% taking	88%	86%	89%	87%	88%
	%>21	42%	46%	44%	48%	51%
	%>25	23%	24%	24%	25%	27%
SAT	% taking	21%	24%	18%	17%	20%
	%>499	5%	7%	6%	5%	7%
	%>599	1%	4%	3%	2%	4%
AP	% taking	7%	8%	9%	10%	12%
	%>2	6%	6%	7%	8%	11%

head decided that a trend analysis of advanced placement participation and results comparing math to English would be instructive. The results are shown in table 4.5.

Table 4.5 provides some good news and some bad news for the math department head. The good news is the upward trend in percentages taking one of the two math subtests of the advanced placement program; the bad news is that they started well behind the English department in this category, and are gaining but haven't caught up yet. Perhaps the most significant information in the table is that the upward trend in math cannot be immediately written off as part of a generalized upward trend in everything.

Finally, the department head obtained cooperation with 38 other high schools, each of whom reported the percentages of seniors in the designated high-performance categories for the last round of testing. These distributions are summarized in table 4.6. In this table, the percentages for the department head's students are identified with an asterisk. (These are real data collected by me in the 1985 High School Comparison Study, which I have been carrying out since 1983.)

In each column, the 39 values are ordered from highest to lowest. The column heading "% Tst" was explained earlier; the number of students shown on the testing report divided by the number of seniors in the graduating class. The other column heading were defined earlier.

The ranks for the school in question are quite variable. The highest rank is for the AP program, where they rank 6th on both percent tested and percent of the senior class with scores greater than 2. The lowest ranks occur with the SAT where they rank 16th on percent tested and 20th on the percent of the senior class in the two defined high-score categories. Since the percents tested on the SAT are generally much lower than those for the ACT, in this instance the ACT is the better choice as a comparative measure for a general scholastic aptitude test. For Midwest high school

Table 4.5. Advanced Placement Test-Taking and Performance for Math and English over a Five-year Period

| Department | Category | *Year of Five-year Cycle* | | | | |
		1	*2*	*3*	*4*	*5*
English	% taking	14%	13%	15%	14%	14%
	%>2	12%	12%	13%	12%	12%
Math	% taking	7%	8%	9%	10%	12%
	%>2	6%	6%	7%	8%	11%

Table 4.6.   How the Department Head's Percentages Compare to Those from 38 Nearby High Schools

Rank	ACT			SAT			PSAT			AP	
	%Tst	>25	>20	%Tst	>599	>499	%Tst	>59	>49	%Tst	>2
1	99	35	61	84	26	52	96	18	43	18	16
2	95	35	57	83	25	51	92	17	40	16	13
3	94	34	57	80	22	50	86	17	36	16	13
4	92	33	56	79	22	47	85	14	35	14	12
5	92	30	55	70	21	39	67	12	32	13	12
6	91	29	55	67	19	38	67	11	28	12*	11*
7	91	28	55	63	18	36	63	10	28	11	10
8	89	27*	54	59	15	33	62	10	27	11	10
9	88*	26	52	58	14	32	61	10	26	11	10
10	87	26	51*	43	14	28	59	10	25	10	9
11	85	25	50	42	14	24	57	9	24	10	9
12	84	25	49	33	13	24	54*	9	22*	10	8
13	82	25	46	33	13	22	47	8*	19	9	8
14	81	25	46	30	10	20	46	7	19	8	7
15	80	24	45	29	10	16	46	7	19	8	7
16	80	24	44	20*	9	16	44	7	18	8	6
17	80	23	44	16	6	12	41	6	17	8	6
18	78	23	42	15	6	12	41	6	17	7	6
19	78	22	41	14	5	10	40	6	17	7	6
20	78	21	40	12	4*	7*	40	5	17	7	6
21	75	20	39	10	3	6	40	5	17	7	5
22	72	19	38	10	3	5	36	5	16	5	5
23	71	18	37	8	3	4	36	5	16	5	4
24	68	18	37	6	3	4	35	4	15	5	4
25	68	17	35	5	2	3	33	4	15	4	4

26	67	17	35		32	4	15	3	3
27	66	16	34	see	32	4	13	3	3
28	65	16	34	note[a]	31	4	13	3	3
29	64	15	34		29	4	13	3	2
30	64	14	31		29	4	13	3	2
31	60	12	28		26	4	13	3	2
32	59	11	27		26	3	11	2	2
33	58	10	26		25	3	11	2	2
34	58	10	25		25	3	10	2	2
35	54	10	22		23	3	10		
36	53	10	21		22	2	9	see	
37	52	9	18		22	2	9	note[b]	
38	52	9	17		19	1	8		
39	47	8	13		17	1	8		

[a] The remaining schools on the list had too few students tested on the SAT to receive a summary report from the publisher.

[b] The remaining schools on the list were too small to have an AP program.

students, participating in the SAT is usually an indication of an interest in an out-of-state school. Since the rationale for seeking an out-of-state school is frequently not totally associated with scholastic aptitude, the lower ranking here is not worth too much attention.

4.2. Discussion

The learning event itself is a good choice. "The high school math program for the college bound" is broad enough to be generally understood, but not so broad that it cannot be defined accurately. Although not all students who say they are going to college actually do, the actual students who participate in this learning event can be named with relative accuracy.

The quality-with-equity issue suggests that a second learning event should also be evaluated: the high school math program for the noncollege bound. Table 4.1 shows that this group is smaller than the college-bound group but nonetheless substantial in size. Remember, however, that table 4.1 reflects information that was collected at different times. The information about college-going behavior was collected as the seniors completed their last year. The decision about highest possible placement was made much earlier. A school cannot have a "noncollege bound sequence level" because, at the time of initial entry into high school, these college-going decisions have not yet been made.

Although this learning event is department-based, this is not a necessary ingredient of all high school learning events. Writing, or more generally communications skills, would cut across departments. So would study skills and most affective learning events, including character education, extensively described in chapter 7. Cross-cutting learning events are worthwhile because they force a look at the relationships among departments and an awareness that there is overlap in what the departments are trying to do. Department-based learning events are nice because that is the way the high school actually is organized for instruction. Neither — department-based or cross-cutting — learning events should be used to the exclusion of the other.

At step 2, the primary decision-making authority is seen as being delegated to the department head who, in most situations, tries to make decisions which conform to a consensus agreement among the teachers. Is there anything wrong with this approach?

That's an empirical question. The answer is that it depends on how things come out. The only sure thing is that somebody in the high school's administration should have it be a regular part of his/her job to check on how things come out.

In support of the current state of things (delegating responsibility to the department), the issue is high school math. Quite obviously, the greatest concentration of knowledge about the content and teaching of math is in the math department. Are they not in the best position to make decisions about text selection, course design and sequencing, and student placement?

On the other hand, this delegation certainly opens the door to abuse. Without external monitoring, there is the tendency toward complacency — following the path of least resistance. Consensus agreements sink to the level of the least able or least willing of the teachers. There is a tendency to let the needs of the teachers take precedence over the best interests of the students.

Just because such a system is open to abuse does not mean abuse will occur. The consensus agreements might be primarily based on the needs of the students. That is why the issue should be resolved on the basis of empirical, not theoretical, evidence. Trend and comparative performance information, of the type gathered to evaluate this learning event, represent the type of empirical evidence that should be brought to bear on this issue. If such comparisons show that the students who come out of this math program attain levels of performance consistent with reasonable expectations, then the administration would be wise to not mess around with a good thing. If this is not the case, then the administration would be wise to intervene.

"Reasonable expectations" is the key phrase in the statement above. It is not fair to look at the outcomes and argue, "These must be reasonable because this is what we got." Once the data are available, it might be wise for the curriculum director or principal to bring in some impartial outside observers to help with interpretation. Likely candidates would be math department heads from respected high schools, or university people known to be knowledgeable about secondary school mathematics programs and the math needs of the college-bound student.

This issue illustrates the importance of step 2. The question is not who *could* make curriculum and instruction decisions in math, but who *does* make decisions. When an administrator responds to the step 2 question with, "Oh, that's a shared responsibility," you can be fairly certain that no one is really in charge and that an informal system has been developed to make the decisions. Now there is nothing wrong with informal systems that work, that is, where the student outcomes conform to the reasonable expectations of expert and impartial observers.

In any event, the dual implication of step 2 is that it is important to know who is in charge of making instructional decisions about a learning event, and that everyone concerned understands that this is where the responsibility has been placed.

In step 3, the rationale for having this learning event is quite clear. In the second part, changes expected in the students because of participation in the event, the response is interesting because it represents a very general response to the question. The students, in this response, are expected to be in the conceptually most difficult program sequence in which they can succeed.

Underlying this statement is the presumption that there exists a body of knowledge roughly called "math for the college bound." This is quite different from the assumption that the learning event consists of the sum of descrete elements with names like Algebra I Regular, Modified Geometry, Algebra II Superior, Analysis, Topics in Math, or whatever. In response to the question, "What do you expect of these students?," the answer is, "I expect them to progress as far as they are capable in this general body of knowledge called 'math for the college bound.' "

A real tendency will exist to respond to the question the other way. That is, the tendency will be to jump immediately to the math courses, and define expectations in terms of specific expected performance outcomes for the many individual courses. This cannot be avoided forever, but the issue of specific learning outcomes is better addressed as part of the continuity-of-instruction and formative measurement issues (measurement questions 3a and 3c). But at this point it is worthwhile to accentuate that the department is trying to offer a coordinated, interrelated math program for the college bound.

In a sense, this explains why this choice of learning event itself is a good one. One could have started with a series of learning events, one for each course (the learning event is Algebra I Regular, the learning event is Modified Geometry, etc.). Each of these is broad enough. Each is understandable, and the students involved are easy to identify. But the broader definition still has these characteristics, and requires a viewpoint that each course does not stand alone. Instead, it requires a viewpoint that each course is part of a sequence of courses that real students take, and that each sequence of courses, irrespective of level, should have continuity internally to that sequence and externally to the broader domain called "math for the college bound."

The issue, as shall be seen, is not trivial. Under the broader definition of the learning event, end-of-course tests are seen as formative, not summative. Course sequences replace the individual course as the primary unit mative. Course sequences replace the individual course as the primary unit of attention. The overall level of high performance for the senior class as a whole is the general outcome measure.

The department head's response to step 4 (What is the mechanism whereby growth occurs for this learning event?) reflects the commitment to highest placement along with some reference to the relationship between time-on-task and amount learned. The department head wants the student in the highest possible course sequence placement in which satisfactory performance can be maintained, and the maximum number of minutes of instructional time.

Once the commitment to maximize student performance levels is coupled with the assumption that there is a knowledge domain roughly called "math for the college bound," highest possible sequence placement is a sensible response. Think of the alternative: the student is *not* placed in the highest possible conceptual level in which s/he could be successful. The same amount of time will be spent in class (each course has the same number of minutes of instruction), but the challenge will be less than if the placement had been at the highest level where successful performance could be maintained. With the less-challenging placement, the student who could have moved further into this domain called "math for the college bound" will not do so. (Of course, there will be students who say, "I know I could handle the next course but I'm not interested in working that hard." Nonetheless, from the perspective of maximizing performance, the student should be aware of highest possible placement and encouraged to participate at that level.)

The other mechanism response, trying to maximize instructional minutes, is a good start. As a general rule, more instructional time leads to more performance. (I'll downgrade the old saw, "Practice makes perfect," to "Practice makes better, usually.") But, as has been discussed elsewhere here, it is not the time itself, but how the time is used, which is causally related to performance. The key is not time-in-the-seat, as the department head's statement implies; the key is opportunity-to-learn time. The shift to opportunity-to-learn time demands that more emphasis be placed on the availability and use of entry-level and formative measures such that opportunity-to-learn time can be maximized. But these will be addressed further under measurement question 3c.

The response to step 5 (content, classroom organization, teacher behavior, and expected student behavior issues) is pretty much what one would expect to find in most high school math programs. It is sort of interesting, in this writer's experience, to find that elementary school teachers are quite willing to regroup for instruction and use peer tutoring so that all students can be brought to mastery on important objectives. Somewhere around junior high school these practices begin to fade, and high school teachers rarely use either approach.

If each course, or each unit in a course, is seen as a discrete element, then the issue above is not so critical. But if each unit or course presumes the presence of entry-level skills necessary if the new material is to be understood, then procedures for bringing underprepared students to mastery before instruction begins are very important. Some math departments try to address this by having available a resource center, staffed by a math teacher, during the students' free periods, or by having before- and after-school review sessions. This might be a fertile area for developing specific remedial units on microcomputers which could be used by the student during out-of-class time.

On the one hand, to think that in the normal context of a class (30 students meeting five days a week for 36 weeks) all students can be brought to equal levels of mastery on all objectives is unrealistic; blindly optimistic might be better. On the other hand, to simply ignore the relationship between degree of mastery of entry-level requirements and amount of later learning is professionally unacceptable.

Although the measurement issues have been serially labeled step 6, the actual measurement transcends the learning event from start to finish. The six questions asked by the department head are coded under the four measurement question headings first developed in chapter 2.

The first question has to do with the accuracy of initial placements. Placement into one of the five ninth-grade, entry-level courses is done through traditional methods; that is, methods which depend heavily on past experiences such as courses, grades, test scores, and recommendations. Chapter 8 has a section that addresses the issue of measures used for groups as contrasted with measures used for individuals. As general group measures, these prior experiences are reasonably good predictors of future performance. This is why people develop confidence in these group measures; in general, they do a fairly good job.

But the individual student deserves better treatment. Some students who jumped through the appropriate hoops (were part of the group scoring over the 90th percentile, got a grade of B or better, and the nod from the junior high teacher) still do not have the entry-level skills for the course in which these experiences would, in general, predict success. Others who stumbled on at least one of the criteria may still have all of the entry-level capabilities for a higher placement than would be predicted, in general, from the experiences they have had.

In both chapters 2 and 3, an "entry-level skills" approach to course placement has been advocated. Under this approach, the department's teachers must take the time to define the knowledge and skills (and possibly study habits) a student must have to successfully *get started* in each course. These are the behaviors upon which the course builds, as new learning units are presented. If the entry-level behaviors have been defined properly (a process which will probably require substantial development time and several iterations), and the students can demonstrate that they have these entry-level behaviors before any new instruction begins, then reasonable diligence by student and teacher should result in satisfactory performance on the material which will follow.

The amount of shifting around shown in table 4.2 is quite substantial. The shifts are generally in an upward direction, indicating that the initial placements were too conservative — in general, students were placed lower than their performance levels later indicated were appropriate.

On the one hand, departmental philosophy is certainly contrary to being slaves of initial placement. Students are not locked into a sequence level. From this perspective, table 4.2 reflects a positive approach.

The cautiousness of the initial placement seems backward. It also seems contrary to the department head's goal of "highest possible placement wherein satisfactory performance can be maintained." As long as the logistics for course level shifts are not insurmountable (and this appears to be the case), it seems reasonable that, with respect to course content, downward shifts in sequence level would be easier for the student than upward shifts. Lower placements are too often based on a misplaced sense of compassion ("Since I cannot make up my mind between these two levels, I'll put you in the easier one and you can work your way up.") From the student's perspective, it would seem that erring on the side of too-high placement would be preferred over erring on the side of too-low placement.

This high level of moving around is only tolerable if one takes the perspective that all courses are independent of one another — an approach that ignores the concept of course sequences. Developing a sensible structure of continuity within each planned sequence seems counterproductive when such a large proportion of students participate in unplanned sequences. Some level of flexibility will always be necessary since no procedure for entry-level course placements will ever be entirely accurate, yet the high level of shifting observed here seems excessive. The entry-level skills approach has much to recommend it, since the placements would then be made on the basis of information (presence of entry-level skills in each individual) which applies directly to what will happen in the course to which the student is assigned.

Defining entry-level requisites for each course is worthwhile for reasons beyond appropriate initial placement. Once these necessary behaviors are defined, and students are placed on the basis of them, they should be assessed once again on the first or second day of class to make sure the performance competence has been maintained. If these are really required start-up behaviors, then instruction on the new material should not begin until all students have been brought to mastery.

That's easy to sit and write about; in practice, as noted earlier, high schools usually are not set up for this sort of corrective effort. With some forward planning, however, it can be done. A high school with which the author has worked implemented a first-day-of-class testing program of this nature with a carefully structured smorgasbord of remediation approaches for the first week. These approaches included microcomputer remediation packages, before- and after-school sessions, a resource center staffed by a teacher, and in-class peer tutoring. This commitment to bringing students to mastery on entry-level skills will pay dividends in higher later performance (Bloom, 1984).

In answer to the question, "Do students know what the performance expectations are for each course and sequence?," the answer found by the department head is, "Well, sort of." Short-term expectations are articulated. The students know what the next day's assignment is, and, generally, when unit or chapter tests will occur. Of course, the students also know about traditional semester testing schedules, and about generalized grading practices at the school. Maybe that's enough.

Still, the concept of total program for the college bound developed around planned sequences of courses keeps coming back. The student is not taking courses for the sake of taking courses; the student is learning mathematics. The student should not be allowed to "lose sight of the forest for the trees"; the student should be kept informed about how these specific units and chapters fit the grand scheme of things, this overall content called "math for the college bound." These links to the bigger picture don't have to occur daily or even weekly, and they don't have to be elaborate things. But some sort of mileposts should be erected as the student moves through this new territory.

The third question, labeled "3a" because it falls under the general heading of a formative measure, has to do with the continuity of the course sequences taken by the students. Once again the focus is on planned sequences, not independent, stand-alone courses.

The data were collected to looking at the math courses taken by the last graduating class at the high school. The students' four-year transcripts were on computer files. Developing the software to select off the math courses and find the frequency of each observed concentration of courses is not a particularly difficult or time-consuming task. Even for a district which does not have these records computerized at this time, the task of data-entry to carry out these analyses is not overwhelming. The results can be very instructive.

For those students who took only 2.0 units of math, 74% were in one of the seven planned sequences. For those with 3.0 units of math, 57% were in one of the prescribed three-course sequences, and for those with 4.0 unit of math, 51% were in one of the required four-course sequences. Turn the data around. Now 26% were in an unplanned two-course sequence, 43% in an unplanned three-course sequence, and 49% in an unplanned four-course sequence. Why?

The reasons have been reviewed before. Inaccurate entry-level placements are certainly a factor. The tendency for these placements to be too low contributes. The rule that students receiving an "A" grade are candidates for upward movement and those with a grade lower than a "C" are candidates for lower placement simply continues inaccurate policies used in initial placement. A grade of "A" in Algebra I Regular does not guarantee that the student has the appropriate entry-level skills for Geometry at the next highest level. Far better, it would seem, to take the time to find out before the shift is made.

The information on the textbooks strongly suggest that the department head make some changes in the procedures for textbook selection. The next time a committee of Geometry-Regular teachers looks for a new geometry text, an additional task should be assigned: determining the extent to which the selected text overlaps, in content, the prior course (Algebra I Regular) and the upcoming course (Algebra II Regular).

The rationale for seeking larger percentages of students in planned sequences and defining areas of overlap in the textbooks used in planned sequences falls under the same general heading: maximizing opportunity-to-learn time. Even in the best case, with two course sequences, 26% of the students were not in a planned sequence. The instructor in that second course cannot assume that students have had common experiences in the prior course. In this sort of setting, each course *must* be viewed as relatively independent of each other course; the instructor begins at the first page of the text and works through to the end, or as far as time allows.

Given that the content of sequences does make some integrated coherence (as it most certainly does in mathematics), this means that a lot of students will be spending seat-time during which they have no opportunity to learn anything — because they already learned the content being presented in a prior course. Both factors — overlapping textbook coverage and large percentages of students in unplanned sequences — contributed to this loss of opportunity time. There are costs to inaccurate placements and shifting students around. The costs are in terms of lost opportunity-to-learn time (note that there are not costs in seat-time), and these costs translate into lower levels of overall learning in this area called "math for the college bound." If the department head is sincere in the move toward attaining the maximum possible overall level of student learning, then this issue of course continuity in planned sequences, and the issue of getting larger percentages of students into the planned sequences, must be addressed.

The second issue of importance has to do with the students' "maintaining satisfactory performance levels" at the mandated highest possible placements. Course grades were accumulated for the last graduating class, and are shown in table 4.3. This fourth question by the department head is coded 3b, emphasizing the concept that courses are part of sequences; thus end-of-course grades are part of the formative measurement system.

If the grades assigned are consistent with actual levels of student learning, then the goal of maintaining satisfactory performance levels has generally been achieved. Very small percentages of students fail; and the percentages of near-failures (except in the Modified track) are also pretty low. Since it is well known that, for high school students, there exist reasons for failure and near-failure other than inability to learn the material — reasons which are often beyond the corrective efforts of the very best teacher — the failure rates cannot reasonably expected to be zero.

The lower grades at the Modified level, coupled with the information in table 4.1 that 47% of the students who enroll in this level of courses do not go on to college, should give the department head something to think about. On the one hand, the school isn't sure who is and is not going to college at the time enrollment in the Modified courses is made. Some students do not make this decision until the summer before, or even the week before, college starts. Thus it is a mistake to cut off the students' college option too early.

On the other hand, if high school is to be the last formal math learning experience a student is going to have, one does wonder about the choice that it will be Modified Algebra, followed by Modified Geometry. Somehow even statistics, emphasizing probability concepts, seems a better choice; but so do construction mathematics, some introduction to the math of economics or banking, or the math required for personal finance. The point is that the low grades in the Modified sequences may reflect a lack of relevance.

Grade weighting is common in high schools that have different course levels. Table 4.3 shows one such scheme. A grade of "A" in Regular

Algebra earns 4.0 grade-units; an "A" in Algebra-Superior, 4.5 units; and in Algebra-Adv.Pl. an "A" receives 5.0 points.

The interesting thing is that the higher-level sequences not only receive higher values for their grades but they also receive more high grades. This does seem like double-jeopardy.

Actually, it's triple jeopardy. The students in the highest level sequences move further into the domain of content called "math for the college bound," receive higher grades for doing it, and receive higher credit for the grades in the process. In the best of all possible worlds, the first ought to be enough.

But of course grades, and the amount of class-rank credit assigned to the grade, do accumulate into something called "grade-point average"; and grade point averages determine class rank; and colleges look at class rank on entrance applications. Never mind that the top-ranked student in one high school couldn't make it out of the lowest quartile in another; colleges still look at these ranks.

So, unfortunately, it isn't the best of all worlds. For too many apprehensive college-bound students and the apprehensive parents of apprehensive college-bound students, the concept of maximizing learning pales in the face of maximizing class rank. There is the fear that without heavily rewarding students for taking the more challenging sequences, students will opt for the "sure A."

That's too bad. Maybe by paying more attention to the measurement concern of keeping the student informed of where s/he is the broader domain called "math for the college bound" some of this short-sightedness could be overcome. At a minimum, however, the triple jeopardy should be replaced by double-jeopardy. That is, if grade-weighting is used, then the distribution of grades should be the same at all levels (the "Avg. Grade" in the last column for table 4.3 should be the same for all levels.) If grade weighting is not used, then the distribution of grades shown in table 4.3 is more appropriate.

The issue of the use of formative measures in instruction (the fifth question asked by the department head, coded 3c because it too is a formative question) overlaps considerably the issue of course continuity. The underlying concept in both cases is the link between opportunity-to-learn time and student performance. Formative measures, by definition, are given during the time of instruction. The results are to be used to inform the instruction, so that teaching is more precise.

The department head made two observations which are fairly typical of high school and college instructional programs. First, chapter and unit tests are given during a course, and the results are returned to the students.

But it is more the exception than the rule when the results of these tests are used to trigger a corrective process; that is, when they are used as formative tests, rather than outcomes tests.

Maybe that's the way it has to be. If the teacher with 30 students in the class slows down to remediate areas of trouble diagnosed by the unit test, the instructional process slows down. Those who didn't need the remediation have no opportunity-to-learn time during these remediation periods. Arlin (1984) calls this the "time-achievement-equality dilemma," and says that educators cannot have it both ways.

As a teacher, the easiest approach is to adopt one of the two extremes. A teacher who adopts what Eckland (1980) calls a "liberal egalitarianism" approach (with appropriate correctives and time, all normal students can be brought to the same mastery levels) will use the chapter and unit tests as formative, and take the time to correct deficits before going on. The other extreme argues that the first approach is contrary to equal opportunity; the students who mastered the material the first time around have no opportunity to learn during the remediation periods. The remediation will slow the pace of instruction down, they say, and performance potential for this group of students will suffer. The teacher who follows this approach uses the unit test as an outcome measure, not for formative information.

Like so many dichotomies, it is likely that few teachers are at either extreme position.

There is an analogy here between an entry-level skills concept for sequential courses and an entry-level skills concept for sequential chapters or units. It isn't that a student moving from Regular Algebra to Regular Geometry needs to demonstrate mastery of every concept presented in Algebra for the matriculation into Geometry. What is important is that the student demonstrate mastery, as Geometry begins, of those previously presented concepts upon which the geometry course will build. In the same manner, it probably is not necessary for the teacher to take time for correctives for every concept not mastered on the unit test; but if a concept not mastered is *critical to understanding a subsequent concept in the sequence*, then of course the time for remediation should be taken. If this is not possible, then the students who have not mastered this critical concept should be moved into a lower course sequence. To do neither is not just unsound educational practice; it is cruel.

Once a course-sequence approach has been adopted, then end-of-course tests are formative, not summative. Obviously, not all of the coverage of an end-of-course test in the earlier course (say in Geometry) will be part of the entry-level prerequisites in the next course (such as Algebra II). And it is likely that many of the entry prerequisites for the following course

(Algebra II) will not logically be a part of the end-of-course test in Geometry. But to the extent these two sets normally intersect, the information should be used for both classes. To carry out this information exchange is not a terribly difficult task, but it does require some front-end planning.

When there is communication across the courses in a sequence, on the first day the teacher has two sources of information about entry-level skills for that course. Some of these would have been tested in the prior exam from the feeder course; remediation on nonmastered skills could being immediately. The entry-level skills needed for the new course, but not part of the feeder course, would have to be tested separately.

Remember that it is the measures taken before (entry-level) and during (formative) instruction which have direct potential for improving the precision of instruction. Outcome measures can only help indirectly; they could improve instruction the next time around, if the teacher is teaching the same course and recalls the prior results. Entry-level and formative measures can improve the precision of instruction. They can be used by the teacher to decide to skip a unit, if the students indicate entry-level mastery, or teach only part of a concept, if the students indicate partial mastery on a formative test, or stay with a unit a little longer, if a lot of trouble is found by the formative measure. Each of these will increase the percentage of time students have an opportunity-to-learn something new, and increased opportunity to learn time will most surely translate into higher student performance.

The last question asked by the department head had to do with outcomes. By definition, the learning event had to do with college-bound students. Thus it was a reasonable choice to use, for this evaluation, the commonly known, national measures used by colleges for purposes of entrance and initial course placement.

Three of the tests listed (PSAT, SAT, AP) are published by Educational Testing Service in Princeton, New Jersey. The fourth (ACT) is published by American College Testing Programs in Iowa City, Iowa.

The measure used in these comparisons is "percent of the senior class at designated high performance levels." This is a good way to make comparisons because, to the extent possible, it puts schools all on the same metric.

High school comparisons are frequently made on the basis of metrics which are far less satisfactory. A common comparison unit is "number of Merit Scholars." Merit Scholars are identified on the basis of results from the PSAT. A certain cutoff score on the PSAT (computed by adding the math score to twice the verbal score) is identified each year (although these cutoffs tend to stay pretty constant). National Merit semifinalists are identified above one score, and letters of commendation are sent to those above a second and lower cutoff, but not at the semifinalist level.

Using "number of Merit Scholars" as a comparison measure has three problems. In the first place, comparing a school enrolling 2,000 seniors to one enrolling 200 seniors on the basis of "number of Merit Scholars" makes no sense at all. In the second place, the cutoff scores are designed to ensure reasonably representative proportions of semifinalist from each state. That is, the cutoffs vary by state. States with very high-performing students have higher cutoffs than states with lower-performing students. Finally, it must be remembered that the PSAT is a fairly short test, and is administered early in the junior year.

So "number of Merit Scholars" is not a good comparison basis; but neither is "proportion of Merit scholars in the senior class." The proportions for nearly all schools would be very small numbers; the numbers would be based on the most extreme end of the performance distribution; the numbers would be based on a very short test, given about halfway through the students' high school program; and the proportions cannot be compared across state lines because the cutoffs differ by state.

Despite all these problems, "number of Merit Scholars" is still, unfortunately, a common basis for making comparisons among high schools. The PSAT itself (upon which the Merit Scholar decisions are based) is still a short test, administered about halfway through the high school program. However, as long as one looks further down the distribution than at the extreme end, and uses the PSAT along with the other three common measures for the college bound, PSAT results can provide useful comparative and trend information.

Another tendency is to make comparisons on the basis of mean scores. These comparisons would be satisfactory as long as all students in every high school took the tests. But of course they don't. Suppose two high schools are of equal size and generally equal performance capabilities. In the first, the best two students take a college entrance test; in the second, all students take the test. Obviously the mean for the first will be much higher than the mean for the second, and comparing means scores will lead to an incorrect inference about overall performance at the two schools.

The decision to take a college-entrance test is between the student and the testing company. (This is at least generally true, although a few high schools known to me administer the PSAT to all juniors during school time and at school expense.) The decision to participate obviously has some relationship to the student's performance capabilitity, but other factors enter as well. These include the student's aspiration level, the socioeconomic status of the student and the community surrounding the school, and the traditions in this school. These other factors can lead an observer to erroneous conclusions if only the means, rather than percent scoring above designated high levels, are used for comparison. Consider data shown in table 4.7 on two schools who were part of a comparison study carried out by the author.

Although substantial proportions of students from both schools attend college, school A is in a more affluent area where the tradition has been to go to (or at least attempt to enroll in) out-of-state schools. School B has never had this tradition; most of its students go to state schools, where the ACT, not the SAT, is the most commonly used entrance test. Thus 5 of 6 students at school A take the SAT, and less than 1 of 20 from school B.

However, those who did take the test from school B were high performers. The mean score ranked them second in the list. Because school A tested nearly the entire distribution of students, their mean score is much lower, ranking them 21st. If, however, a common metric is used, namely "the proportion of the available seniors who scored 500 or above on the SAT," then school A is ranked first, and school B 21st.

This is the type of error commonly made by the media as they compare mean SAT scores for states. The reasons for taking or not taking the test are based on factors other than performance capabilities.

Developing a tradition of making comparisons based on means presents a second problem, a problem which is essentially an equity issue. If a small percentage of students is tested, they are obviously not chosen at random from the entire distribution; to some extent, at least, they are students from the upper end of the performance distribution. One fairly easy way to keep means high, or raise them, is to keep the group tested small, and concentrate improvement efforts on those students whose performance levels at the time of entry place them at the upper end of the distribution. Intensive efforts directed at a relatively small percentage of high performers could lead to high group means and, probably, to relatively high numbers

Table 4.7. Comparison of Ranks of Two Schools on the Basis of SAT Results using Two Comparison Methods

| | | | Rank (out of 39 high schools) | |
| | | | --- | --- |
School	*Test*	*% Tested*	*Based on Mean*	*Based on % >499*
A	SAT	84%	21	1
B	SAT	5%	2	21

of Merit Scholar semifinalists, since this measure looks only at the most extreme end of the distribution.

The other approach, maximizing performance capabilities for students at the entire range of performance distribution, certainly is more in the spirit of equity. Thus comparing on the basis of "proportion of senior scoring in certain high-performance categories" is superior to "mean score" on the basis of a better comparison metric and causes the school to pay attention to the entire distribution of students, and not just those at the upper end.

Of the four measures summarized in table 4.4, three (PSAT, ACT, and SAT) are basically aptitude tests, used to make decisions about the future. Only the AP test is an achievement test, designed to assess previously learned and fairly specific material. Of course, all tests measure previously learned material; no one comes from the womb hard-wired to do integral calculus. The ACT math subtest score is based on previous math experience. If the department head's goal of "highest possible placement under which satisfactory performance can be maintained" is fully implemented, then students will spend three years in high school, prior to taking the ACT math subtest, operating at their highest possible level. An increase in the number of students in the high-score categories should follow.

Although all four measures are sensitive to the conceptual level of the experiences the student has had in high school, the advanced placement program is the one over which a department head has the most direct control. Although some students can study for and take these tests in the absence of a formal advanced placement sequence in the school, the availability of courses is clearly the more effective approach. Not only must the courses exist but the "pipeline" to AP tests should be as full as it possibly can be, given the entry-level characteristics of the student body. And these decisions about who will at least start on the long, arduous road to scoring "3" or better on an AP test cannot be delayed, at least in mathematics, until the junior year. At the latest, the student must start this path as s/he enters high school. And it has been strongly argued previously that these decisions (who should at least be started in the path which eventually leads to the AP level course) should be based on the measurement of necessary entry-level skills for the sequence, and not be based only on past courses, test scores, or recommendations.

In table 4.4, the ACT and AP comparisons are most useful for this department head. Of the three general aptitude measures, the ACT is routinely taken by the greatest percentage of seniors. The percentage is fairly stable over the five year comparison period. The AP tests are useful for reasons cited above.

Both measures indicate an upward trend for this school. This is not so surprising because these are alterable variables. A school which has not adopted a policy of "highest possible placement where satisfactory performance can be maintained," and switches to this philosophy, should experience observable performance gains over a five-year period.

The information in table 4.5 suggests that the growth in math cannot be routinely written off as part of a generalized higher-performance trend across the entire school. The English department's proportion of those taking an AP test and scoring a passing grade is steady, not rising.

Table 4.6 indicates that for the AP and ACT measures, this school tends toward the top of the distribution of 39 schools in the comparison study. How the department head interprets this information will depend on two factors:(1) what was expected and (2) whether or not the trend line is moving down, holding steady, or moving up.

If everyone in the surrounding community thinks this school is the best possible high school in the area, the department head is going to be a little disappointed with the results. Given that the identities of the other 38 high schools is known, the department head ought to have a pretty good general sense of where this school should fall in the distribution.

But these generalized levels of expectations are not too precise; convincing oneself that "that's good enough" is too easy. The other approach, monitoring the trend lines, is preferable.

Two-point trend lines (e.g., comparing only this year and last) are not of much value. Two sequential graduating classes can differ substantially even though they are both drawn from the same, stable community of families. The department head should not respond too quickly to one-year changes. A two-year "trend" is not trend at all; a five-year trend is long enough; under certain conditions, a clear trend over three years is enough. There is a tendency to want to appeal to inferential statistics at this point, to test hypotheses about the significance of the slope of the trend line. One problem with this approach is that the students are obviously not randomly assigned to graduating classes (a whole variety of possibly interesting other factors, occurring about 18 years and 9 months earlier, accounts for these assignments). The second problem is that if the classes are reasonably large, small changes will be labelled "statistically significant" even when they don't have any real practical significance. It is interesting that, in this country, billion-dollar decisions are made on the basis of "eye-balling" trends in the Consumer Price Index, unemployment percentages, or the Gross National Product, without any demand for statistical tests of the significance of trends. But educators, so very often, seek the comfort of these tests, which so often provide precious little useful information.

All in all, the evaluate-your-instruction process with this learning event has turned up some interesting information. At the outcomes level, the department head sees the trends in the right direction for the two key measures, the ACT and the AP. While these upward trends might be coincidental, in the absence of knowledge about other external factors, it is reasonable to conjecture that the upward trends are caused by the philosophy of "highest possible placement." The task now is to continue monitoring the trends, to make sure they at least don't go down, and hopefully continue in the upward direction.

The evaluate-your-instruction process also uncovered some areas where improvements would be appropriate. Initial course placement does not seem to be very accurate, and improvements should be made. Grading practices might be improved.

Given that students are so frequently seen in unplanned sequences, and that little use of entry-level and formative measures was found, there is good reason to believe that the percentages of students in the highest performance categories have not yet been maximized. With better placement and more precise instruction within each leveled sequence, it is reasonable to expect that the upward trend lines can be maintained for some time to come.

Whether or not this can occur is an empirical question. It certainly is worth striving for, however.

References

Arlin, M. (1984). "Time, equality, and mastery learning."*Review of Educational Research* 54(1):65–86.

Bloom, B.S. (1984). "The search for methods of group instruction as effective as one-to-one tutoring."*Educational Leadership* 41(8):4–18.

Eckland, B.K. (1980). "Education in the meritocracy."*American Journal of Education* 89, 76–85.

5 The Learning Event: The Reading Comprehension Program in a K–8 Elementary School

Step 1

The learning event (step 1) is defined in terms of "reading comprehension", not just "reading." Reading comprehension means just what the title says: a student reads some passage for the purpose of comprehending what the passage means. Reading comprehension is generally measured by presenting a reading passage to the student and following the passage with questions such as "What is the main idea of this passage?," "Why did the woman need more money?" (an inference question), or "Which of the animals is Tom's favorite?" (probably a literal comprehension item). Questions about cause-and-effect relationships or the mood or purpose of the passage are also frequently asked.

Other important skills are frequently included under the general title of "reading."Shepherd and Ragan (1982, p. 229) include under "Forms of Reading" the ability to use maps, charts, graphs, tables, indexes, tables of content, dictionaries, and card files, as well as study skills such as skimming, outlining, summarizing, and note taking. These are important, but they are not reading comprehension skills. The first list consists of reference skills, the second of study skills.

Listening, along with reading comprehension, falls under the heading of "decoding skills" (speaking and writing are "coding skills"). Listening is not reading comprehension. Listening obviously helps one learn to be a better reader, first when sound-letter relationships help the beginning reader, then when discussions help confirm interpretations of printed material. For the new, inexperienced, or poor reader, listening is more efficient than reading. Such a reader can learn more, minute for minute, from listening than reading. Somewhere during the upper elementary school years, for those whose reading comprehension progress is normal, reading "catches up" with listening. Good readers can learn difficult information much faster by reading than by listening, a fact which has been lost on many univeristy professors who insist on lecturing on the material found in assigned texts. (For further elaboration of the concept of the relative effectiveness of reading and listening for reading levels, see Chall [1983, p. 85–87].)

The point is that reading comprehension, while obviously closely related to listening comprehension, is not totally dependent on it, especially as one learns to read better. Advanced readers can read and understand words they have never spoken or heard spoken. For the purposes of this chapter, it is important not to mix the evaluation of listening comprehension and reading comprehension in an evaluation.

The learning event is the K–8 program in reading comprehension. If the learning event had been defined as the grade 3 to 8 program then the initial acquisition stages, for most students, would have been bypassed and the issue simplified. But the issues are related; the method used for first learning to read is related to how well independent reading is facilitated (Chall, 1983, p. 43). Thus "learning to read" should not be treated as a separate learning event with an outcome of its own. Reading for comprehension includes the formative step of learning to read.

Thus the learning event is a good choice. Most adults have an intuitive understanding of the term "reading comprehension." Including in this learning event techniques to facilitate initial reading is necessary since learning to read for comprehension is certainly a part of a reading comprehension program. Excluding listening, reference skills, and study skills from the learning event also make sense. Obviously, taking notes, using a dictionary or table of contents, or appropriately interpreting charts can help one comprehend text better. Reading comprehension, in a literate society, is the key to cognitive development.

Too often, educators turn these two around. That is, they presume that a child is a poor reader because of inadequate cognitive capacity when the reverse is more commonly the case; the child does poorly on measures of cognitive capacity because s/he has not been appropriately developed as a good reader.

Step 2

What person or group of persons, closest to the classroom, can independently make decisions about content, classroom organization, teacher behavior, and expected student behavior?

The learning event is set in a self-contained school housing 670 students in grades K through 8. There are three teachers per grade level. Kindergarten and the first six grades are structured as self-contained classroms, and the junior high (grades 7 and 8) is departmentalized. Through grade 6, a portion of each day is set aside for a reading class; at the junior high, a unified language arts approach is used.

The principal is a female in her early 40s. Before arriving at this school six years ago, she spent 12 years as an elementary school teacher. This school is her first principalship.

At the time of her appointment, responsibility for the reading program was implicitly assigned to three teacher committees. The first, consisting of primary teachers, devoted itself to techniques for initial reading acquisition. The second committee, consisting of teachers from grades 3 to 6, met only when the adoption of new text materials was imminent. The junior high committee selected its own materials, generally without consultation from other staff.

The principal, during her first year in the school, observed two disconcerting pieces of evidence about the overall outcomes of this approach. Performance scores on locally developed and standardized measures taken at the end of grade 2 were excellent, indicating outstanding mastery levels of word analysis skills. That was good. However, relative levels of performance at grades 4 and 5 fell off substantially, and were not regained. Despite initial performance levels which were very impressive, the students exited junior high school at a much lower level relative to their national cohort. Additionally, the junior high teachers were uniformly critical of the students' capabilities to read and critically respond to the literature program developed for them.

With this evidence in hand, and responding to the growing literature extolling the virtues of schools in which the principal functions as instructional leader, this principal decided to take direct and personal control of the K–8 reading program. This chapter reflects the evaluation results which have accrued over the five-year period of her program leadership. (Again, as in chapter 4, the information in this chapter is not based on any one school, but is a composite of observations made by me over the past 15 years in quite a number of different school districts.)

In this case, given the evidence at hand, it seems reasonable that the principal would exercise this type of leadership. Sometimes educators generalize too far about matters like this. There must be many cases where a committee of teachers is a better choice for the primary decision-making role; where putting a weak or poorly trained principal in this position would cause serious damage to a good program; where each teacher, working independently, does precisely the right thing without enforced structure; or where a system like the one which this principal initially found was working quite adequately. To say, "It is always best to have . . ." is silly. A good way to operate is to find a way that works; a better way is to find a way that works better. The standard of practice (the best teacher-learner model) for one school may differ in another. The evaluate-your-instruction process should help in efforts to find the standard of practice for a given situation.

Step 3

Why is this learning event being held in the first place?

That is, what changes are expected in students because of their participation in this learning event? The answer to the first part is pretty obvious. Reading is inextricably entwined with the three general purposes of school: to function as a citizen, for vocational preparation, and to strive for self-actualization. Additionally, as Stroud (1964, p. 113) says in his usual direct manner, "In seeing how a child learns to read and in observing how the ability to read grows from the preprimer and the primer to Carlyle, Darwin, Shakespeare, Gibbon, or Einstein, we can understand a great deal about mental development."

The response to the second question is a little less obvious. Shepherd and Ragan suggest these outcomes for a reading program (Shepherd and Ragan, 1983, p. 222): "(1) Extending and enriching the experiences of the child; (2) broadening interests and tastes in reading; (3) fostering the personal social adjustment of the child; (4) providing worthwhile recreational interests and skills; (5) encouraging critical analysis of ideas; (6) developing resourcefulness in locating information; (7) promoting self-direction; and (8) achieving satisfactory progress in such basic reading skills as word recognition, vocabulary development, comprehension and speed."

The principal, in reviewing lists like this, decided that items (1) through

(7) are the essence of what integrates all of the programs in this building; they are not uniquely reading issues. Math, science, art, music, and physical education programs would legitimately include items (1) through (7), as long as the last word in item (2) were appropriately changed for each area. Additionally, item (8) gives equal recognition to "word recognition, vocabulary development, comprehension, and speed." Believing that word recognition and vocabulary develpment do not precede but follow better reading, the principal decides to concentrate on comprehension with adequate speed.

Although it was earlier argued that including initial reading acquisition and reading comprehension in the same learning event was appropriate, the mechanism, organization, and evaluation issues will be facilitated by keeping them separate at this time. Chall (1967), in addressing the issue of optimum ways of approaching initial reading acquisition, comments that the "code-emphasis method, i.e., one that views beginning reading as essentially different from mature reading and emphasizes the learning of the printed code for spoken language, produces better results than 'meaning emphasis' methods." She cautions that this may not be true of every child. In her later book (Chall, 1983) she addresses the dangers of pursuing this philosophy too long. Once the child has "broken the code," reading, not code, must be emphasized (although more advanced decoding skills can still be taught in context).

The principal separates her response to the question "what changes are expected of the student because of participation in this learning event" into more levels than just the "learning to read" and "reading comprehension" levels mentioned previously. Generally following the stages of reading development proposed by Chall (1983), she states these expected changes.

Level 0

In the most efficient and direct manner possible, the children will be brought to a mastery of necesssary prereading skills. This includes recognition of what letters are, that combinations of letters are called words, that a word means something, and that groupings of words mean something, too. Later this level includes identifying and naming the letters and reproducing at least those letters which appear in the child's name. Cawley, Cawley, Cherkes, and Fitzmaurice (1980) measure aspects of prereading (which Cazden [1974] calls metalinguistic awareness) under headings like Letter

Recognition, Picture-to-Picture Rhymes, Sound-Picture Relations, Visual Synthesis, and Auditory Picture Rhymes.

The principal's objective is for each student to move from level 0 to level 1 as quickly as possible, consistent, of course, with each child's capabilities.

Level 1

In the most efficient and timely manner, each student is to master a series of requisite decoding skills. This initial reading or decoding stage includes specific objectives about the sounds of initial and final single consonants and common consonant blends; a small sight vocabulary corresponding to the first stories in the basal reading series used; matching a dictated phoneme (teacher says "those" or "with" for initial or final sound of "th") to the appropriate grapheme (the printed "th"); matching words which have the same vowel sounds; and using common prefixes, suffixes, and compound words. Based on the textbooks used in the district, the principal identifies 47 specific skills of these types.

Chall (1983) points out that at level 0 children, faced with a book which includes pictures and print, draw meaning from within themselves. The print offers little help, since they don't know what the words mean. But as the code of level 1 is presented and internalized, the child begins to pay very close attention to the print (particularly if there are inadequate pictures and the material is unfamiliar). This is where her term "glued to the print" emanates.

As before, the principal's main objective is to move out of level 1, where the child is not yet really reading, into level 2 as quickly as the child is capable of making this shift.

Level 2

Level 2 has the purpose of ungluing the child from the print. The principal's objectives now shift to maximizing each student's experience with stories which are known to the child. Repeated exposure to a core sight vocabulary, used in sequences so that the meaning confirms something already known by the child, is the vehicle to this "confirmation and fluency" (Chall, 1983, p. 18).

At this level, the child is still dealing with reading skills, not really reading comprehension. The principal's objective once again is to have the child move to the next level as quickly as each child's capabilities allow this shift. This is particularly true here, for at level 3 the child can begin reading independently.

Level 3

Level 3 presumes sufficient sight vocabulary, confidence, and fluency so that the student can use reading to find out new information through reading. At the outset, the child still learns more efficiently by listening than by reading (Chall, 1983, p. 86), but this situation will reverse during the transition through level 3. The material itself is new to the child and should be presented from a single viewpoint. Normatively, Chall places level 3 at roughly grades 4 to 8.

The principal of a K–8 school might be tempted to stop here. However, even if her school were "normal," there would still be some segment of the group who, even as early as grade 4, are well beyond the type of material needed at level 3. Thus she establishes one more objective: that the proportion of children who exit grade 8 reading beyond level 3 will be maximized.

Level 4

Level 4 material abandons the restriction of a single viewpoint. The multiple viewpoints require the student to do some analyzing (breaking things apart to see how they differ) as well as some synthesizing (seeing how the material fit into what the student already knows).

Overall, the principal's response to "what do you expect them to learn in this event called reading comprehension?" has two dimensions. First, the road to being a competent, adult reader consists of the phases or levels defined in a manner corresponding to Chall's (1983) levels, and second, that each student should progress through the levels as quickly as possible consistent with his/her capabilities. The principal is interested in having each child maximize his/her level of reading comprehension.

Now, there are those who will disagree with one or both of the principal's two dimensions. The author has had the opportunity to present this philosophy of reading comprehension improvement to many groups of teachers. There are always those in the audience who nod their agreement and affirmation; those who just nod sleepily; and then those who disagree, sometimes fervently. And that is one of the strengths of the evaluate-your-instruction approach; now each reader has a pretty clear idea of the principal's basic philosophy about reading comprehension. A foundation for further discussion has been established. Unambiguous communication has much to recommend it. One might conjecture that ambiguity might be better in the short run, for staff harmony is facilitated if no one states a specific point of view.

As was stated in the introductory chapter, the viewpoint taken in this book is that clarity of communication is central to the process of improvement of instruction in schools. Now the teachers, parents, school board, university professors, and any other interested party have a basis for task- and problem-centered discussions about what the purposes of a reading program are, and about the changes expected in children because they participate in the program. For this particular situation the discussions will focus on at least three issues.

First, the technique used at level 1, where the child is seen as "glued to the print," learning the specific decoding objectives in a code-emphasis method. Some common current practices have more of a meaning-emphasis than a decoding-emphasis. Basal readers and initial reading approaches that let the child prescribe, in some manner, the type of material most meaningful to him/her fall under the heading of meaning-emphasis. Phonics is a code-emphasis approach.

At this time, a somewhat different orientation to what should happen at level 1 is surfacing. Some researchers (Smith, 1983; Clay, 1979) propose that reading and writing represent a language of their own, related to but not totally dependent on the language of speaking and listening. With the recognition that written language is a language parallel, not secondary, to oral language, theories about the acquisition of written language become more focused on the language acquisition process itself. In this view meaning is everything. Decoding, for the sake of decoding, is out. Meaning is the driving force behind language acquisition.

A second area of disagreement will be generated from the principal's dismissal of the first seven general reading objectives listed earlier. Included here were objectives dealing with enriching experiences, developing tastes, fostering personal social adjustment, and promoting self-direction. In presentations to teacher groups, the author always finds one group of teachers who fear that this approach is too achievement-, growth-, and performance-oriented. They fear that the overall objective of maximizing individual performance capability will take the enjoyment out of reading. By implication, those with this perspective are urging that the process be slowed down; that children be allowed to stay at certain levels for some time period after they have achieved mastery so they can read comfortably.

An absurd way to restate this issue is as follows: Is the goal of a reading comprehension to produce mediocre, happy readers or excellent, less-happy readers? Put in that manner, the issue no longer makes any sense at all. Is it not more reasonable to believe that those who read best are more positive about reading than those who read less well? Are these well-meaning teachers really doing the children a long-term favor by *not* maximizing performance? After all, the better one reads, the larger the wealth of printed materials available. Change and improvement, obtained at the cost of being fed a steady reading-class diet of material which is a little beyond the current functioning level, is difficult, sometimes painful. But it will always be that way, whether or not a delay is built into the system. The joy of reading, one can conjecture, is threatened more by boredom than challenge.

The point of this elaboration is that the school cannot have it both ways. If the principal responds, "Well, if you think I'm pushing too hard, slow the process down," than the goal of maximizing reading comprehension performance is seriously compromised. Chall (1983, p. 84) comments: "To reach the most mature stages of reading is of value to both the individual and to society. No evidence suggests that too many highly literate and highly educated people are a burden to society." If the principal believes that the overriding concern of a reading comprehension program is maximization of performance for each individual, then that should be the program all teachers implement.

Step 4

What is the mechanism whereby the person in charge believes growth occurs in this learning event?

There are actually two mechanisms involved here. At levels 0 and 1, and to a certain extent in level 2, the material constitutes a "finished system." Addition and subtraction are finished systems; so also are the common punctuation and capitalization rules. A finished system is a specific and defined body of content that the teacher knows and about which the student must learn. There is no real reason for discussion, at level 0, about which shapes represent letters and which do not; or that the shape "B" is called "bee" and, in fact, is called "capital bee"; the "B" comes between "A" and "C" in the alphabet. At level 1, the initial and ending sounds of the consonants, the sounds of blends like "th" need no discussion.

The mechanism for a finished system is to maximize opportunity-to-learn time, a concept which has been distinguished in this book from the more-common "time-on-task." Maximizing opportunity-to-learn time means not teaching a skill the child has already learned; teaching only until mastery is indicated, and not thereafter; not moving into an area until the child has shown the necessary entry-level skills. Maximizing opportunity-to-learn time demands good measurement and record keeping.

Operating parallel to these finished system objectives are what might be termed "pure reading comprehension objectives." A "B" in English is always a "B"; when used initially in a word it always has that sound. In computation, "6 + 4" is always "= 10," as long as the operation is in the common base-10. Once mastery is attained by the student, neither of these will adopt a new meaning from the context that surrounds it. Once these kinds of objectives are mastered, the child moves on to bigger (and hopefully better) objectives.

Reading is quite different. One of the first words a child learns is "cat." At that point, this simple word signifies an animal; presumably a lovable little animal. "Cat" doesn't fall away as bigger things are mastered; it cannot become automatic like "6 + 4 = 10" because its meaning expands and the reader must infer the meaning from context. "Cat" can be a tiger or a lion; a fast-talking, classy dresser; a large tractor; a way of behaving.

Finished systems are objectives-driven; they are based on a known, and usually logically sequenced, set of specific objectives. Reading comprehension is difficulty-driven. Once the student has become "unglued from the print" (has moved through level 2 above), that student is a reader. The task now is incrementally to keep ever more difficult material in front of the student.

Thus the mechanism still involves opportunity-to-learn time. The principal's response at step 3 consistently involved moving the student to higher levels in minimum possible time (consistent with the each student's capabilities). She is trying to maximize opportunity time. Holding a student at a reading level which is already mastered is equivalent to spending three more class periods on reading a clock after a student already knows everything which will be "taught" in those three days. A student cannot become a better reader unless the student has a chance to do so.

It is important, in terms of this mechanism, to keep separate the concept of "becoming a better reader" and "reading something which has never been read before." Many excellent readers use simple novels about cowboys, detectives, or romances for diversion. Each provides a new plot, some new characters, some new diversions; but if they are already excellent readers and frequent readers, then this type of reading is unlikely to improve seriously their reading level or expand their vocabulary. In a similar manner for a student, just because the material is new does not necessarily mean it will "stretch" the student into being a better reader.

To the question of mechanism for growth in reading comprehension, the principal stresses once again maximizing opportunity-to-learn time. With reading, this means keeping material in front of the student which is at a challenging enough level that the student has an opportunity to grow, as a reader. Chall (1983, p. 5) says, with respect to reading growth, that it depends on ". . . how much the reading program stresses language and vocabulary growth and provides sufficiently challenging reading materials." Addressing the principal's observed problem of high performance early which does not keep up as the years go by, Chall (pp. 7–8) comments, "Each stage of reading development has its own tasks and crises, but the 4th grade seems to present a major hurdle. . . . Evidence points to the need for more challenging instructional materials. Materials in reading textbooks (basal readers) have tended to focus on enjoyment and fun, presenting narrative fiction almost exclusively even during the middle and upper elementary grades."

Of course, the idea is not to expose the students to difficult material and back away. This would lead to frustration and take away the fluency gained at level 2. The student, faced with challenging material, needs to take some risks about the meaning of unfamiliar words and the inferences to be drawn from conceptually more-difficult passages. The teacher needs to draw the student out and reinforce or correct, as appropriate. But these will be covered further as part of step 5.

One more comment before moving on: A student does a lot of reading in school for purposes other than becoming a better reader. The reading material which is part of math, science, or social studies will (hopefully) represent new information but not necessarily at a challenging reading level. In these areas it is the information and concepts presented, not growth as a reader, which are of primary concern. Here opportunity-to-learn time is maximized by trying to keep the redundancy of the concepts and information to a minimum, not by making sure the reading level is "stretching" the child.

Step 5

What combination of content, classroom organization, teacher behavior, and expected student behavior is to be used?

For this learning event, there are five issues which are interlocking and transcend the reading levels proposed earlier. These have to do with "finished system" objectives; reading comprehension objectives; a "previewing" need at the first four levels; the interaction among the student's age and developmental level, test methods, and reading level; the choice between listening or reading as the more efficient learning mode; and the issue of increasing ranges of performance within a cohort group as the students progress through the grades.

1. Finished system objectives can be listed and monitored. There is a finite number of them (this principal identified 47, but the number depends on the materials used and how groupings are done) and, generally, there is a logically defensible way to sequence them. The trick is to get the task done as efficiently as possible. In chapter 9, information system needs and criterion testing needs for this type of system are described in some detail. The process involves making sure that the grade of initial instruction is agreed upon by the teachers, and that the grade at which all normal students are expected to enter at mastery is defined similarly. Measures have to be in place to monitor performance on the objectives, as will summary programs to provide the instructional leader with a basis for assuring that satisfactory progress is being made.

The organization would involve what is generally termed "direct teaching," if this is taken to mean a teacher-dominated and -controlled environment, drill and practice, and redundancy until mastery is shown by the student. The teacher is the expert; the students' opinions are not necessary in this setting. For the words these beginning readers will see, a "b" used as an initial consonant always has the same sound; no discussion is necessary. If this is giving a picture of a dull, authoritarian classroom, consider these comments from Sirotkin (1983, p. 25): "The good news is that this monotonous scenario of teacher talk to total class and student work on written assignments is consistent with the recommendations emerging from current research on effective schools."

However, this classroom organization, teacher behavior, and expected student behavior combination is not always the best, as shall be seen presently in the reading comprehension situation. But for finished system areas, like word analysis skills, computation, or common punctuation skills, the mechanism is to maximize the opportunity-to-learn time for each student. That means keeping the student working at areas the student is ready for but has not yet learned, and keep at it until the student can demonstrate mastery on that objective, and then move on. The teacher should be in control and get the job done; there is time for interaction and socialization later.

2. Reading comprehension objectives. In this instance, the principal has stated that the mechanism for becoming a *better* reader is first to identify the student's current reading level and then provide material which is incrementally more difficult. By design, this material is not easy for the student, but the student is encouraged to persevere, make some estimatations, and take some risks in an attempt at understanding. The teacher's

role is to reinforce those instances where the risks and estimates were the right ones, and correct those instances where the student has headed down a blind alley. The teacher needs to question the student about issues of comprehension. Did the student appropriately interpret the main idea, the mood of the author, the next logical thing a main character will do? The students now need to interact with the teacher, and listen to one another, for reinforcement and confidence-building. If the reading range in the class is not terribly heterogeneous, reading groups would be a satisfactory organization to accomplish this. The children would read a story silently and alone; the group function would be for confirmation, reinforcement, and diagnosis of problems that exist.

Once again, there may be readers who are saying, "Wait a minute! That's contrary to what the noted expert Ghadzomoskov (or whomever is doing a speaking tour about this year's theory of reading salvation) recommends!" After all, this is not a reading book, it's an evaluation book. The evaluate-your-instruction model draws out, from the person in charge of the learning event, how s/he believes growth occurs in an area. The principal has stated what she believes. If any part of this is contrary to the teachings of this year's international expert, a basis for a professional discussion has been established. Now Ghadzomoskov will be pinned down too; pitted against "reading comprehension grows best when the student is consistently faced with material designed to stretch his/her reading level," a response like "language acquisition must be viewed as a schemata representing a theory of knowledge" is pretty pale. "I didn't ask how the watch was built; I asked you what time it was!" — the principal doesn't want to know how the English language developed; she wants to know how to direct the teachers to develop in the students' maximum levels of reading comprehension. If someone can propose a mechanism for maximizing reading comprehension empirically verified as more effective, then that alternative should be discussed. As in faculty meetings at a university, issues don't seem to be seriously discussed until there is a motion on the floor.

The issue is not "much ado about nothing." It is obvious, from observation, that teachers do not agree on these mechanisms; it is likely that most teachers never seriously consider which mechanisms would maximize growth in reading comprehension. Some have no reading groups; reading is individualized or else the class is treated as a single, homogenous group. Some use the reading group for oral reading. Many believe students should never be frustrated, never be faced with material so difficult that have to take risks and make estimations to get a sense of meaning. Many believe vocabulary and word knowledge growth precedes comprehension growth, and they have the students learning words, not reading passages. Many think study skills and paragraph analysis techniques are the route to better reading. Unless someone, preferably the person in charge of the learning event, states with some clarity what s/he thinks is the standard of practice (the best presentation method) for this learning event, then there is no basis for discussion. Unless there exists an agreed-upon standard of practice in the district, someone will hear Ghadzomoskov (I hope the reader knows this is a purely fictional name.) speak and jump on the bandwagon. That doesn't mean the district sticks to the current standard of practice as if it's one of nature's fundamental building blocks; if evidence indicates that some changes are sensible, then the standard of practice is redefined.

3. Previewing needs as the student makes the transition from level to level. The student at level 0 is just developing the necessary prereading capabilities; but even before level 0 is completed, level 1 should be anticipated. At level 1, the student will need to have had experiences with the sound relationships in the word analysis objectives. This experience can only come from being read to. At level 2, the student needs to have very familiar material such that the confidence and fluency can be developed so the child can "unglue from the print." The teacher can establish this familiarity by oral reading while the student is at level 1. At level 3, the student begins reading new material, with unfamiliar words and a one-dimensional new idea. These should be previewed in level 2. Finally, at level 4, the student will begin seeing multiple views, and can be previewed in level 3.

The content here is obvious: the appropriate material for the next level. The organization is whole-group. The teacher reads and the students listen. Discussion is not as critical, since the material, while beyond the student's current reading capabilities, should have been selected such that it is not beyond their listening capabilities.

4. The interaction of testing and age/development of the student. In chapter 8, an appeal is made to bypass, with children in kindergarten and grade 1, the normative testing of outcomes. The rationale was based on substantial age, experience, and developmental ranges within a group of students grouped as a class.

This should not be taken to include entry-level and formative testing. These, after all, are the key to precision teaching and maximizing opportunity-to-learn time. When the students have attained level 3 and above, the usual reading comprehension measures (a new passage followed by questions) are appropriate. These can be administered in a group setting. When the students are at levels 0 and 1, which usually corresponds to the time they are in the early primary grades, testing becomes more tedious.

Young children have a short attention span; the tester will have to have a variety of tasks available if attention is to be maintained. Young children have a fairly limited set of response capabilities. They can point, listen, make a mark with crayon, or manipulate physical objects. They have the tendency to want to please — to mark the first thing they see, or the largest or smallest, or anything that has a touch of familiarity around it. And they have not yet developed an experience base with testing; they aren't familiar enough with this area to be able to say, "Oh, that's just another test." The most difficult element, in terms of logistics, is that testing with the young children will have to be done individually, or with groups small enough so each can be carefully monitored.

None of the above is presented to support an argument that the formative evaluation step should be bypassed with young children. The tester, usually the teacher, only needs to be aware of these issues. The testing is for the purpose of diagnosis; the testing is done for the purpose of finding out what is needed next in the development of the child. This type of testing is based on an expectation of success; an expectation that each child is on an upward path. The teacher diagnoses to know the times at which to move the child along, for the purpose of maximizing opportunity-to-learn time.

Earlier, the statement was made that at levels 3 and above, reading comprehension could be measured by the usual techniques (silently reading a new passage and the questions which follow it). Group measurement can be used. This, too, will likely generate some controversy. Some of the basic assumptions of group reading tests are sharply criticized by current writers. These critics disagree because the teacher (or tester), not the child, selects the materials, and that the passages are disconnected and not part of a longer discourse. Harste, Woodward, and Burke (1984, p. 226) argue that under the usual reading comprehension conditions, ". . . such data give us a picture of what reading looks like under unnatural conditions. Under normal conditions we read things for which we have a background and in which we are interested, go to materials with a host of expectations about what we will find there, locate the materials in a situational context rich with signs to help us access appropriate anticipatory texts, and use colleagues and friends to discuss and clarify our understandings."

The viewpoint is appealing but the teacher still needs help making decisions. If children work together how does the teacher know each is contributing and learning? If the passage must be embedded in a much longer discourse the time needed for assessment will be greatly increased. Is there evidence that testing the usual way (disconnected, short passages) provides different information than testing short passages in the context of a longer one? Additionally, the testing task, already difficult logistically, becomes even more so if each student is to be tested over materials in which s/he has an interest.

5. The range of performance in reading comprehension increases as the students move through the grades. For most students, growth in mathematics computation or concepts is closely associated to the instruction which occurs in school. One doesn't generally learn long division, addition of fractions with unlike denominators, or (unless one is Newton or von Leibniz) differential calculus independent of the school setting. Since the amount of time available for mathematics instruction is limited by the need to teach in other areas as well, one can expect mathematics growth to be somewhat controlled.

Reading comprehension is different. Once the student becomes a reader, printed information is part of life in and out of the school on a fairly constant basis. The range of independent reading done outside of the time period called "reading class" will probably vary between "an awful lot" to "almost none." When the author tested students (testing done in March) such that the conceptual level of the passages conformed to each student's current functioning level (see Wick [1983] for a further description), in a district where the average student, on a nationally normed test, read at about the 60th percentile, the ranges shown in table 5.1 were recorded. (Section 9.4 shows how these kinds of data can be gathered quite easily through computer-adaptive testing procedures.)

The ranges shown are actually underestimates since the students at percentile ranks 5 and 95, not 1 and 99, are used for the comparisons.

Table 5.1. Range of Reading Performance by Grade When Students are Tested at Their Functioning Reading Levels

Grade	*Reading Level for a Student at*		*Range*
	PR = 5	*PR = 95*	
1	Nonreader	Middle 3	3 years
2	Middle 1	End 4 — Beg. 5	3.5 years
3	End 1 — Beg. 2	Middle 6	4.5 years
4	Middle 3	Middle 8	5 years
5	End 3 — Beg. 4	Middle 9	5.5 years
6	End 4 — Beg. 5	Middle 11	5.5 years
7	Middle 5	Beyond gr. 12	7+ years
8	End 5 — Beg. 6	Beyond gr. 12	7+ years

(This smaller comparison range is used because the extreme scores frequently are unstable.) Additionally, the tests used to gather these data only included passages up to a mid-high school difficulty level. College-level passages probably were needed to challenge the best readers in grades 7 and 8. Nevertheless, even with these conservative estimates, the increasing range by grade is quite clear. This increasing range has some obvious implications for content, teacher behavior, expected student behavior, and measurement.

By grade 3, a class is likely to have students operating at different levels. By grade 6, students in the same room might be two levels apart. In these middle grades, some students will learn more efficiently if instruction is oral; others are better off with printed instruction. If the testing is to match the current level, then test materials must differentiate within a room (striking still another blow at the common practice of testing all students at a grade level with the same level of a standardized achievement test).

If one crudely interprets the onset of level 4 as "high school level reading," then table 5.1 shows that level 4 readers begin appearing around fourth grade (remembering that the data for the table were collected in March). These readers, according to Chall (1983), need material from a broad range of fiction and nonfiction with varying styles and content, and which frequently presents a multiplicity of different viewpoints. Students at this level can deal with articles in *Time* magazine or the *New York Times*.

Thus, at the same grade level, different levels of reading exist. From another viewpoint, a given reading level appears across a wide range of grades. A reading program which is a slave to its basal reading series can hardly respond to these ranges. The instructional program needs to be organized such that other materials (trade books, newspapers, magazines, etc.), coded to the correct reading level, can be matched to student needs in the face of these wide variations.

But this leads to the issue of measurement.

Step 6: Measurement issues.

As usual, the measurement issues will be covered under the general headings of entry-level measures, student expectations, formative measures, and outputs. The first three — and in particular the first and third — inform instruction and are therefore of particular importance to an ongoing instructional program. All of the preceding mentions of maximizing opportunity-to-learn time and efficiency have presumed satisfactory measures.

1. Entry-level measures are necessary at each developmental reading level. They become less well-defined as the principal's developmental level (patterned after Chall's, 1983), gets higher.

The entry-level measure for level 1 would include some common pre-reading skills. These were discussed earlier, and include alphabet knowledge, rhyming capabilities, demonstrated understanding between words and sounds, and some gross motor skills for printing and marking. The principal, as noted earlier, has listed these necessary skills. In this instance, the actual measures are less difficult than the logistics of obtaining the information. All of the warnings about special problems with testing young children need to be heeded in gathering these data.

The entry-level measure for level 2 is the demonstrated mastery of the list of word analysis objectives. The precise number of these would vary with instructional materials and with techniques used to consolidate some objectives; this principal identified 47. This transition would be occurring, for the average child, about the middle of grade 2. Some of the limitations on testing young children can now be relaxed, since standardized tests have long tested groups at grade 2, but for children who are making the transition earlier, or seem to have trouble attending for long periods, a more individualized approach would be needed.

Now these first two transitions are not all that precise. Additionally, not all students move into level 2 via a word analysis route. Some children who have mastered almost none of the 47 objectives might demonstrate they can read — one hopes the teacher is flexible enough to back off from the word analysis at that point. Others will master the objectives but still be unable to become "unglued from the print." Another way will be needed. But it is reasonable to expect that the entry-level measures for levels 1 and 2, described above, will be satisfactory for most. The interpretive judgment of a teacher familiar with the child is critically important at these points.

If the first levels were not all that precise, the remaining transitions are even less so. Instructional materials do not come at discrete levels, like the energy levels of the electrons in an element. The principal establishes the following rules for obtaining rough judgments about reading progress in her school. (The entry levels for levels 3 and above are modeled after suggestions by Chall [1983, pp. 98–100.])

Enter level 1: Mastery of prereading objectives; teacher recommendation.

Enter level 2: Mastery of all 47 word analysis objectives and/or teacher recommendation.

Enter level 3: Demonstrates normative performance on a reading comprehension test designed for use toward the end of grade 3. That is, in percentile ranks, score at the 50th percentile or above on norms for the end-of-year in grade 3.

Enter upper half of level 3: Demonstrates normative performance on a reading test designed for use toward the end of grade 6.

Enter level 4: Demonstrates normative performance on a reading test designed for use toward the end of grade 8.

Enter level 5: Demonstrates normative performance on a reading test designed for use at the senior level of high school.

Please note the phrase "designed for use toward the end of grade . . ." To illustrate, using grade equivalent scores, if a student scores 6.8 on a commonly known standardized reading test designed for grade 6, the implication is that this student is moving into the upper half of level 3. However, if a student scores 6.8 on a reading test designed for fourth graders, the same statement *cannot be made*. The fourth grade test contains no sixth grade material. This issue will be developed further later in this chapter.

2. Measuring to determine if the student understands what the teacher's expectations are of him/her. Under the principal's philosophy of maximizing reading comprehension by keeping challenging material in front of the student (during reading classes), the student is going to develop a sense that reading is a hard area. The principal, as instructional leader, needs to make sure the students' parents are aware of this approach. The teachers need to make the students aware that the level of challenge is expected. The students need to be rewarded for persevering and taking some interpretation risks, even when those interpretations are not correct. Properly handled, the other reading the student does — for example, in social studies — will be at a more comfortable level, and the student should be made aware of this.

The measurement of the extent to which students understand these expectations can be somewhat informal. Through the eyes of the teachers, the principal watches for any indication that a student is being "turned off from reading" and should intervene to make sure the student understands why reading is so constantly challenging.

3. Formative measures and outcome measures. These two categories have been pooled because for this learning event, reading comprehension development in an elementary school, all measures are formative. There is not some performance level where the school will say, "There. That's enough. Let's stop here and measure the outcome." No matter how proficient the student becomes, there is still room for growth.

Of course, one could take cross-sectional snapshots at fixed intervals (say annually) and argue that, at that moment, the snapshot is an outcome.

But for instruction purposes, it seems advantageous to adopt the posture that all measures are formative; that is, they are given primarily to provide information about what should be done next instructionally.

Given that reading comprehension development is a continuous process through the elementary school, the principal's first instinct was to use the district's annual standardized every-pupil-testing program as the primary formative measure for this learning event. This is not a good decision.

Risking redundancy, the term itself needs to be defined because conflicting definitions make discussions about "reading" confusing. In a reading comprehension test, the student is given new material (fiction, nonfiction, poetry) which s/he has presumably not seen. The items address the student's performance when asked to extract details, analyze characters, or give the main idea of the passage; judge the mood of the article or the author's apparent reason for writing it; or generalize beyond the content of the passage.

Frequently, at the lower grades, a word analysis (or a test of the same purpose with another name, like word attack or phonics) is also included. Word analysis is objectives driven. Word analysis is different from reading comprehension. Pooling a word analysis score with a reading comprehension score and calling it "reading" or "reading total" is, to say it most kindly, not very diagnostic.

At the upper grades, and in many research projects, reading *skills* are sometimes confused with reading comprehension. The title of an article by Walberg and Tsai (1983), "Reading Achievement and Attitude Productivity Among 17-Year-Olds," gives one the impression that reading capability, which most people connote to mean reading comprehension, is the topic. However, the article defines reading (p. 44) as, "Fifteen items . . . (for) example, what is the best place to find the meaning of a word you do not know?" (The multiple choice answer is "dictionary.") This questions taps a study skill, not reading comprehension. Naming the topic sentence of a paragraph, using sources of information, choosing the sentence in a paragraph which does not belong, and developing outlines for book reports are all study skills. This is not to argue that they are unimportant; they just should not be confused with reading comprehension.

What about reading comprehension monitoring with standardized tests? All standardized achievement batteries designed for the elementary school or high school have reading comprehension items. Almost always the same level of the test is given to all the students at a particular grade level — a procedure open to question given the broad reading comprehension performance ranges found in the typical classroom. Think about this proposition: The material contained in a reading comprehension subtest for a particular grade (e.g., grade 4) will almost entirely be written for that grade level or lower. The corollary is that a substantial percentage of students taking the reading comprehension test at a particular grade level are not seeing material written for their current functioning reading level.

If that proposition can be satisfactorily defended, it has important implications for the use of standardized reading comprehension tests in monitoring student performance. The evidence to support the proposition is difficult to gather, because in a test the conceptual level of the material and the difficulty of the items interact. The questions associated with a very easy passage might demand very subtle generalizations; the items associated with a conceptually difficult passage might be developed entirely at a literal comprehension level.

However, there are two reasons why test publishers keep most material in a reading comprehension test at, or below, the grade level for which the test is intended. These have to do with the needs of test selection committees and the compassion of the usual classroom teacher.

Consider these two together. Test publishers need to sell tests to stay in business. The biggest unit sales come from state adoptions or from large districts, the largest of which are urban centers. Test selections are generally made by committees; and many of the seats on these committees are reserved for classroom teachers. Whether it be a state adoption or a large city adoption, teachers representing urban schools will almost certainly be present. Generally speaking, average performance by students in these large cities will be at least somewhat lower. Since a substantial proportion operate at or below grade level, these teachers will be unenthusiastic about material which they perceive to be written beyond the grade for which it is designed to be used.

But the above scenario is at a more general citywide or statewide level. At the classroom level, even in a district where the students are *on the average* at or above national averages, some percentage of the students (given the usual range of individual differences in a group) will be operating below grade level. It will be difficult to convince a teacher that the psychometric necessity of having a wide difficulty range in a test is more important than avoiding the anguish of those lower-performing members of the class who find the majority of passages well beyond their comprehension level. Again, publishers are in business to sell tests, and this type of feedback ("ABC test is all right for the average and above-average, but much too hard for some of my class") is unwelcome. Both of these issues, the problem on a statewide or large city selection committee, and the concern of the classroom teacher for the lower performers, can be solved by keeping the conceptual level of material at or lower than the grade being tested. And that, according to the proposition above, is exactly what test publishers do. (A personal anecdote: In 1979, while developing the *Comprehensive Assessment Program* for Scott, Foresman and Co., for which I was the lead author, the then-president of the company called me into his office and said, "We don't publish material here with a reading level beyond the grade for which it is intended." I recall the comment as being unambiguous.)

The proposition that publishers use mostly at-grade-level or below-grade-level material in reading comprehension tests cannot be rigorously defended, but logic and experience suggest it is reasonably accurate. What about the scores reported for a grade level?

Publishers, of course, report a whole stable of scores — percentile ranks, stanines, standard scores, grade equivalent, and NCE (normal curve equivalents). Most (percentile ranks and stanines, for example) indicate a student's relative ranking compared to a national norm group for that student's grade. The grade equivalent score shows the estimated grade level at which the average student nationally had the same score on this test as a given student. Suppose, for example, a student in fifth grade took the test designed for fifth grade and received a grade equivalent score of 8.8. This means that this fifth grader scored as well *on this fifth grade test* as the average eighth grader, after eight months of eighth grade.

Compare, in table 5.2, the conceptual level of the material at grades 4 and 5 with the range of grade equivalent scores delivered for three standardized tests.

The table shows quite clearly that the ranges of scores delivered is much beyond the conceptual level of the material in the test — at both the high and low ends. Now, what has all this to do with the principal's thought of using her district's standardized reading comprehension test to monitor this learning event?

The grade equivalent scale is not the point; the point is that the stand-

Table 5.2.   Comparison of the Conceptual Level of Material and Scores Delivered for Three Standardized Tests

Grade	Range of Material	ITBS Form 7	CAT Form C	CAP Form A
		(Grade Equivalent Range Shown is from Percentile Rank 5 to 99)		
4	3rd, 4th grade	2.9 — 8.3	1.9 — 12.2	3.0 — 10.4
5	4th, 5th grade	3.6 — 9.6	2.4 — 12.2	3.2 — 12.9

ardized reading comprehension test has material which matches the student's current functioning level only if the student is functioning at, or a little above, or a little below, grade level. Again using fourth grade as an example, all students whose current functioning reading level is beyond the middle of grade 5 or lower than grade 3 will see no material at their current functioning level. For those fourth graders who are now operating two grade levels above grade 4, this fourth grade material was child's play; for those operating below a grade 3 level, the material was probably excruciatingly difficult. For a district whose average student is scoring near the 60th percentile on reading comprehension tests, more than half of the students will be functioning above the conceptual level of the material in the standardized reading comprehension test. Even for a district whose average student is at grade level, about one-fourth of the students will be functioning above the conceptual level of the material in the test.

The school should be looking for information to help in the instructional process. Instead of reporting, "Dickie Smith, in fourth grade, took a reading comprehension test and scored a grade equivalent of 8.3, which places him in the 99th percentile compared to other fourth graders," the report should read, "Dickie Smith took a fourth grade reading comprehension test and it was too easy for him." That latter statement is really all of the diagnostic information provided for a student like Dickie; and that's not much, if the principal is trying to use this information to find appropriate material or plan for instruction.

Again, the above is not to argue that a standardized reading test has no value. A district administers such a test for other reasons having to do with monitoring average cross-sectional and longitudinal growth and providing validity information to the school's constituencies. The thrust of the preceding was to argue that the standardized test provides some useful diagnostic information, but not enough to stand alone. The standardized reading comprehension test provides very little useful diagnostic information about the outlying groups — the high and low performers.

The principal has, however, continued to have the standardized test administered. She has gathered data for the five years of the reading comprehension improvement program, summarized as suggested above. The data are shown in table 5.3.

The information for this table was provided by the standardized test. District summaries are shown as frequency distributions, so that tabulating the data in this manner is not difficult. The data, which are real, not hypothetical, say some interesting things about the principal's program as well as some seldom-understood things about the scales of a reading test.

The upper category most directly informs the principal about the success

Table 5.3.   Percentages of Students at, above, or below the Conceptual Level of the Test over a Five-Year Period.

Category	Year	2	3	4	5	6	7	8
% of students whose score is	1	25	30	28	28	30	32	33
higher than the conceptual	2	25	31	29	29	32	36	37
level of the standardized test	3	29	34	33	36	40	39	42
	4	27	35	37	39	45	44	47
	5	28	34	36	41	47	45	49
% of students functioning at the	1	60	53	55	46	43	37	34
test's conceptual level*	2	58	53	55	48	41	36	38
	3	61	57	53	47	42	39	38
	4	62	58	51	49	43	37	36
	5	61	58	51	48	41	38	36
% of students whose score is	1	15	17	17	26	27	31	33
lower than the conceptual level	2	17	16	16	23	27	28	25
of the standardized test	3	10	9	14	17	19	22	20
	4	11	7	12	11	12	19	17
	5	11	8	13	11	12	17	15

* The conceptual level of the test is defined as the grade for which it was planned, plus and minus one-half year. Thus the conceptual level of the grade 5 test would be from grade equivalent scores 4.5 to 6.5.

of her efforts. At grade 8, the proportion of students scoring about the conceptual level of the tests (for grade 8, defined as a grade equivalent score of 9.5) has increased from 33% in year 1 (about what one would observe for a group scoring at about the national average) to 49% over the five year period. These increases at the upper category are matched by decreases in the lower category (below the conceptual level of the test; defined for grade 8 as below 7.5). The pattern repeats at the other grades, with the least dramatic gains at grade 2, where, as reported earlier, the students already were doing very well in year 1.

This type of summary is a start. It's the type of data which would be understood by the press and the public. Instructionally, it defines the limits of the problem. The principal has estimates of the proportions above and below the grade level in which they are enrolled; but the principal doesn't know how much above and below they are. In addition to these diagnostic weaknesses, these data still reflect results from an annual program, and feedback is delayed until five to eight weeks after testing. More information is needed if the principal or other instructional leader is going to plan for providing material which is at the current conceptual level of each child.

The tabled data also give some interesting information about the test scales themselves. Look only at year 1 for the three categories. Notice how, from grade 2 to 8, the proportion of students in the middle category (i.e., at the conceptual level of the test) decreases, and the proportions at the two extremes increase toward the higher grades. This is simply a reflection of the increased range of performance at each grade as the students progress through the school. The conceptual level of the test continues to focus on the grade for which it is designed; but the range of performance for the students tested gets larger and larger as the grades go by.

So the standardized test obviously does not provide nearly enough of the information needed if information is to drive instruction. What is needed is an information system with two characteristics: The students must be tested with test material developed for their current functioning level, and the reports must be available to the teachers in a timely manner.

Consider "timely" first. The term addresses two issues: How frequently does a reading comprehension assessment need to be repeated, and how quickly does the teacher need the data after the assessment?

The frequency of necessary testing decreases as the student moves up in the developmental levels. At the beginning, when the child has just "broken the code" and is a reader, growth can come very fast. Later, as the student moves through level 3 and into level 4, growth is slower. If one looks a the mean scaled score (not the grade equivalent score) in a national norming study of a reading comprehension test, the greatest increment is between grades 1 and 2, the second greatest between grades 2 and 3, and so forth, so that the smallest growth increment appears between grades 7 and 8. (Recalling the prior discussing about the ranges of performance by grade, it is a little confusing that as the rate of growth decreases from grades 2 to 8, the range of performance within each grade increases.)

The slowing growth rate across grades suggests that assessment should be more frequent at the early grades, when the growth rate is steeper, and less frequent at the upper grades. The next question is: How much time must go by before it is reasonable to expect perceptible gains in performance? In math, and even in word analysis skills, one might expect to see clearly perceptible changes as the result of instruction in just a week; in reading comprehension, this is too short a time period.

A testing schedule of six testings per year at grade 2 (about every six weeks) is reasonable. This figure would be reduced to four testings per year at the junior high school grades. Grades 4, 5, and 6 were to test five times per year.

After each testing, the results, summarized so they are easily used, need to get back to the teachers as quickly as possible. A four-week turnaround time would render the process essentially useless; one week is the outside limit for this; one-day turnaround, or immediate feedback, would be much better. As quickly as the information goes to the classrooms, the principal, as instructional leader, needs easily understood summary information to monitor progress and intervene as necessary.

The task of choosing the appropriate functioning level is not as complicated as it sounds. The task is actually only troublesome the first time it is done; after that, one need only make reasonable corrections based on prior performance and growth estimates.

One approach to this assessment need, presented in more detail in section 9.4, would be to use computerized adaptive testing, since with this mode one does not need to estimate the student's current functioning level — the computer does that for you. With computerized adaptive testing, the student sees the test items on a computer monitor and responds by using the computer's keyboard. The "adaptive" part is in the program for the test; the program keeps adjusting the conceptual level of the test material to the student's responses. Quite quickly, the material is brought to the functioning level of the student and the student is tested with a number of passages at that level. (A description of computerized adaptive testing can be found in McBride [1985]. Although this is such an obvious use of microcomputers such that eventually a multitude of packages will be inexpensively available, at this time the only one I know of on the market is from Lagniappe Testing, Inc., 953 Oak Drive, Glencoe, IL 60022.)

But computerized adaptive testing is not the only way these timely estimates of the student's functioning level can be made. Most publishers of standardized tests will provide reading "separates" — the reading comprehension section of the test printed alone. Many publishers provide sequential reading tests, leveled from grade 1 through high school. At the lower grades, there is often more than one test per grade (e.g., a beginning second and end second grade level).

Most schools do not completely individualize reading instruction in the elementary school. The pattern of three reading groups (high, average, and low performers) seems pretty pervasive. Table 5.4 below provides some conservative estimates of median functioning reading level for the high and low group, by grade. The column headed "Average Percentile = 65th" is for schools where the reading comprehension percentile rank of the average student is 65. There is also a column for schools where the percentile rank of the average student is 50, and where it is 35. The estimates are made for midyear, and are based on the assumption that about 25% of the students will be in the high and low groups, and 50% in the middle. The term "conservative estimate" is used because the medians are purposely estimated on the low side.

Table 5.4 is designed to be used only as a starting point in situations

Table 5.4. Conservative Estimates of Median Functioning Reading Level, by Grade, for Three Median School Performance Levels

| | Avg. PR = 65 | | | Avg. PR = 50* | | Avg. PR = 35 | | |
Grade	High	Mid	Low	High	Low	High	Mid	Low
2	E3B4	E2B3	E1B2	3	1	E2B3	E1B2	B1
3	E4B5	E3B4	E2B3	4	2	E3B4	E2B3	E1B2
4	6	E4B5	E3B4	E5B6	3	E4B5	E3B4	E2B3
5	7	E5B6	E4B5	E6B7	4	E5B6	E4B5	E3B4
6	8	7	E5B6	E7B8	E4B5	E6B7	E5B6	E4B5
7	E9B10	8	E6B7	9	E5B6	8	E6B7	5
8	11	9	E7B8	10	E6B7	9	7	E5B6

* The midyear estimates for PR = 50 on, by definition, on grade level.

where no other information is available. As an exercise in using the table, look at the grade 5 numbers. If the percentile rank of the average student in your district (in reading comprehension) is 65, then a first estimate of median functioning level for the high reading group is grade 7 material; for the middle group material designed for the end of grade 5, beginning of grade 6; and for the low group, material designed for the end of grade 4, beginning of grade 5. Remember, these are midyear estimates for the average child in the group. For a district like this (percentile rank of average student is 65) there will most likely be some fifth graders in the high reading group whose functioning level is already well beyond grade 7 material by the middle of fifth grade. The estimates are based on the needs of the median child in the high reading group.

If the principal is to be the instructional leader, she needs more information about student performance than that gathered through anecdotes and occasional classroom visits. The testing schedule called for testing replications ranging from six tests per year at the lower grade levels to four tests per year at the junior high. The principal's first summary of results is ready on October 15, and is shown as table 5.5 below.

The table shows:

. . . ranges at a grade level. A look at the column below grade 4 shows that 11% are at developmental level 2, 51% at the first part of the long process of level 3, and 38% in the second half of level 3.

. . . the range of grades represented in the school at a particular developmental level. Look at the row for level 4. This shows that 15% of the students in this K–8 school are, already in September, operating at the high school level. This 15% is spread over four grades: 22% of the fifth graders, 41% of the sixth graders, 28% of the seventh graders, and 43% of the eighth graders.

This information provides the principal with a technique for monitoring the extent to which her proposed mechanism for growth in reading comprehension

Table 5.5. Principal's Summary of Reading Comprehension Performance Levels by Grade (Summary of Results Gathered Between the First and Fourth Weeks of School)

Development Level	Functioning Level Estimates (see Note * Below)	Grade (% at grade shown in cells)									Distr. Totals	
		K	1	2	3	4	5	6	7	8	%	N
0	Preschool — End K.	81	11								10	65
1	Beg. 1 — 1st half 2	9	67	38	7						13	87
2	2nd half 2 — End 3	5	15	40	42	11	5				13	86
3A	Begin 4 — End 6		7	22	33	51	44	18	9	5	21	141
3B	Begin 7 — End 8				18	38	29	51	48	23	23	155
4	Begin 9 — End 12						22	41	28	43	15	102
5	Beyond end 12								15	29	5	34
	Number	71	73	72	75	74	77	71	77	80		670

* This estimate is based on the average functioning reading comprehension level of an average student nationally at the designated grade level.

(making sure the students are being faced by material which "stretches" their capabilities) is being implemented. Obviously, the teachers cannot give the students material at the appropriately challenging level if they don't have such material; as instructional leader, the principal needs to make sure the appropriate material, in sufficient quantity, is in place. Additionally, as the principal visits classrooms, she can make sure that the grouping patterns conform (with some variation due to teacher judgments) to the distributions in the summary report.

Since some of these definitions are rather imprecise and arbitrary, and since all measures have error associated with them, it is really progress and growth, rather than the absolute levels, which should be of primary interest to the principal. The principal is interesting in monitoring growth within a year, while at the same time making comparisons between the current year's performance levels and prior ones. Summaries are prepared for the principal four times each year, after the 4th, 14th, 24th, and 35th week of instruction. Table 5.6, prepared after the 35th week in instruction, shows what a summary looks like.

The table has a lot of numbers and takes a little study to dig out some meanings. The table shows a composite picture of reading comprehension performance, and growth, for one year in one school building. The grades are collapsed into this table. The data from the middle levels are difficult to interpret, since students are moving both in and out of those levels between summary periods. The high and low extreme levels, however, can be used to chart progress. The table shows that the proportion of students in the lowest two levels, 0 and 1, is moving down as the year progresses, and the proportion in the highest two levels, 4 and above, is moving up. To get a visual display of this movement, the principal keeps a graph on her office wall like the one shown in figure 5.1.

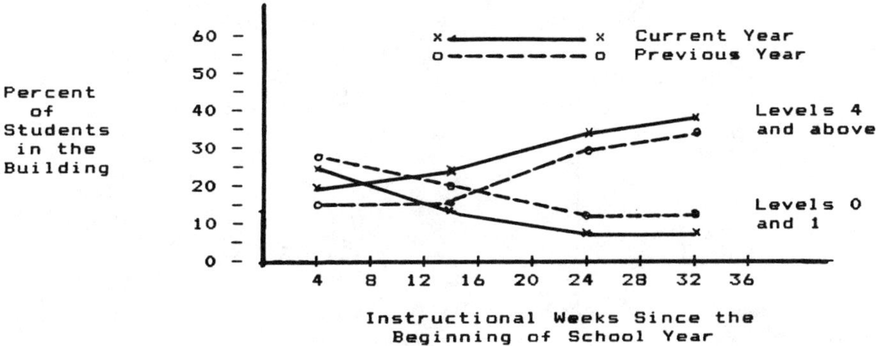

Figure 5.1.   Progress of Upper and Lower Developmental Levels for First Three Reporting Periods

Table 5.6. Principal's Fourth Summary Report of Testing Done During the School Year, with Prior Year's Results for Comparison

Developmental Level	Functioning Level Estimates (see note * below)	Year	Testing Done During Weeks			
			1–4	*5–14*	*15–24*	*25–35*
0	Preschool — End K	Current	65(10%)	27(4%)	7(1%)	2(0%)
		Previous	80(12%)	40(6%)	27(4%)	13(2%)
1	Beg. 1 — 1st half 2	Current	87(13%)	80(12%)	47(7%)	54(8%)
		Previous	100(15%)	100(15%)	60(9%)	67(10%)
2	2nd half 2 — End 3	Current	86(13%)	94(14%)	100(15%)	100(15%)
		Previous	67(10%)	100(15%)	87(13%) 107(16%)	
3A	Begin 4 — End 6	Current	141(21%)	147(22%)	134(20%)	134(20%)
		Previous	174(26%)	141(21%)	141(21%)	127(19%)
3B	Begin 7 — End 8	Current	155(23%)	168(25%)	147(22%)	127(19%)
		Previous	147(22%)	174(26%)	154(23%)	114(17%)
4	Begin 9 — End 12	Current	102(15%)	80(12%)	114(17%)	107(16%)
		Previous	87(13%)	60(9%)	107(16%)	127(19%)
5	Beyond end 12	Current	34(5%)	74(11%)	121(18%)	147(22%)
		Previous	13(2%)	54(8%)	94(14%)	114(17%)

Figure 5.1 shows two things: first, increased membership in the two highest levels, and decreased membership in the two lowest levels as the year progresses. Second, it shows that the overall performance levels for the current year exceed those of the previous year. The same interpretations can obviously be made from table 5.5; but most people find visual displays easier to interpret than charts of numbers.

In interpreting these kinds of data, it is important to state again that the measures themselves (the reading comprehension tests) are not perfect. Even tests which are very reliable have what measurement people call a standard error of measurement. In addition, the transitions between developmental levels are not precisely defined. The two add some random variation to the observed results; and this randomness suggests two cautions.

First, the user should not over-respond to two-point trends; that is, to two subsequent measures. It's much better to keep baseline data and monitor trends over fairly substantial time periods. A school couldn't survive a climate which institutes a new program every time a random "blip" occurs on the trend chart. In the second place, the absolute levels, headings like "Begin 7 — End 8," do not have a guaranteed common meaning to different observers. Actually, a person reading at this level can function quite satisfactorily in adult society in this country. In a sense, the levels are like the Gross National Product (GNP), defined as the market value of the goods and services produced in the country during a period. People pay almost no attention to the actual GNP number reported, but they pay a great deal of attention to the trends and amount of change which the current number reflects compared to prior reports. The analogy is a little strained, but the point is the comparative data are the easiest to interpret and respond to.

Quality-with-equity differs from just quality in the degreee of attention paid to the entire distribution of students, and through consideration of the incoming characteristics of the student body. Quality-with-equity comparisons are based on programs designed to bring about growth for students, independent of the baseline measures in the district. Table 5.6 and figure 5.1 show the types of comparsions envisioned as a basis for making quality-with-equity comparisons. The principal defined a problem, charted a solution, gathered baseline data, and continues to monitor to see if the expected improvement is occurring.

The teachers need immediate feedback, too, to help them respond to the growing performance levels of the students. Table 5.6 shows a class output listing for one round of reading comprehension testing. Please note that the scores in this table are based on material near the functioning level reported. The students have not all taken the same test; the test difficulty is adjusted to match the performance level of the student. (The data were collected in a computerized adaptive format; the table is patterned after one used by Lagniappe Testing, Inc.)

The report gives the current functioning level of each student. The last column, "*Easy Level*," reports the passage difficulty of a passage about which the student got every answer correct. The teacher can choose the number of reading groups used in that class, and the output tries to separate students at the greatest scale separation points and provides an estimate of the level of material which would be appropriate for the average student in each group. (Although these data were collected in a computerized adaptive format, the same information could be gathered in a paper-and-pencil format. With something like 40 or 45 reading passages scaled in difficulty from a beginning reading level to a high school level, accompanied by five to seven questions for each passage, a testing system to provide these kinds of reports could be implemented.)

References

Cawley, J.F., Cawley, L.J., Cherkes, M., and Fitzmaurice, A.M. (eds.) (1980). "Beginning Educationnoal Assessment." In J.W. and J.K.Smith, *Comprehensive Assessment Program*. Iowa City, IA: American Testronics, Inc.

Cazden, C.B. (1974). "Play with language and metalinguistic awareness: One dimension of language experience." *Urban Review*, 2:28–39.

Chall, J.S. (1967). *Learning To Read: The Great Debate*. New York: McGraw-Hill.

Chall, J.S. (1983). *Stages of Reading Development*. New York: McGraw-Hill.

Clay, M. (1979). *Reading: The Patterning of Complex Behavior*. Exeter, N.H.: Heinemann Educational Books.

Harste, J.C., Woodward, V.A., and Burke, C.L. (1984). *Language Stories and Literacy Lessons*. Portsmouth, N.H.: Heinemann Educational Books.

McBride, J.R. (1985). "Computerized adaptive testing." *Educational Leadership* 43(2):25–8.

Shephard, G.D. and Ragan, W.B. (1982). *Modern Elementary Curriculum*. New York: Holt, Rinehart and Winston.

Sirotkin, K. (1983). "What you see is what you get — consistency, persistency, and mediocrity in classrooms."*Harvard Educational Review* 53(1):16–31.

Smith, F. (1983). *Essays Into Literacy — Selected Papers and Some Afterthoughts* Exeter, N.H.: Heinemann Educational Books.

Table 5.7. Classroom-Level Output Form for One Round of Reading Comprehension Testing

Diagnostic Reading Test

Class List for: Dewey   *Date: Sept. 22, 1985*

Rank	Student Name	Grade	Reading Level	Easy Level
1	Calvin, Marie	5	Grade 9	Middle 7
2	Ming, Kunki	5	Grade 9	Middle 7
3	Moore, Bruce	5	Grade 8	Middle 7
4	Roberts, Helen	5	Grade 8	End 6 — Begin 7
5	Janus, Lois	5	End 7 — Begin 8	No Info
6	Holzimer, Debbie	5	Grade 7	Middle 6
7	Anderson, Paul	5	Grade 7	End 5 — Begin 6
8	Weller, Louise	5	Grade 7	No Info
9	Klee, Dale	5	Grade 7	End 5 — Begin 6
10	Fleishman, Peter	5	Grade 7	End 5 — Begin 6
11	Sellers, Nancy	5	End 6 — Begin 7	No Info
12	Demorray, Jerry	5	Middle 6	Middle 4
13	Monroe, Sheila	5	Middle 6	End 4 — Begin 5
14	Fellows, Walter	5	Middle 6	Middle 4
15	Riley, Martha	5	End 5 — Begin 6	Middle 4
16	Dillon, Bill	5	End 5 — Begin 6	Middle 4
17	Clayworth, Mark	5	End 5 — Begin 6	Middle 4
18	Steele, Patricia	5	Middle 5	No Info
19	Simpson, Adam	5	End 4 — Begin 5	Middle 3
20	Tyler, Elaine	5	End 4 — Begin 5	No Info
21	Black, Ruth	5	End 4 — Begin 5	Middle 3
22	Young, Jacob	5	End 4 — Begin 5	No Info
23	Singh, Balbir	5	Middle 4	No Info
24	Feldmeir, Sam	5	Middle 4	Middle 2
25	Ulzeisz, Emil	5	Middle 4	No Info

Note: A "No Info" under easy score means student did not get a perfect score on any passage.

Suggested Breakdown for Three Reading Groups

Group	Ranks Included	Number of Stnts.	Average Reading Level
High	1–10	10	End 7 — Begin 8
Middle	11–17	7	Middle 6
Low	18–25	8	End 4 — Begin 5

Stroud, J.B. (1964). *Psychology in Education*. New York: David McKay Co., Inc.
Walberg, H.J., and Tsai, S. (1983). "Reading achievement and attitude productivity among 17-year-olds." *Journal of Reading Behavior* 15(3), 41–53.
Wick, J.W. (1983). "Reducing the proportion of chance scores in inner-city standardized test results: Impact on average scores." *American Educational Research Journal* 20:461–463.

6 AN OBJECTIVES-DRIVEN EXAMPLE: Certain Language Arts Basic Skills

The learning event (step 1) for this chapter is the basic skills areas of punctuation, capitalization, grammar and usage for an elementary school, grades K to 8.

Language arts is a very broad area in the elementary school curriculum. Stewig (1983) includes listening, speaking, drama, writing, handwriting, spelling, literature, vocabulary, and grammar and usage. Shepherd and Ragan (1981) include all of these, and add reading. Petty, Petty and Becking (1973) add study and library skills.

It is interesting that the Stewig book has a short section on punctuation and capitalization (pp. 200–204); the others make almost no mention of these two topics. Standardized tests in common use at the elementary school level include, under the language arts heading, punctuation, capitalization, grammar and usage, and spelling. This rather major difference between what language arts curriculum books tell teachers to teach, and what standardized tests actually measure under the language arts heading, certainly provides a sound basis for misunderstanding.

Actually, grammar and usage are frequently used interchangeably. For the purposes of this book, grammar has to do with the stucture of the language; usage is usage. The question, 'What is the simple subject of,

'The big tree is beautiful'?" is a grammar question. If the student were to identify the noun, verb, and adjectives in the sentence, they are grammar questions also. Appendix B gives a list of 230 objectives, of which about three-fourths deal with usage and the rest grammar. Although standardized tests frequently use the term "grammar" with one of the subtests under the language arts heading, almost no grammar is tested; the items are almost entirely usage items.

In charge of this learning event (step 2) is the superintendent of a small unit district with three elementary schools and one middle school. The district is too small to maintain a full-time assistant for curriculum and/or instruction. The superintendent is a grandfatherly veteran who assumed these responsibilities into his own job description. He has decided on this learning event in the face of internal criticism that such a mechanistic approach inhibits creativity, is certain to be unsuccessful, and will be seen as boring by the students.

His critics probably learned these areas of complaint in college methods courses. The language arts curriculum books are critical of the structured approach to the learning of punctuation, capitalization, and grammar and usage implied by the short description of this learning event. In the usage area, teachers are urged to correct usage errors as they occur in oral language. This is a limited perspective if one considers those who now argue that reading and writing represent a language distinct from listening and speaking. Punctuation and capitalization errors are to be corrected only as they appear in the students' writing. Petty (1973, p. 200) writes, ". . . the introduction and reinforcement of skills cannot be accomplished effectively in isolation from genuine communication activities." Earlier (p. 51), these authors lament extensive "grammatical rules, definitions of terms, exercises calling for pupils to fill in blanks with their choices of a word or phrase from among two or more possible choices, and activities calling for analyzing or restructuring sentences." They continue, "Not much of this can be defended as good. In fact, little of it is of value." This harsh analysis is difficult to reconcile with their later statements (p. 68) that "Every person is judged at some time or other in his lifetime by the way his language conforms or does not conform to the accepted dialect of the community . . ." and ". . . the person whose language differs markedly from standard will find that the social, economic, and educational opportunities available to him will be limited." Stewig (1983), after arguing strongly that usage errors should only be corrected as they occur naturally (pp. 436–437), nonetheless concedes that "Like it or not, language is one way American society makes class distinctions, and less-acceptable usage choices are heavily penalized by those in power." He concludes these contradictory messages with this "definitive" summary statement that (p. 447) "It would be folly for a writer to prescribe what an individual school system ought to do, without knowing intimately the nature of that system."

So this dilemma exists: The books advise the teacher that basic punctuation, capitalization, grammar, and usage skills cannot be taught in an isolated manner. They need to be taught in context; as the child needs them, the skill is taught. At the same time, however, the teacher is told of the devasting impact of not learning appropriate skills. "Us boys went . . . ," "He clumb up . . . ," "Her and me went . . . ," and "He hisself . . ." are bad enough when a teenager applies for a job at the supermarket or pizza shop, but used in a college entrance interview, any one of them is likely to be devastating. If errors are to be corrected only as they occur, these issues are troublesome:

> . . . What if the cautious student, unsure of the appropriate punctuation, capitalization or usage skill, simply makes sure s/he never uses these troublesome skills in the presence of the teacher? (A prolific writer well known to the author cannot, for some reason, spell the word "occasionally," never remembering which consonants are doubled and which are not. Rather than look the word up time after time, the writer goes around the word, using "now and then" or "once in a while" in its place.) Young people are as clever as this writer. If they are not sure, they will write or speak around their uncertainties in situations where it is important to avoid errors.
>
> . . . What if the student makes the error and the teacher, for whatever reason, doesn't identify it as an error and set about correcting it? The superintendent isn't positive all the district's teachers are diligent in seeking out and correcting errors which will eventually embarrass the student and, ultimately, the school.
>
> The superintendent isn't going to count on chance learning. He wants to establish responsibilities for instruction, including the grades at which each student is first introduced to each important skill, and the grade at which mastery is to be expected of all normal students. He has been known to comment to his board, "I don't think I can make a good teacher out of a bad one; but I can make bad ones follow the rules." The students have the right at least to be exposed to the rules which can have such an important impact on their future.

Step 3 asks, "Why is this learning event being staged? What are the expectations for the students?"

The areas of punctuation, capitalization, and grammar and usage are objectives-driven — what has here been termed a "finished system." This simply means it is a body of content which is not changing rapidly. (This body of content changes slowly with changing language patterns. For example, try using "gay" in the same way it was used when the author was born, in the mid-1930s.) and where there is minimal controversy among content scholars over what is "correct." This is not to say there is no disagreement among experts in these areas, but the disagreements usually occur on fine points which are not normally part of an elementary school curriculum. The superintendent is asking that the march through the sequence be orderly, following a known pattern; he has rejected the call for serendipitous learning, where correctives are applied only as errors are observed. As shall be seen presently, the teachers in the district will make the decisions about which of the skills will be presented in the district, so it is fair to call this a finished system for this district.

This chapter then is provided as an example of an objectives-driven area which has been termed a "finished system." Other objectives-driven areas include math computation, math concepts, certain references skills, the content parts of science instruction, and word study skills.

Chapter 5 covered a learning event involving reading comprehension. Reading comprehension was not termed a "finished system." Reading comprehension is not objectives-driven; it is difficulty-driven. Once a student is a reader, the objectives remain the same throughout school. The objectives continue to deal with the main idea, making cause-and-effect connections, serially ordering events, making inferences, and picking out details.

The second part of the question at step 3 deals with expectations on the part of the student. The expectation is quite simple: that all normal children shall demonstrate mastery on the punctuation, capitalization, grammar and usage objectives which are part of the instructional system in this district. The year at which mastery will be demonstrated will be determined by the teachers.

In a sense, the superintendent is functioning as the curriculum director; the instructional decisions are being left to the teachers. The superintendent has decided that the basic skills in punctuation, capitalization, grammar and usage will be presented in an orderly manner. The decisions concerned precisely which objectives are to be included in this learning event, and the years of initial instruction and mastery, will be left to the teachers.

Chapter 9 outlines some different approaches to putting this type of objective-flow system in place in a school or district. The superintendent has implemented his system in the following manner.

As a first step, the teachers need to choose the objectives which will be included. Rather than work with the entire faculty, which would be cumbersome and expensive, he has asked each grade-level committee to identify a teacher representative for a districtwide committee. The representative is expected to have prior teaching experience at that grade.

A committee like this needs a list of objectives. There are a number of ways to approach this need. One way would be to have the committee begin assembling such a list. They might look for guidance at the language arts series in use in the district or from the objectives listed with the district's standardized testing program.

Either of these approaches, as discussed in more detail in chapter 9, is limiting. The primary interest of publishers of texts and tests is sales, not coverage.

Establishing a committee and giving them, as a first task, the responsibility to develop an exhaustive, nonredundant objective list is of questionable value. The committee will take substantial time completing this task; any initial enthusiasm will be spent. Unless the process of going through this exercise is deemed very important, it makes more sense to start with someone else's list and refine it to conform to local needs. Others have considered the issue of basic skills in language arts!

One such list is included in Appendix B of this book. This list was begun by the author in the mid-1970s and has been refined over the years. It is still not totally exhaustive, and some people may find redundancies in it, but it is a good place for a committee to start.

It is unlikely that any district, particularly an elementary school district, would choose to include all of the 230 objectives in this list. Some might leave out most of the grammar objectives; how important is it for a student to differentiate the meanings of "intensive" and "reflexive" pronouns? Some schools do want to go into this level of detail, and that's why certain objectives which might be termed obscure are retained on the list.

The openness and clarity issues are seen here once again. Rather than have a general objective that the district will "bring the students to mastery on those language arts basic skills deemed necessary for student success," the teacher committee will be asked to define precisely what that very general statement means. The committee is asked to select from the list those objectives which will be taught. Obviously, they also have the opportunity to add objectives not included on the list.

This brings the definition out in the open for discussion. Once the selections are made, those objectives included and excluded are clearly identified and are subject to discussion. How important is it in this district that the student distinguish the use of "can" and "may" or "shall" and "will" or the triad "who-that-which"? The decision process is moved from a teacher-by-teacher preference issue to a consensus statement by a teacher committee. All students will now receive the same program. In the short run, there might be a tendency to leave things alone to avoid the possibility of controversy (although one has trouble envisioning a parent group packing a board of education meeting over the issue of "shall" and "will"), but in the long run consensus seems preferable to pot luck.

Once the committee has decided which objectives will be included in the system, they are asked to decide also on how instruction is to flow through the grades. Specifically, they are asked to agree, for each objective, on the grade at which *initial instruction* will occur, and on the grade at which all normal students are expected to demonstrate *entering mastery*.

"Initial Instruction" means just that; taught, not just familiarized. The kindergarten teacher who writes on the blackboard "Today is January 22, 1986" is not yet teaching capitalization or punctuation skills. The grade of initial instruction refers to the time the skill is presented as an issue itself, with the expectation that the students will begin demonstrating mastery on it.

The term "normal students" has been used to exclude those with special learning problems (perhaps up to 10% overall), including those who have been mainstreamed. "Entering Mastery" means just that; as they enter the grade in question, prior to review, they are capable of demonstrating mastery. Hopefully this monitoring would take place on the first day or two of class. Chapter 9 goes into more detail on these issues, including why entering mastery is preferred to exiting mastery, and the rationale for testing for mastery before having any review activities.

This process of selecting objectives and identifying the grades of intial instruction and entering mastery will take a diligent committee about one day. If the committee is particularly talkative, or contains a member or two who are quite cantankerous, the process can be stretched into a second day.

The output of this meeting becomes the instructional program for the district for the upcoming school year. With this in mind, the superintendent schedules the session for spring of the prior year, finding that logistically it was easier to have the sessions after school had been dismissed for the summer. By having the committee meetings in June, plenty of time was available to disseminate the results to all teachers prior to the coming year, and develop the entering mastery measures necessary when school opens again in the fall.

"Wait a minute," the reader is saying, "don't these clarity and openness issues naturally lead to feedback and change? Is it appropriate to put the system in place immediately?" Good point; but the opposite observation is that improvements in education too often are tied up in committee so long they never are implemented. The superintendent is a pragmatist about this issue. Better, he feels, to take this first approximation of the teacher committee and put in in place, for all teachers, for a full school year. During that year, data are collected concerning student performance and the teacher committee continues to serve, this time as a liaison to the other teachers at their grade level regarding anecdotal evidence about the current coverage and placements.

At the end of the first school year of implementation, the committee, possibly with some new membership, is reassembled to review the evidence and the original placements. Chapter 9 provides some reasons why evidence would suggest to the committee how placements might be changed, why certain objectives originally included should now be dropped, or why certain objectives originally excluded should now be included.

The superintendent designs the system to be a dynamic one. Each June, a committee is assembled to review the evidence and the placements. The committee has the authority to make changes. Their decisions, of course, continue to be very specific and out in the open for review; any committee would have difficulty defending the exclusion of skills most parents would consider to be very basic. Whatever the teachers decide becomes "the" program for the coming year. In the author's experience, after two or three years of this approach, the percent of objectives actually changed by a teacher committee becomes fairly small. The system becomes quite stable.

What information should be disseminated to the classroom teacher? Table 6.1 shows a grade-level report. The report is for grade 4. Please note that tables 6.1 and 6.2 have been developed around the assumption that all 230 objectives listed in Appendix B are part of the district's instructional program. This would indeed be unusual. In general, the lists shown in tables 6.1 and 6.2 would be much shorter.

The objectives in table 6.1 are summarized under four headings:

Entering Mastery Objectives (the objectives which are to be mastered by all normal students as they enter grade 4).

Pretest Objectives (objectives still in the instructional system at grade 4, but which have been initially taught prior to grade 4. The term "pretest" is used to suggest to the teacher that these objectives be pretested prior to instruction, to determine the extent to which mastery already has been attained from the prior instruction).

Initial Instruction Objectives (the objectives on which initial instruction responsibility has been designated for fourth grade).

Entering Mastery Objectives for the next year. (If these students are expected to demonstrate mastery as they enter grade 5, they will need to get one last push before leaving grade 4, since one cannot count too heavily on summer learning).

Table 6.1.   A Typical Grade-Level Report of Instructional Responsibilities in Punctuation, Capitalization, and Grammar and Usage

Grade 4	*Summary of Instructional Objectives*

Entering Mastery Objectives:
122.   Capit.-Calendar related: Months of year.
123.   Capit.-Calendar related: Common holidays.
131.   Capit.-Geog. location: Streets, avenues, . . .
132.   Capit.-Geog. location: Cities, states, countries.

Table 6.1.   continued.

142.   Capit.-Specific rules: Salutation, closing of letters.
153.   Overcapitalization: Second word in closing of letter.
201.   Punctuation-Comma: Separate city and state.
211.   Punctuation-Comma: Friendly letter, after salutation and closing.
242.   Punctuation: Period in initials and after titles like Mr., . . .
243.   Punctuation: Period with abbreviations (except Mr., . . .)
261.   Punctuation: Colon in standard time notation.
271.   Punctuation: Apostrophe in common contractions.
435.   Identify run-on sentences.
461.   Grammar Usage: Use posi., compara., superla. w/ reg. adjectives.
471.   Grammar Usage: Subj.-verb agreement, simple structure.
615.   Gram. Usage: Correct form irregular verb *come.*

Pretest Objectives:
112.   Capit.-Titles: Common (King, President, Captain, . . .)
134.   Capit.-Geog. location: Rivers, lakes, mountains, . . .
143.   Capit.-Specific rules: Titles of works.
245.   Punctuation: Use exclamation point.
273.   Overpunctuation: Apostrophe inserted in words ending with 's'
401.   In context, identify nouns.
402.   In context, identify verbs.
404.   In context, identify adjectives.
451.   Grammar Usage: Correctly use articles 'a,' 'an,' 'the.')
452.   Identify sentence element modified by an adjective.
457.   Grammar Usage: Properly use *good, well.*
491.   Gram. Usage: Regular verbs, present-past tenses.
492.   Gram. Usage: Regular verbs, perfect and past perfect tenses.
493.   Gram. Usage: Regular verbs, future and future perfect tenses.
531.   Grammar Usage: Pronouns use, nominative case for subject.
554.   Gram. Usage: Place 'I' last in compound sentences.
561.   Gram. Usage: Do not use double negative.
571.   In context, identify the noun for which a pronoun stands.
573.   In context, identify personal pronouns.
581.   Gram. Usage: Form plurals of regular nouns.
601.   Gram. Usage: Correct form irregular verb *be.*
616.   Gram. Usage: Correct form irregular verb *do.*
620.   Gram. Usage: Correct form irregular verb *eat.*
621.   Gram. Usage: Correct form irregular verb *fall.*
628.   Gram. Usage: Correct form irregular verb *give.*
629.   Gram. Usage: Correct form irregular verb *go.*
641.   Gram. Usage: Correct form irregular verb *ride.*
643.   Gram. Usage: Correct form irregular verb *run.*
644.   Gram. Usage: Correct form irregular verb *say.*

Table 6.1.   continued.

---

645. Gram. Usage: Correct form irregular verb *see*.
651. Gram. Usage: Correct form irregular verb *sleep*.
652. Gram. Usage: Correct form irregular verb *speak*.

Initial Instruction:
103. Capit.-Names: Family relationships.
104. Capit.-Names: Bldgs., organiza., . . .
135. Capit.-Geog. location: Continents, oceans, planets.
144. Capit.-Specific rules: First word in direct quotation.
151. Overcapit.: Relationship preceded by possessive (My father . . .)
152. Overcapitalization: Generic product or institution.
155. Overcapit.: First word, continued section, interrupted quote.
203. Punctuation-Comma: Separate words in a series.
212. Punctuation-colon: Business letter, after salutation.
221. Punc.-Comma: Set off nominative of address (Dad, can I . . . ?)
222. Punctuation-comma: To set off quotation from rest of sentence.
231. Overpunctuation: Comma separates subject and verb.
235. Extra commas: Inserted in phrases
251. Punctuation: Quotation marks direct quote, continuing quote.
253. Overpunctuation: Overuse quotation marks (indirect quotes, . . .)
403. In context, identify pronouns.
405. In context, identify adverbs.
411. Select simple subject of a sentence.
412. Select simple predicate of a sentence.
413. Select complete subject of a sentence.
414. Select complete predicate of a sentence.
431. Distinguish between sentences and non-sentences.
453. Identify sentence element modified by an adverb.
462. Grammar Usage: Use posi., compara., superla. w/ reg. adverbs.
463. Grammar Usage: Use posi., compara., superla. w/ irreg. adjctves.
555. Gram. Usage: Misuse of 'them' to modify a noun.
574. In context, identify interrogative pronouns.
575. In context, identify demonstrative pronouns.
582. Form plurals of irregular nouns.
583. Grammar Usage: Apostrophe to form regular possessives.
605. Gram. Usage: Correct form irregular verb *begin*.
607. Gram. Usage: Correct form irregular verb *blow*.
609. Gram. Usage: Correct form irregular verb *bring*.
611. Gram. Usage: Correct form irregular verb *buy*.
612. Gram. Usage: Correct form irregular verb *catch*.
617. Gram. Usage: Correct form irregular verb *draw*.
623. Gram. Usage: Correct form irregular verb *find*.

Table 6.1.   continued.

624.   Gram. Usage: Correct form irregular verb *fly*.
627.   Gram. Usage: Correct form irregular verb *get*.
630.   Gram. Usage: Correct form irregular verb *grow*.
635.   Gram. Usage: Correct form irregular verb *know*.
636.   Gram. Usage: Correct form irregular verb *lead*.
637.   Gram. Usage: Correct form irregular verb *lose*.
638.   Gram. Usage: Correct form irregular verb *meet*.
650.   Gram. Usage: Correct form irregular verb *sink*.
660.   Gram. Usage: Correct form irregular verb *take*.
663.   Gram. Usage: Correct form irregular verb *throw*.
666.   Gram. Usage: Correct form irregular verb *write*.

Entering Mastery Objectives for Grade 5:
112.   Capit.-Titles: Common (King, President, Captain, . . .)
143.   Capit.-Specific rules: Titles of works.
245.   Punctuation: Use exclamation point.
401.   In context, identify nouns.
402.   In context, identify verbs.
404.   In context, identify adjectives.
431.   Distinguish between sentences and non-sentences.
451.   Grammar Usage: Correctly use articles 'a,' 'an,' 'the.')
452.   Identify sentence element modified by an adjective.
491.   Gram. Usage: Regular verbs, present-past tenses.
492.   Gram. Usage: Regular verbs, perfect and past perfect tenses.
531.   Grammar Usage: Pronoun use, nominative case for subject.
554.   Gram. Usage: Place 'I' last in compound sentences.
561.   Gram. Usage: Do not use double negative.
571.   In context, identify the noun for which a pronoun stands.
573.   In context, identify personal pronouns.
581.   Gram. Usage: Form plurals of regular nouns.
601.   Gram. Usage: Correct form irregular verb *be*.
616.   Gram. Usage: Correct form irregular verb *do*.
620.   Gram. Usage: Correct form irregular verb *eat*.
621.   Gram. Usage: Correct form irregular verb *fall*.
628.   Gram. Usage: Correct form irregular verb *give*.
629.   Gram. Usage: Correct form irregular verb *go*.
641.   Gram. Usage: Correct form irregular verb *ride*.
643.   Gram. Usage: Correct form irregular verb *run*.
644.   Gram. Usage: Correct form irregular verb *say*.
645.   Gram. Usage: Correct form irregular verb *see*.
651.   Gram. Usage: Correct form irregular verb *sleep*.
652.   Gram. Usage: Correct form irregular verb *speak*.

Each classroom teacher needs a list like table 6.1 for the grade level at which s/he teaches. Each teacher might also have reason to check, at some time during the year, on the complete grade placement history of a particular objective. For this reason, a matrix of all objectives taught in the district is prepared. Such a matrix is shown in table 6.2.

In this table, the objective numbers in the left-hand column conform to the objective numbers found in Appendix B. The first objective, 101, is shown in Appendix B to be, "101 Capit.-Names: The pronoun 'I.' " The grade levels, K through 10, are shown across the top. The grade level headings are repeated frequently so the matrix is not so difficult to read. The letters (I, P, and M) stand for Initial Instruction, Pretest, and entering Mastery.

Table 6.2. A Summary of Grade Placements Selected by a Teacher Committee for Appendex B Objectives

Default grade placement of instruction:
  M   Entering mastery expected.
  P   Pretesting, before review, suggested.
  I   Grade of initial instruction.

No.	K	1	2	3	4	5	6	7	8	9	10
101		I	P	M							
102		I	P	M							
103					I	P	P	M			
104					I	P	P	M			
105								I	P	M	
111			I	M							

No.	K	1	2	3	4	5	6	7	8	9	10
112				I	P	M					
113						I	P	P	M		
121			I	M							
122			I	P	M						
123			I	P	M						

No.	K	1	2	3	4	5	6	7	8	9	10
124								I	P	P	M
131			I	P	M						
132			I	P	M						
133								I	P	M	
134				I	P	P	M				

Table 6.2. continued.

No.	K	1	2	3	4	5	6	7	8	9	10
135					I	P	M				
136							I	P	P	M	
141		I	P	M							
142			I	P	M						
143				I	P	M					

No.	K	1	2	3	4	5	6	7	8	9	10
144					I	P	M				
151					I	P	M				
152					I	P	P	M			
153			I	P	M						
154							I	P	P	M	

No.	K	1	2	3	4	5	6	7	8	9	10
155					I	P	M				
156		I	P	M							
201			I	P	M						
202			I	M							
203					I	P	M				

No.	K	1	2	3	4	5	6	7	8	9	10
204						I	P	M			
211			I	P	M						
212					I	P	M				
221					I	P	M				
222					I	P	M				

No.	K	1	2	3	4	5	6	7	8	9	10
223							I	P	P	M	
224								I	P	M	
226								I	P	M	
231					I	P	M				
232							I	P	P	M	

No.	K	1	2	3	4	5	6	7	8	9	10
233								I	P	P	M
234								I	P	P	M
235					I	P	P	M			
236								I	P	P	M
241		I	P	M							

No.	K	1	2	3	4	5	6	7	8	9	10
242			I	P	M						
243			I	P	M						
244		I	P	M							
245				I	P	M					
251					I	P	P	M			

Table 6.2. continued.

No.	K	1	2	3	4	5	6	7	8	9	10
252							I	P	M		
253					I	P	P	M			
254							I	P	M		
255									I	P	M
261			I	P	M						
No.	K	1	2	3	4	5	6	7	8	9	10
262								I	P	M	
263								I	P	P	M
264								I	P	P	M
271			I	P	M						
273			I	P		P	M				
No.	K	1	2	3	4	5	6	7	8	9	10
275									I	P	M
291						I	P	M			
292							I	P	M		
293							I	P	M		
301								I	P	P	M
No.	K	1	2	3	4	5	6	7	8	9	10
311							I	P	M		
312							I	P	M		
313							I	P	M		
314							I	P	P	M	
315									I	P	M
No.	K	1	2	3	4	5	6	7	8	9	10
316									I	P	M
401				I	P	M					
402				I	P	M					
403					I	P	M				
404				I	P	M					
No.	K	1	2	3	4	5	6	7	8	9	10
405					I	P	M				
406							I	P	M		
407						I	P	M			
411					I	P	M				
412					I	P	M				
No.	K	1	2	3	4	5	6	7	8	9	10
413					I	P	M				
414					I	P	M				
415						I	P	M			
431					I	M					
432							I	P	P	M	

Table 6.2.   continued.

No.	K	1	2	3	4	5	6	7	8	9	10
433							I	P	P	M	
434						I	P	M			
435			I	P	M						
436								I	P	P	M
441								I	P	P	M

No.	K	1	2	3	4	5	6	7	8	9	10
442									I	P	M
443									I	P	M
451				I	P	M					
452				I	P	M					
453					I	P	M				

No.	K	1	2	3	4	5	6	7	8	9	10
454						I	P	P	M		
455									I	P	M
456									I	P	M
457				I	P	P	M				
461				I	M						

No.	K	1	2	3	4	5	6	7	8	9	10
462					I	P	M				
463					I	P	P	M			
464						I	P	P	M		
465						I	P	P	M		
466								I	P	P	M

No.	K	1	2	3	4	5	6	7	8	9	10
471				I	M						
472								I	P	M	
473								I	P	M	
474								I	P	M	
475								I	P	M	

No.	K	1	2	3	4	5	6	7	8	9	10
476								I	P	P	M
477							I	P	P	M	
478							I	P	P	M	
479							I	P	P	M	
480									I	P	M

No.	K	1	2	3	4	5	6	7	8	9	10
491				I	P	M					
492				I	P	M					
493				I	P	P	M				
501							I	P	P	M	
502						I	P	M			

Table 6.2.   continued.

No.	K	1	2	3	4	5	6	7	8	9	10
503								I	P	M	
504							I	P	P	M	
505									I	P	M
531				I	P	M					
532							I	P	M		

No.	K	1	2	3	4	5	6	7	8	9	10
533							I	P	M		
534							I	P	M		
535								I	P	M	
536								I	P	M	
537								I	P	M	

No.	K	1	2	3	4	5	6	7	8	9	10
541						I	P	M			
543						I	P	M			
544							I	P	P	M	
545							I	P	P	M	
546							I	P	P	M	

No.	K	1	2	3	4	5	6	7	8	9	10
551							I	P	P	M	
552								I	P	M	
553							I	P	M		
554				I	P	M					
555					I	P	M				

No.	K	1	2	3	4	5	6	7	8	9	10
561				I	P	M					
562								I	P	P	M
571				I	P	M					
572							I	P	M		
573				I	P	M					

No.	K	1	2	3	4	5	6	7	8	9	10
574					I	P	M				
575					I	P	M				
576									I	P	M
577							I	P	M		
578								I	P	M	

No.	K	1	2	3	4	5	6	7	8	9	10
579								I	P	M	
580								I	P	M	
581				I	P	M					
582					I	P	M				
583					I	P	M				

Table 6.2.   continued.

No.	K	1	2	3	4	5	6	7	8	9	10
584							I	P	P	M	
591							I	P	M		
592							I	P	M		
593							I	P	M		
594						I	P	M			

No.	K	1	2	3	4	5	6	7	8	9	10
595							I	P	M		
596							I	P	M		
597							I	P	M		
601				I	P	M					
602							I	P	M		

No.	K	1	2	3	4	5	6	7	8	9	10
603						I	P	M			
604									I	P	M
605					I	P	M				
606						I	P	M			
607					I	P	M				

No.	K	1	2	3	4	5	6	7	8	9	10
608						I	P	M			
609					I	P	M				
610						I	P	M			
611					I	P	M				
612					I	P	M				

No.	K	1	2	3	4	5	6	7	8	9	10
613								I	P	M	
614								I	P	M	
615				I	M						
616				I	P	M					
617				I	P	M					

No.	K	1	2	3	4	5	6	7	8	9	10
618						I	P	M			
619						I	P	M			
620				I	P	M					
621				I	P	M					
622						I	P	M			

No.	K	1	2	3	4	5	6	7	8	9	10
623					I	P	M				
624					I	P	M				
625					I	P	M				
626					I	P	M				
627					I	P	M				

Table 6.2.   continued.

No.	K	1	2	3	4	5	6	7	8	9	10
628				I	P	M					
629				I	P	M					
630					I	P	M				
631							I	P	M		
632							I	P	M		

No.	K	1	2	3	4	5	6	7	8	9	10
633						I	P	M			
634						I	P	M			
635					I	P	M				
636					I	P	M				
637					I	P	M				

No.	K	1	2	3	4	5	6	7	8	9	10
638					I	P	M				
639						I	P	M			
640							I	P	M		
641				I	P	M					
642						I	P	M			

No.	K	1	2	3	4	5	6	7	8	9	10
643					I	P	M				
644					I	P	M				
645					I	P	M				
646							I	P	M		
647							I	P	M		

No.	K	1	2	3	4	5	6	7	8	9	10
648								I	P	M	
649						I	P	M			
650					I	P	M				
651				I	P	M					
652				I	P	M					

No.	K	1	2	3	4	5	6	7	8	9	10
653							I	P	M		
654						I	P	M			
655							I	P	M		
656						I	P	M			
657							I	P	M		

No.	K	1	2	3	4	5	6	7	8	9	10
658							I	P	M		
659						I	P	M			
660					I	P	M				
661						I	P	M			
662						I	P	M			

Table 6.2.   continued.

No.	K	1	2	3	4	5	6	7	8	9	10
663					I	P	M				
664						I	P	M			
665							I	P	M		
666					I	P	M				

Step 4 addresses the mechanism whereby the person in charge (here the school superintendent) believes growth occurs in the learning event.

This is an objectives-driven area. The superintendent believes that the mechanism involves maximizing the opportunity-to-learn minutes available to the students during the class periods designated for language arts. In this situation, the mechanism and the measurement issues are so closely related that much of step 6 will necessarily be included in this discussion.

The distinction between time-on-task (assigned class time) and opportunity-to-learn has been made before. The superintendent has not made any changes in time-on-task; the same number of minutes of weekly instruction in language arts have been scheduled each year. The program he has put in place is designed to increase the efficiency ratio of opportunity-to-learn minutes divided by time-on-task minutes. He is convinced that increasing the size of this ratio (increasing instructional efficiency) will inevitably lead to increased student performance in this area. He believes the efficiency increases will come in three phases:

> First, when the teacher committee attains consensus for each objective on the grade of initial instruction and entering mastery.
>
> Second, when a monitoring system is put in place to use paper-and-pencil criterion-referenced measures four times per year.
>
> Third, when a computer-interactive monitoring system is put in place such that testing can be on demand, and not artificially constrained to four testing times.

He was able to institute the first of these during the first year of his program; the second took another year before it was ready. The third has not been put in place yet, due to inavailability of an appropriate number of microcomputers per building to manage this process. (See section 9.4, p. 232, for a further discussion of computer-interactive testing conditions.)

Why would the first step, getting the teachers to come to consensus on what is being taught, and the grades of initial instruction and entering mastery, lead to increases in instructional efficiency? Take a minute to look at table 9.1, found in chapter 9. Prior to implementing this program, the teachers in the superintendent's district were given lists of objectives and asked to identify the instructional responsibility at the grade they were currently teaching. The objective in table 9.1 is number 462, the positive, comparative, and superlative form of regular adverbs. Table 9.1 shows the state of confusion about which grade level has initial instruction responsibility. Seven of nine second grade teachers, five of nine third grade teachers, three of nine fourth grade teachers, and one of nine fifth grade teachers believe instruction occurs initially at that grade. Claims for entering mastery begin as early as grade 4; at grade 4, three teachers believed the objective was first taught there, while one believed all normal students should begin the grade with mastery.

This type of situation is terribly inefficient. The concept is not difficult to learn. If a student is taught, and attains mastery, on the concept in grade 4, the re-instruction in grades 5, 6, 7, and possibly 8 will involve a situation where time-on-task passes but no opportunity-to-learn exists. How can the student learn something when the teacher is reteaching what the student already knows?

Additionally, it is important for the teacher to know, when an objective appears in the language arts text, whether or not this objective has been taught before. If the teacher knows s/he is responsible for initial instruction, the teacher is likely to organize for instruction differently than if the objective is known to have been taught before. After all, if it has been taught before, the logical first step would be to determine if this prior instruction "took"; to what extent have the students maintained mastery?

The annual meeting, when the teachers get together again to review the prior year's data and determine if changes should now be made in grade placements or objectives, will continue this move toward more efficiency. Generally speaking, the grade of initial instruction of an objective is tied fairly closely to the first time the objective appears in the textbooks in use in the district. The grade of entering mastery, however, does not have an anchor that is quite so obvious. Teacher committees will tend to be a bit conservative in their first estimates of the entering mastery grade. Teachers don't like to see students faced with tests that are very difficult; they will tend to place entering mastery at a grade level such that they, the teachers, are almost certain entering mastery will have been attained.

This tends to leave some objectives in the system too long. As time goes by, and testing data accumulate, the teachers will become convinced that entering mastery can be achieved in shorter time periods. The grade of initial instruction probably won't change, since it is tied to the texts; but, as experience in this system accumulates, the grade of entering mastery will tend to move closer to initial instruction.

Each of these, getting a first consensus on grade placements of initial instruction and entering mastery, followed by a gradual moving of mastery closer to initial instruction, addresses the issue of improved instructional efficiency. Instructional efficiency is defined as the ratio of opportunity-to-learn minutes to time-on-task minutes. The superintendent believes that increasing this efficiency ratio will lead to higher student performance.

There really isn't much sense having a curriculum guide or an instructional system if no attempt is made to monitor it. There is no professional shame in being monitored; bank presidents, salespeople, pizza clerks, and bus drivers are all monitored in one way or another to see if they are doing their job. There exists a very important distinction between the monitoring system usually in place for this list of workers and the one the superintendent puts in place for language arts. For each of these, from the bank president to the bus driver, the monitoring is primarily based on outcomes: the "bottom line." The superintendent is less directly interested in outcomes than process. The information from the monitoring system is to be used to increase instructional efficiency — to help avoid teaching students things they already know, or teaching them a concept long after they have learned it, or going onto new material which depends on unmastered prerequisite skills.

So the purpose of the monitoring system is to improve instructional efficiency, not to measure output. The improved outcomes will naturally occur as the instructional program becomes more efficient.

Once the teachers have selected the objectives, the superintendent has a consultant develop a three-item criterion-referenced test for each objective. (A consultant is not really necessary here. There exist item banks from which most of these items could be obtained. For names and addresses, see Gronlund [1985, p. 509].) The definition of mastery, as discussed in chapter 9, varies among educators. Some want 80% mastery, based on 4 out of 5, or 8 out of 10, or 16 out of 20 items on the objective. Others settle for 75%, demanding three out of four. Some standardized tests have adopted a policy of using two items per objective, with two-out-of-two defined as mastery.

The superintendent weighs the options and selects a definition of three items per objective, with three-out-of-three defined as mastery. For four-response, multiple-choice items, a student is not very likely to get three items correct entirely by chance (the probability is 1 in 64). If the student knows the underlying rules for the objective, scoring all three correct should not be difficult. By holding the number of items per objective to three, the logistics of testing will be substantially easier to handle than if the more common 3 of 4 or 4 of 5 rules were adopted.

The first tests assembled are the entering mastery tests. The teacher committee completes its annual meeting in June, which allows the superintendent's staff almost three months to assemble the entering mastery tests for each grade level. The tests themselves, answer sheets, keys, and recording forms are delivered to the teachers' classrooms a few days prior to the first day of school in the fall.

The tests are to be administered as early as is logistically possible in the classroom. For certain, they are to be administered prior to any review activities. The purpose of the monitoring system, remember, is to increase instructional efficiency. The tests need to be scored immediately; the results will be needed the very next day. If the school is fortunate enough to have a scoring device which can turn all of the tests around immediately, that's fine; if not, the tests should be scored by the teachers. By administering the tests prior to any instruction, and having the results available the very next day, the following three areas of instructional information can be obtained.

1. If the students demonstrate mastery on the objectives tested before any instruction occurs, this indicates that prior instruction would have been a waste of time. In efficiency terms, time-on-task would have gone by without any opportunity-to-learn time.

2. To the extent that some portion of the students do not demonstrate mastery, the entering mastery test can be used to determine which parts of the objective caused the difficulty. Instead of reteaching the entire concept, the correctives can be directed only at the parts on which difficulty was observed.

3. The teacher gets an idea of how much long-term learning has occurred. To some, long-term may not equate to over-the-summer; but it certainly is a better indicator than drilling for an hour directly before giving the test.

The results from this entering mastery testing should not be relegated to the "gee whiz" category. The results have immediate instructional meaning. If the students have demonstrated mastery, then the objective should *not* be retaught, even if it does appear in the textbook for that year. That would reduce efficiency. If the students have not demonstrated mastery, a system should be in place to bring all normal students to mastery prior to beginning the rest of the instructional year. This type of remediation, termed by Bloom (1984) as "enhanced prerequisite mastery," pays performance dividends. And it should pay dividends, again from a viewpoint of improved instructional efficiency. Learning in an objectives-driven area is at least somewhat sequential; later objectives depend on earlier ones. By bringing all normal students to mastery prior to beginning the instructional year, the likelihood that a student will face an objective without a necessary prerequisite objective is reduced. With the necessary prerequisites for a new objective safely mastered, the student has an opportunity to learn the new one. Without the prerequisite, there may have been no opportunity.

The next round of testing is scheduled for late September or early October of the school year. This allows plenty of time for other necessities during the language arts classes. Language arts, as was noted at the outset, is much broader than just punctuation, capitalization, grammar and usage. The October testing is to cover the objectives which are still in the instructional system at a grade level, but which have been initially taught at a prior grade. Since the teacher committee finished its meetings the prior June, the superintendent's staff has plenty of time to assemble these measures.

The purpose is the same; to increase instructional efficiency by avoiding teaching concepts the students know without any review, and, where some difficulty is encountered, to use the tests to identify the areas wherein the students are having trouble. For these benefits to occur, just as with the entering mastery testing, the testing needs to occur prior to any review of these previously taught objectives.

A January round of testing is scheduled shortly after the winter holidays. This round is set aside to retest those objectives, first tested in September and October, where the performance levels were not up to agreed-upon levels. These levels can vary by district; some might ask for 95% of the students at mastery, others 90%, some 85%. The retesting round is set aside more for the students than anyone, to demonstrate that previously unmastered objectives have now been mastered.

The March testing round is set aside to begin the final push for mastery on those objectives designated for "entering mastery" the following fall. With all of the other things happening in a language arts classroom as the year closes down, it is well to have a diagnosis of the extent of the remediation task as early as possible. No useful information will be provided if the teacher first reviews the objectives, then retests. The fall testing is designed to assess long-term learning, with no prior review. The diagnosis in March should conform to the same format.

By mid-May, most of the initial instruction objectives for a grade should have been presented. The May testing covers these initial instruction objectives. This is the only round of testing which does not lead to direct improvements in instructional efficiency. The testing is done to see the extent to which the initial instruction "took" — the proportion of students demonstrating mastery at the end of the year of initial instruction. This round of testing is carried out primarily to provide data for the teacher committee which will meet less than a month later. As the committee attempts to adjust the grades of initial instruction and entering mastery, these data giving proportion at mastery after the first initialization will be useful. The data might show that the grade of initial instruction is too early; that the instructional materials are inadequate; or, conversely, that one instructional session is enough, and entering mastery can be expected the following fall.

As soon as it is financially feasible to equip each school with a microcomputer lab with 30 positions, the superintendent intends to shift the criterion-referenced testing from paper-and-pencil measures to computer-interactive testing. He argues that the change can be justified by a combination of improved logistics, instructional efficiency, teacher support, and coordinated monitoring.

The fall entering mastery testing would be done in the same manner, except the test would be administered on a computer screen, and the students would respond at the keyboard. Five minutes after the last student in a class was tested, the summary report would be ready for the teacher. The software for this report would not only show outcome listings for each student but could also regroup students according to observed difficulties. Additionally, the data from each student would be captured permanently, with no record keeping or scoring expected by the teacher. This certainly would make the monitoring system more palatable to teachers, particularly a seventh grade English or math teacher with five sections of 30 students each.

With computer-interactive testing, the October (pretesting), January (review testing), and May (initial instruction testing) would not have to be done in batches. The teacher could pretest objectives previously initiated close to the time the review section appears in the instructional material. Monitoring initial instruction could occur shortly after the instruction was given. Retesting could occur anytime. Of course, theoretically, all of these are also possible using paper-and-pencil systems. In the author's experience, with very large school districts and with small ones, the logistics of maintaining the paper-and-pencil system is overly intrusive on the teacher's instructional time. Each time a test is needed, the teacher needs to find it in the files, make appropriate copies, find the key, score the tests, organize results to improve instruction, and keep the records. Replicating this task 50 to 150 times a year eventually makes a serious dent in the time available for instruction.

This is why the superintendent, not yet having the 30 computer lab in each building, opted for batch testing four times per year. With the computer lab, however, the problem of intrusion into the teacher's time is eliminated. The teachers now select objectives to be tested interactively at the keyboard; from that point on, the computer tests, scores, regroups, and maintains the files. The testing can be done at the time it is most appropriate toward the improvement of instructional efficiency.

Step 5 in the evaluate-your-instruction process asks for the combination of content, classroom organization, teacher behavior, and expected student behavior which is consistent with the mechanism believed to bring about student growth.

For an objectives-driven area like this, the superintendent believes that what is usually termed "direct instruction" is most appropriate. The content is the textbook, supplemented by the placements determined annually by the teacher committee. The teacher is the authority. For initial instruction, the classroom is organized as a whole group. When data indicate that certain groupings of students have not yet attained mastery, the students are reorganized into groups to correct specific deficiencies.

Step 6 has to do with measurement. Much of this discussion seemed to fit quite naturally with step 4 regarding the proposed mechanism for growth. In a sense, with objectives-driven areas like these, the mechanism is the measurement.

The entering mastery testing does not equate fully with the need for entry-level skills, discussed first in chapter 2. The teacher committee set an entering mastery grade for all objectives taught in the school district. These are tested at the beginning of each school year. Entry-level skills have been defined in terms of skills necessary to make a satisfactory start in a course or unit of instruction. One might argue that some of the entering mastery skills may not be fully necessary for the language arts program during the impending year.

However, the superintendent feels that if an objective is in the instructional program, it should eventually be taught to mastery, and that mastery should be demonstrated by the student. For a K–8 program in punctuation, capitalization, grammar and usage, maintaining separate records for necessary entry-level skills as (possibly) contrasted with entering mastery skills seems unduly cumbersome. The need to monitor all of the objectives in the system takes precedence.

The measurement issue, "Do the students know why this event is being staged, and what is expected of them?" is important in a program like this. Errors in these areas, in both speaking and writing, can have serious repercussions. It isn't fair to prejudge the students, identifying in advance those who will need appropriate usage in their speech, correcting punctuation, capitalization, and usage in their writing to make sure this select group masters the objectives. The students need to know what is expected of them, and why.

The formative measures are primarily the pretest measures, and, to a certain long-term degree, the measures of initial instruction taken after the instruction has been completed. The annual meeting of the teacher committee, to adjust grade placements of initial instruction and entering mastery, is a formative measure, since it is making corrections to improve instruction the next year.

In the broader sense, the fact that the superintendent defined the learning event as the coordinated K–8 program, instead of breaking it into nine separate learning events (the kindergarten program, the first grade program, and so forth) forces all of the instructional measures discussed thus far into the formative category. The grades are not independent; the teachers and students participate in one integrated program.

These data need to be reported to the teachers after each round of testing. They also need to be summarized for overall analysis by the administration and by the teacher committee which meets each June.

Table 6.3 is a summary document for any given round of testing by one teacher. Across the top, reading down, are the objective numbers tested. The selection of objectives should be a flexible event, consistent with the instructional flow in each particular classroom. (See section 9.4 for difficulties which occur when objectives-driven areas like punctuation or math computation are treated, in computerized adaptive testing, as if they were difficulty-driven areas like reading comprehension.) This teacher is obviously on a unit about grammar, for all 16 objectives shown are consistent with this theme.

The student names are given, followed by their performance on each objective. The superintendent has chosen to define mastery as three items correct out of three items tested. A " + " on this form indicates the student mastered the objective; if a number appears, this indicates the number, out of three, the student did get correct.

The students are ordered vertically from the one with the most masteries to the student with the least. The objectives are ordered from left to right from most to least mastered.

The following pages of the summary show, objective by objective, the students who did not demonstrate mastery. The list begins with the easiest (most mastered) and continues to the hardest (least mastered) objective. This type of output could be easily developed if the testing were done at computer terminals, or if the testing were done on machine-readable answer sheets using paper-and-pencil tests.

If neither of these situations exists, the data from each student would have to be keyed into a computer before the report form of table 6.3 could be generated. This technique for source-data acquisition, a fancy way for saying "get the information into some sort of electronic memory," is

Table 6.3 A Class Summary Report for One Round of Testing

Diagnostic Language Arts Achievement Test Analysis
Class List

School: Eisenhower *Teacher: Nomellini* *Last Test Date: 10–31–85*

Objectives tested (Read 3-Digit Number Down.)

Student Name	405	408	407	401	402	406	403	404	412	415	433	411	413	431	432	414
Yung Alexander	+	+	+	+	+	+	+	+	+	+	+	+	+	+	+	0
Martha Arnold	+	+	+	+	+	+	0	+	+	+	1	+	+	+	+	+
Stacey Yager	+	+	+	+	+	+	+	+	+	2	+	+	+	+	+	1
Les Munch	+	+	+	+	0	+	+	+	+	+	+	+	+	+	1	+
Louise Held	+	+	+	+	+	+	+	+	+	0	+	1	2	+	+	+
Quint Walheim	+	+	+	1	+	+	+	+	+	+	+	2	0	+	+	+
Heather Koosma	+	+	+	+	+	+	+	+	+	+	+	0	0	1	1	+
Jim Barber	+	+	+	+	+	+	+	+	0	0	+	2	+	+	1	+
Jill Meagher	+	+	+	+	+	+	+	+	+	1	+	+	+	1	2	0
Pete Lundquist	+	0	+	+	+	+	+	+	+	+	1	+	+	0	1	+
Marissa Peters	+	+	+	+	+	2	+	+	+	+	+	+	+	0	1	0
Zeke Chrnak	+	+	+	+	1	+	+	2	+	+	+	0	+	+	+	0
David Nunn	+	+	+	+	+	+	+	+	1	+	0	+	1	+	+	2
Janet Sholl	+	+	+	2	+	+	+	+	0	+	1	+	+	+	1	0
Bobby Martinez	+	+	+	+	+	0	+	+	1	+	0	+	+	2	+	1
Adam Andover	0	+	1	+	+	+	+	+	+	+	0	+	1	+	2	+
Rachel Newsome	+	+	+	1	+	+	2	0	+	1	+	+	+	1	+	0
Amy West	+	+	+	+	+	+	2	0	+	1	+	+	+	1	2	0
Bob Adams	0	+	+	+	+	+	0	+	+	+	0	1	1	+	+	2
Bill Nielsen	+	1	1	+	+	+	+	0	+	1	+	2	0	+	+	0
Ann Saunderson	+	+	+	+	+	1	+	+	+	1	+	2	0	1	2	0

Pete Nelson	+	+	1	+	0	+	1	+	2	+	+	+	0	0	1	+
Bruce Olseth	+	+	+	1	+	+	+	+	+	0	2	2	+	1	1	0
Eric Olberg	+	+	+	+	0	1	+	0	2	+	1	1	0	0	+	+

An entry of + indicates mastery (student got three items correct out of three). An entry of 0, 1, or 2 indicates the actual number of items gotten correct.

Students are ordered from most to fewest objectives mastered. Objectives are ordered, left to right, from easiest to hardest.

Diagnostic Language Arts Achievement Test

Below is a listing of the tested objectives along with a description of each. Also shown is the name of each student who did *not* demonstrate mastery.

405.   Identify adverbs.
Adam Andove,   Bob Adams,
408.   Identify interjections.
Pete Lundqu,   Bill Nielse,
407.   Identify conjunctions.
Adam Andove,   Bill Nielse,   Pete Nelson,
401.   Identify nouns.
Janet Sholl,   Rachel News,   Quint Walhe,   Bruce Olset,
402.   Identify verbs.
Zeke Chrnak,   Eric Olberg,   Les Munch,   Pete Nelson,
406.   Identify prepositions.
Marissa Pet,   Bobby Marti,   Eric Olberg,   Ann Saunder,
403.   Identify pronouns.
Martha Arno,   Rachel News,   Amy West,   Bob Adams,   Pete Nelson,
404.   Identify adjectives.
Zeke Chrnak,   Bill Nielse,   Rachel News,   Amy West,   Eric Olberg,
412.   Select simple predicate.
Jim Barber,   Janet Sholl,   David Nunn,   Bobby Marti,   Eric Olberg,   Pete Nelson,

Table 6.3.   continued.

415.   Identify prepositional phrases.

Stacey Yage,	Jim Barber,	Louise Held,	Jill Meaghe,	Bill Nielse,	Rachel News,
Amy West,	Ann Saunder,	Bruce Olset,			

433.   Differentiate between compound and complex sentences.

Martha Arno,	Pete Lundqu,	Janet Sholl,	David Nunn,	Bobby Marti,	Adam Andove,
Eric Olberg,	Bob Adams,	Bruce Olset,			

411.   Select simple subject.

Heather Koo,	Jim Barber,	Louise Held,	Zeke Chrnak,	Bill Nielse,	Eric Olberg,
Quint Walhe,	Ann Saunder,	Bob Adams,	Bruce Olset,		

413.   Select complete subject.

Heather Koo,	Louise Held,	David Nunn,	Adam Andove,	Bill Nielse,	Eric Olberg,
Quint Walhe,	Ann Saunder,	Bob Adams,	Pete Nelson,		

431.   Differentiate between sentences and fragments.

Heather Koo,	Jill Meaghe,	Pete Lundqu,	Marissa Pet,	Bobby Marti,	Rachel News,
Amy West,	Eric Olberg,	Ann Saunder,	Pete Nelson,	Bruce Olset,	

432.   Differentiate between simple and compound sentences.

Heather Koo,	Jim Barber,	Jill Meaghe,	Pete Lundqu,	Janet Sholl,	Marissa Pet,
Adam Andover,	Amy West,	Les Munch,	Ann Saunder,	Pete Nelson,	Bruce Olset,

414.   Select complex predicate.

Yung Alexan,	Stacey Yage,	Jill Meaghe,	Janet Sholl,	Marissa Pet,	Zeke Chrnak,
David Nunn,	Bobby Marti,	Bill Nielse,	Rachel News,	Amy West,	Ann Saunder,
Bob Adams,	Bruce Olset.				

too cumbersome. Hand scoring would be better under this condition.

Table 6.4 shows objective-by-objective output after a number of rounds of testing. The examples shown presume that all five of the rounds of testing described earlier have occurred, and the teacher committee is now reviewing the results for potential changes during the following year.

The objective was tested in May of the year of initial instruction and only 11% were still at nonmastery at this time. Some dropoff occurred over the summer; the nonmastery figure increased to 14%. However, when pretested the next October, in sixth grade, the nonmastery percentage was very low, where it remained for the March testing of the next grade's entering mastery objectives.

The data suggest that the students had mastered this objective as they entered sixth grade. Carrying the objective through sixth grade makes little sense; entering mastery should be moved down to grade 6.

Table 6.4(b) shows a somewhat different result. In this situation, the grades of initial instruction and mastery are further apart; students seem to be "limping up to mastery."

This objective deals with an error which is pretty pervasive in usual conversation. "He did real good" or "Get the job done quick" are commonly heard. Maybe the school should give in to common usage. This particular teacher committee thought otherwise; the objective is part of the program, and therefore it should be taught to mastery.

Perhaps initial instruction is placed too early. At grade 5, there may not yet be a basis to convince students that what is common in oral exchanges is not appropriate for formal written communications. Perhaps by the junior high school years students can begin to see a reason for being

Table 6.4(a). Percent Not Passing Objective 103 (A Situation Where Entering Mastery May be Delayed Too Long)

	Obj. 103: Capitalization — Names: Family Relationships								
	Initial Instruction Grade: 4				*Entering Mastery Grade: 7*				
					Grade				
Mon.	*1*	*2*	*3*	*4*	*5*	*6*	*7*	*8*	*9*
Sep							5%		
Oct					14%	3%			
Jan									
Mar						4%			
May				11%					

Table 6.4(b).   Percent Not Passing Objective 454

Obj. 454: Grammar-Usage: Correctly choose between adjectives, advebs.
Initial Instruction Grade: 5   Entering Mastery Grade: 8

| | | | | | *G r a d e* | | | | |
Mon.	1	2	3	4	5	6	7	8	9
Sep								14%	
Oct						36%	22%		
Jan						21%	11%		
Mar							11%		
May					33%				

Table 6.4(c).   Percent Not Passing Objective 435

Obj. 435: Grammar: Identify run-on sentences
Initial Instruction Grade: 2   Entering Mastery Grade: 4

| | | | | | *G r a d e* | | | | |
Mon.	1	2	3	4	5	6	7	8	9
Sep				8%					
Oct			64%						
Jan			21%						
Mar			10%						
May		67%							

more precise in their written communications. The data indicate that the students eventually do master the objective. It might be more sensible to not have the objective in the system quite so long by delaying formal initial instruction a year.

Table 6.4(c) is an example of a situation where initial instruction just didn't seem to take hold.

The data suggest that initial instruction came a little early. It isn't that the students cannot master the concept; by the time they enter grade 4, 92% demonstrate mastery (and 8% do not). Identifying a run-on may be closely associated with independent reading, and Chall (1983) suggests this stage does not normatively occur until grade 3. Whatever the reason, it doesn't make much sense to perpetuate bad results. The third grade teachers are clearly doing the instruction for most students anyway. Third grade looks like a more logical placement.

The three tables above are chosen because they are atypical. After a year or two of this type of system, most of the tables will simply confirm that the current placements are correct.

There will be a temptation to presume that the same sort of information shown in table 6.4(a) to 6.4(c) can be taken out of results from the district's standardized testing program. Section 9.2.1 covers this issue in some detail. In short, the standardized test is inadequate. There are four reasons for this developed more fully in section 9.2.1.

1. The coverage is incomplete. The score on a subtest called Punctuation is derived from a sample of items in this domain. Time constraints prevent testing all objectives. Differences across texts and schools in the way instruction flows make the match between any test and the flow in a given district an incomplete one.

2. Diagnostic feedback needs to be more often than annually. Each of the five testing times described earlier is scheduled for a purpose; the purpose of increasing instructional efficiency. Even if the standardized test were ten times as long, to get adequate coverage, the timing would be wrong.

3. The feedback from a standardized test is delayed. If information is to drive instruction, the teacher needs the information quickly — immediately or the next day. For standardized tests, the time between when the last child is tested and the results appear is generally in the five- to eight-week range.

4. Finally, even for those objectives tested in the standardized battery, the number of items tested per objective is quite variable. Objectives are usually sampled with one item; sometimes two are used; and in rare instances, as with common objectives like capitalization of proper names, comma between city and state, or use of the articles, more than two items. The consistent three-items-per-objective selected by the superintendent gives a much better basis for comparison.

The last measurement category is the outcomes measures. The standardized test, noted above as having very limited value as a formative measure, serves the outcome purpose a little better. However, items 1 and 4 above still apply. A standardized test coverage is not exhaustive, may not conform to the instructional flow in the district, and inconsistently saturates the objectives it does include. Nonetheless, it does represent a sample from a domain and the publication of the results is a type of validation understood by communities.

Table 6.5 below shows the standardized test results for language arts

Table 6.5.   Standardized Test Monitoring of Performance in Language Arts during the Period of This Learning Event's Evaluation (Scores shown are standard scores)

Year	*Grade*							
	1	*2*	*3*	*4*	*5*	*6*	*7*	*8*
0	432	551	623	695	706	744	774	809
1	444	569	623	702	724	756	774	809
2	459	590	646	730	733	783	792	815
3	509	581	664	728	761	786	819	812
4	482	590	676	733	768	780	823	827

for a district which implemented the essential elements of the program described in this chapter. The implementation covered a four-year period, which began in the 1979–80 school year. (Data are based on the standard score scales of the Metropolitan Achievement Test [1978], Form JS, published by the Psychological Corporation. Testing is done in February each year. The district involved is the public schools of Geneva, Illinois. The program continued past year 4 shown in the table; however, the district changed standardized tests at that time. The new testing program approximated the same percentile ranks as the old, and performance has continued to improve through the 1986 testing program.)

The publisher's standard score scale is used to demonstrate the extent of growth that occurred (grade equivalents could have been used just as easily). Note for year 4, for fourth grade, the average standard score was 733. This score is higher than the average fifth grade score had been before the program began. This improvement continues at each of the subsequent grades, where the average fourth year score surpasses the average pretest score of the next grade. One way to state this result is as follows: The improved instructional efficiency has caused the basic skills program in language arts (at least as measured by this test) to be taught to a higher level one year faster.

A standardized testing program, while providing external validation of growth, is not a very thorough monitor of this type of program. The superintendent set out to raise student performance. The mechanism he proposed was an increase in instructional efficiency. The standardized test data suggest that more is being taught in less time. Table 6.6 shows a more

Table 6.6.   Instructional Flow at the Beginning of the First Year and End of the Fifth Year of the Program

Grade	Ent. Mstry		Init. Instr.		In System		Avg. % Pass	
	Yr.1	Yr.5	Yr.1	Yr.5	Yr.1	Yr.5	Yr.1	Yr.5
1	0	0	8	6	8	6	—	—
2	0	0	13	16	21	22	—	—
3	5	9	39	35	55	48	88%	96%
4	8	16	46	48	93	80	73%	91%
5	19	29	32	32	106	83	86%	94%
6	36	44	46	50	116	89	89%	88%
7	45	35	34	31	105	85	88%	93%
8	45	37	12	12	72	60	88%	91%
9	44	36	0	0	28	24	94%	92%
10	28	24	0	0	0	0	92%	90%

direct way to accumulate the data to investigate the extent to which efficiency and performance have increased. (This table is patterned and mirrors the results from the program in Geneva, Illinois. However, the number of objectives has been expanded to include all of those shown in Appendix B.)

The table shows the number of entering mastery and initial instruction objectives, by grade, at the beginning of the program and after five years. The columns headed "In System" show the number of objectives at each grade which have been taught (including initial instruction for that grade) but have not yet been tested for mastery. The last two columns show the percentage of objectives mastered by the average student.

One increase in instructional efficiency can be seen by studying either the columns under entering mastery or "In System." The data show that, over the years, the teacher committee moved mastery to lower grades. In the first year, the number of objectives piled up in the fifth to seventh grade; the mastery test was longest in the seventh to ninth grade. By the fifth year, the mastery tests in all of the upper grades were shorter; the system had been smoothed out and mastery responsibilities shifted generally to lower grades.

The outcome columns show that while this reduction in time between intial instruction and mastery was taking place, the performance level of the students was not decreasing. In fact, the last two columns indicate a general increase in the percentage of objectives mastered by the average student.

Table 6.6 is the more direct measure of growth. It is more appropriate to say that the standardized test data are a validation of table 6.6 then to argue the reverse. Table 6.6 reflects performance on all of the instruction done in this learning event in this district. The standardized test is just a sampling.

References

Bloom, B.S. (1984). "The search for methods of group instruction as effective as one-to-one tutoring." *Educational Leadership* 41(8):4–18.

Chall, J.S. (1983). *Stages in Reading Development*. New York: McGraw-Hill Book Co.

Gronlund, N.E. (1985). *Measurement and Evaluation in Teaching*. New York: Macmillan Publishing Co.

Petty, W.T., Petty, D.C., and Becking, M.F. (1973). *Experiences in Language*. Boston: Allyn and Bacon, Inc.

Shepherd, G.D., and Ragan, W.B. (1982). *Modern Elementary Curriculum*. New York: Holt, Rinehart and Winston.

Stewig, J.W. (1983). *Exploring Language Arts in the Elementary Classroom*. New York: Holt, Rinehart and Winston.

7 A CROSS-CUTTING, INTERDISCIPLINARY LEARNING EVENT: The Character Development of the Students in a K–12 District

Step 1. What is the Learning Event?

The learning events in the prior three chapters, addressing reading comprehension and language arts at the elementary school, and the math program for college bound students at the high school, have fit quite nicely a traditional view of the way content is organized in schools. This chapter makes some sharp breaks. Character development generally falls under the affective column, if one dichotimizes cognitive and affective goals. Character development is not usually a class or a course of study; it is, as shall be seen, difficult to define so that all will agree; and it cuts across the entire school program.

By the way, the topic of this chapter is an example of why the term "learning event" has been used here instead of "instructional program." The school's impact on the student extends well beyond formally developed instructional programs and, as shall be seen, much of this impact falls under the general heading of character development. The distinction here is that the student is indeed learning, but not necessarily as part of the traditional interpretation of a planned instructional program.

Character development would generally be assigned to the affective side

159

of a cognitive-affective dichotomy. Such a dichotomization implies the two are unrelated, which is foolishness. McKown (1935, p. 53) wrote, "The process of developing moral character parallels, in general, the process of developing thinking ability." Beane (1986, p. 27) states more directly that "The cognitive domain involves not only the acquisition of knowledge, but its use in increasing complex thought processes. At its highest level the cognitive domain involves evaluation, the determination of value or worth, which obviously includes value preferences and appreciation." Wynne and Walberg (1986) continue, ". . . character development depends on the school treating its academic program seriously." Schaps and associates (1986), commenting on a specific implementation, write, ". . . academic and character education . . . often can be achieved simultaneously." Beane (1986) argues that to consider higher-order thinking skills as entirely within the purview of the cognitive domain is foolish, particularly with adolescents. He writes (p. 27), "Given youths' preoccupation with personal and social issues, might not higher order thinking skills be promoted more successfully through their application to these issues, rather than limiting their application to academic subjects?" .

It is difficult to address the evaluation of a learning event without establishing a context. Perhaps this learning event, more than any other described here, is situation specific. Indeed, many private schools have been established precisely because they have the goal of developing character in a specific manner. To this point Peshkin (1986, p.41) writes that in such schools, ". . . there is but one standard, one outlook, one code of conduct, . . . students are taught to see all of life as one, with no warrant for spiritual adjustments. Right behavior does not vary with time and place."

But it is not only between private and public schools where differences of opinion would be found on this issue. Regional differences, rural-urban-suburban differences, and differences in long-standing traditions within schools near one another suggest that establishing a context for this learning event is necessary.

Therefore:

> The learning event is in a K–12 school district enrolling about 5,000 students. The district has one high school, one junior high school, and six elementary schools. The elementary schools are neighborhood schools, where all children walk to school.
>
> The district is in a community separated by 40 miles from an urban center. The community was, at the close of the World War II, a small village. Over a

25 year period, it grew to its current size. Enrollment in the schools reached its maximum in the early 1970s and has been fairly stable since then. The residents of the community are generally on the younger side, upward mobile, moving to more affluent areas as their own affluence increases. The median income and median home value place the community in a broad category called "middle class."

Justifying the existence of a reading comprehension, language arts, or high school math program was not necessary. In this case, however, some might ask, "Is character development a learning event which a school should formally address, or should the school just let things happen without specific guidelines and measures?" The superintendent of the district is male; has been in the district for five years; generally has the support of the board of education; and aspires for a larger district superintendency in the near future.

The superintendent has observed, over his tenure in the district, that more of the community's attention seemed to be directed toward the general topic of character development. Some community members are upset by changes in behavior of young people not only in the community but in general. Many put the responsibility for these undesirable behaviors at least partially on schools. Wynne (1986) echoes these people, arguing that there is a relationship between student conduct and moral learning. As examples, he states, "Within the recent past, American education substantially disassociated itself from . . . the deliberate transmission of moral values to students." As evidence of this decline he cites, ". . . increase since the early 1950s of youth disorder: suicide, homicide, and out-of-wedlock births." The superintendent thinks this is going a bit far, but he is generally a proactive type, feeling that if things are going to change, he'd just as soon control the change than be pulled by it.

But those are not the only reasons the issue keeps coming up. Shane (1975) includes these under headings like "frustration stemming from permissiveness" and "fear that the fabric of our society is coming apart." He also mentions a heightened consciousness, to a certain extent triggered by events of Watergate and the Viet Nam war, and that people are beginning to realize that the "good life" is more than material possessions and "things."

The superintendent asks first, Should the schools be involved with character development?

Wynne (1986) argues that the question itself is not viable. The world will turn on its axis; snow will fall in Minneapolis; and character education will occur in the school. He would argue that the question is not whether or not the event occurs; the question is rather the extent to which the school chooses to intervene with that which is occurring anyway. Beane (1986) supports this viewpoint in his discussion of the "hidden curriculum." He says (p. 29), ". . . young people learn a great deal about themselves and others from the institutional features that govern day-to-day life in the school — the methods of decision making and control, system of rewards and punishments, the nature of interactions, patterns of grouping, rituals of grading, and other procedures used for labeling, sorting, and processing students." The content and values built into these usually routine administrative procedures are powerful lessons. He continues these issues are ". . . more likely to be a living example of intentional affective education than an unplanned accident of institutional convenience."

So the answer to "Should the school be involved with character education?" is, "Don't be silly. The school is involved whether it likes it or not." From Beane's (p. 29) perspective, the schools character education program has two elements: intentional programs (e.g., on substance abuse, citizenship, family living) and institutional policies (many mentioned above). He feels intentional programs tend toward the humanistic, developmental side, whereas institutional policies frequently show a less humane side.

Step 2. Who is in charge of this learning event?

Now there's the rub. Lockwood (1986, p. 10) says, "If there are moral experts to whom we should appropriately defer, I'm not sure how to spot them." But that's a trap which sets up this circular, no-win argument:

> . . . Character education is going to occur in your school no matter what you do about it.
> . . . And, by the way, if the students don't behave in a manner which is within society's accepted normative boundaries, the school will be held accountable.
> . . . But since people differ on the meaning of "accepted normative boundaries" the school better not act.

Primack (1986) thinks the school should lead, with these admonitions (p. 12). "(The school) must be able to (1) justify its selection of values to the community at large; (2) justify itself as the appropriate institution, or at least one of the institutions of choice, to convey these particular values, and (3) design an effective means to propagate them."

The school might just establish some broad general goals (have good citizenship, be sensitive to others, be considerate, work hard, etc.) and hope for the best. The superintendent believes the district should go further than this and accept a more active leadership role. However, he views character development as a cooperative program involving the students themselves, their parents, the teachers, other community members, and significant other community groups (churches, service clubs, scouts, etc.) involved in this area.

The superintendent's district has eight schools. Should there be a central committee, with representation from each school; or should there be eight relatively autonomous separate committees, one for each school, with looser coordination?

The superintendent adopts the viewpoint that the school is the appropriate unit of intervention. Having eight separate committees will be administratively more difficult; yet the schools, albeit part of the same community, are different. The six elementary schools serve subtly different neighborhoods; the social situation at the elementary, junior high, and senior high levels are obviously different. He reasons that eight separately functioning committees will develop different viewpoints, varying emphases, a range of creative responses, and a broader picture of what character education is. Through coordination, the committees will learn from one another; eventually, a single, coordinated program might be attained by consensus. Additionally, having eight committees will give each of the eight principals, along with a substantial number of teachers, students, parents, and community members an opportunity to participate actively in the process of developing a character education program for the district.

To start off with, however, the learning event is in charge of the eight committees, one for each of the schools. Membership includes students and teachers from the school, parents of students at the school, other adults who live in the school's attendance area, and representatives from other community groups interested in the topic. The principal of the school chairs the committee. Each group is asked to elect their representatives.

Step 3. Why is this learning event being staged in the first place? What are your expectations for the students?

The first question has already been answered. Character development is going to happen as a normal part of schooling. The only issue here is that the superintendent has decided that instead of taking a laissez faire attitude, the district will address the issue under the direction of a broad-based committee from each school.

A temptation will exist to define character development in terms of discreet traits. Standardized, published measures of achievement and aptitude are much more common than their counterparts in the affective areas. What affective measures do exist are usually measures of traits, such as motivation for schooling, academic self-concept, sense of mastery, authoritarianism, or introversion. Closure sometimes suggests that the program be defined in terms of what is available to serve as a measure. Why not define a trait area considered to be part of character development (say, work habits) and then redefine that in terms of subtraits (purposefulness, sustained effort, punctuality, persistence, responsibility), and top it all off with some standardized measures of each?

Chapter 10 addresses in some detail the problems of these affective measures, termed measures of "acquired behavioral dispositions," of traits. There are problems of commonly accepted definitions and problems in interpretation. Sugarman (1973) acknowledges that one advantage of a trait approach is that (p. 42) "it has the advantage of being more manageable in scale" but overrides the advantage by saying, "but the disadvantage that there are not many single attributes which stand out as being intrinsically interesting or outstandingly important in themselves."

A trait is a name given to some set of behaviors. At best, it represents an average. Around the average, the meanings assigned by different people vary a great deal. A measure, after all, is a number assigned to people or constructs according to rules. For a measure to be reliable, the rules have to be interpreted the same way by all of the people. With traits, like self-concept, motivation for schooling, punctuality, courtesy, or patriotism, the rules differ with each beholder. An important example of this is at the extremes, where many traits become vicious. Patriotism that leads to a Calley or an Eichman, loyalty that leads to a Haldeman or Dean, are examples. Traits are undependable indicators.

An emphasis on traits can divert the school from their real goal; behaviors that are consistent with the expectations of the community. Do all punctual students have good work habits? Is a good work-habit student necessarily punctual? In fact, if the student manifests "satisfactory" performance on all of the traits used to describe "good work habits," will the student's behavior be pleasing to the community? The trait approach can focus on the intervening measure at the expense of the ultimate goal.

Additionally, the trait approach has a tendency to focus the program inward, intrapersonally, instead of outward, interpersonally. Manifestations of behavior, good or bad, in the school setting mostly occur in situations where the student is interacting with others. A trait like "responsibility" is difficult to address intrapersonally. McKown (1935) wrote over 50 years ago, "It is not teaching a child anything new to teach him a code of standards. What he needs is help in seeing the implication of such matters for daily living."

The superintendent decides that, working through the principals who will chair the eight committees, he will try to lead discussions away from the trait approach. Sugarman's (1973, p. 43) "character-type" approach, in which ". . . one can specify a collection of attributes which represent a cultural ideal . . ." seems more appropriate. But this is pretty vague. It has some definition problems too.

Competing viewpoints exist over the way such a program should be structured. One approach is to stress conduct; the other is more taxonomic and developmental. Proponents of the two groups do not always speak highly of one another. The developmentalists accuse the conduct people of preaching indoctrination and an absolute position. The conduct people view the developmentalists as avoiding the real issues of behavior: of teaching young people to always treat behavior as relative and to learn to always say, "Yeah, but what if. . . ."

For example, addressing conduct, Wynne (1986) advocates (p. 6) ". . . concern with good habits of conduct as contrasted with moral concepts or moral rationales." These conducts, he continues, occur day-by-day — telling the truth, being polite, recognizing legitimate authority. He contrasts ". . . good habits of conduct" with "moral concepts or moral rationales" which, he continues, ". . . sought to emphasize the scientific base . . . these approaches disavowed . . . persistent concern with affecting conduct." In other words, these programs worked on the students' thinking and reasoning, but not directly on practices.

Lockwood (1986, p. 10) responds that "Wynne holds in particular disdain school programs that permit young people to exercise reasoning and judgment on ethical issues. He believes such programs contribute to alarming rates of youth disorder." In a broader sense, Lockwood (1986, p. 30) writes that ". . . absolutists believe in indoctrination and inculcation of their beliefs; developmentalists emphasize the process of continuous questioning of beliefs." He thinks the two viewpoints are irreconcilable and that public schools have the obligation to present the developmentalist viewpoint.

The developmentalist or scientific viewpoint is best expressed by Kohlberg's six stages of moral development (Sugarman, 1973, pp. 50–51). Crudely put, the first stage (with a little child) involves prescribing to an imposed standard to avoid punishment, followed by doing what is "right" because it satisfies personal needs. At stage three, a person is "good" because this is pleasing to family and friends. At the next stage, people do "right" out of respect for authority and because this is one's duty — some people never get beyond this stage. At the next stage, the focus moves somewhat to the situation. Although laws are necessary for a society to function, there are times when moral needs supersede these specific rules. At the final stage, the person ". . . makes moral judgments on the basis of general moral principles which he has chosen to be his moral pole stars and his incentive for sticking to these principles lies in not wanting to endure the self-reproach which he must suffer if he fails."

The superintendent decides he doesn't want to be labeled absolutist. He does not want to be accused by anyone of advocating indoctrination. He has already rejected trait as definitions, and along with them any extensive dependence on questionable paper-and-pencil measures. But he is interested in behavior — in conduct. An interest in behaviors does not have to equate to a support of indoctrination. The more scientific developmentalist approaches sound too scholarly. He wants the committees to concentrate on programs and expected behaviors which relate to things that happen in schools.

The superintendent decides that the ". . . moral experts to which he will defer . . ." will be a broad-based committee representing each school in the district. Working through his eight principals, he is going to discourage a concentration on traits, discourage a totally scientific approach, and concentrate on behaviors which are associated with what happens in schools. Additionally, he wants to emphasize that character development is not a topic which is separate from the academic programs of the schools. He is convinced that character development and academics are inseparable.

The eight committees, working independently, will most certainly define their task in different manners. What ground rules should be established to facilitate their task? How does one make "character education" out of this difficult construct called "character development"?

The underlying philosophy of the evaluate-your-instruction process is that things happen for a reason; that the reason events occur should relate to the way they occur; and that outcomes should be measured in a manner consistent with the driving philosophy and the process of implementation. The three — philosophy, practice, and outcomes — are linked to one another in both directions. Practice changes outcomes; but outcomes change practice too. Philosophy impacts practice; but practice impacts philosophy. Outcomes obviously impact philosophy. The superintendent wants to make sure the committees do not focus only on outcomes, particularly undesirable outcomes, without looking at the entire picture. And this involves both cognitive and noncognitive elements in the schools' programs.

In chapter 5, dealing with a learning event involving certain basic skills areas in language arts, the point was made that it is better to give a faculty committee an exhaustive listing of objectives, and let them select from the list those presented in that school, than to ask them to develop such a list from "scratch." Character development is obviously not as neat as basic skills in language arts; but people have spoken on the topic over many years. The superintendent feels it would be useful for each committee to have a compendium of definitions of character development in terms of expected behaviors.

Many of the descriptions simply do not suggest associated behaviors. For example:

. . . Brandt (1986, p. 3) defines moral values as "the specific values that particular cultures generally hold in regard" and later ". . . proper family conduct or nature of reciprocal relations." Sugarman (1973) is probably addressing Brandt's "reciprocal relations" when he says the morally educated person is ". . . competent at knowing other people's feelings and good at knowing and expressing own."

. . . Lockwood (1986) says, ". . . the morally educated person possesses virtuous dispositions and can reason justly." "Reasoning justly" is more directly stated by McKown (1935, p. 53) as the need "to develop an increasing ability to discern causes and to relate effects." Sugarman (1973, p. 49) puts this as, ". . . (is) objective in sizing up situations and unafraid to proceed with the plan of action intended." Ultimately, when faced with an unfamiliar situation, the morally educated person, ". . . thinks in terms of universalistic moral principles based on concern for the rights of other people as well as himself."

. . . Wynne and Walberg (1986): ". . . displaying commitments."

. . . Beane (1986) argues against ". . . hazy phrases like 'developing self-worth' or 'understanding others.' " McKown (1935, p. 58) expresses self-worth as "the harmonious development, adjustment, and integration of one's personality."

. . . Schaps and colleagues (1986): ". . . concern for other people, understanding of others, and concern for balancing one's own needs and rights with those of others." More generally, McKown (1935, p. 56) believes the goal should be to "develop a recognition and acceptance of one's responsible membership in society and an increasing success and satisfaction in discharging that membership effectively." Sugarman (1973, p. 49) says the morally educated person ". . . has concern for others such that their feelings, wants and interests count with one and are not lightly overridden for the sake of one's own goals."

These are a little less general, do suggest behaviors, but are beginning to approach a trait philosophy:

. . . Telling the truth in the face of evident temptation (Wynne, 1986; Primack, 1986), including "stick(ing) to a set of principles" (Coles, 1986).

. . . Being polite (Wynne, 1986); common courtesy (Lockwood, 1986); helpful, considerate (Schaps et al., 1986).

. . . Obeying legitimate authority (Wynne, 1986), obedience to legitimate authority (Wynne and Walberg, 1986). Examples of obedience to legimate authority include "arriving on time to class, paying attention in class, applying themselve during recitation . . ." More gently, "To develop an intelligent respect for the conventions of society" (McKown, 1935).

. . . Orderly environment (Lockwood, 1986); discipline (Coles, 1986). "Suppress destructive peer groups" (Wynne and Walberg, 1986).

. . . Responsibility (Primack, 1986).

. . . Courage (Primack, 1986); courage "to be himself, herself" (Coles, 1986).

. . . Absence of arrogance and self-importance (Coles, 1986).

. . . Hard work (Coles, 1986). To the faculty: "assignment of substantial and relevant homework, giving tests and otherwise evaluating, and treating teaching and academic learning as important" (Wynne and Walberg, 1986).

Then there are organizational behaviors which have been associated with the way students develop character. Generally, the implication is that supposedly routine operating practices in the organization can have a detrimental effect on behavior. Included in this list, with some thoughts on how the effect can be detrimental, are:

. . . The way decision are made and potential for appeal. (Students cannot be expected to learn decision-making and legitimate means of questioning authority without having experience in these processes.)

. . . The control function, including systems of rewards and punishments. (The long term goal is self-control. A school that needs extensive control mechanisms is not allowing the students to move toward self-control.)

. . . Grouping, grading, sorting of students. (When there exists a strong emphasis on individual competition in these practices it is difficult to work toward cooperation and concern for others.)

The three lists certainly cannot be termed "expected outcomes from the learning event." They are not the equivalent of the specific list of performance statements used to select language arts objectives for punctuation, capitalization, and grammar-usage. But in a manner similar to the language arts objectives, the lists define a range and some parameters. Each of the eight committees will have the difficult (and interesting) job of sorting through to identify elements which are central to its perception of the important elements of a character education "curriculum." In a real sense, the committees will not really define character education until they begin addressing specific programs. Now, however, the issues of practice and outcomes need to be addressed.

Step 4. What is the mechanism whereby growth is believed to occur on this learning event?

Part 1. Group socialization

One mechanism is to move the locus of control as far from the adult in charge and as close to the peer group as possible. In objectives-driven areas (math computation, learning to fly an airplane) the teacher in charge is the expert. Control remains with the teacher. Many goals of character education will be best served if the peers themselves are viewed as the "experts." Unknowingly, until they start talking to one another, a group of students will probably represent a range of potential responses to issues. Cooperative learning will occur when the environment is designed to facilitate free expression among the students.

Opportunity-to-learn is once again relevant. The mechanism of cooperative learning will only work if the students have a sense that they are in control, such that they freely express their opinions. No member can be allowed to dominate; no honest expressions can be termed "dumb." The teacher's role is to provide a realistic stimulus to get the discussion started, and then monitor to see that the discussion doesn't get out of control. This is essentially socialization by peers. Let them learn from one another the full range of responses, and, through discussion, work toward the group's definition of "good" behavior, which might also be termed "normative," at least for that group.

Sugarman (1973), citing Kohlberg, stresses the need for the student's having a range of opportunities for social interaction and role-taking. Role-taking involves seeing another person as someone like yourself, and the tendency to begin seeing how your behavior is interpreted by another person. He continues, "The more democratic the group, the more role-taking both members and leaders do in accommodating to each other's varied points of view." (The superintendent's decision to use eight broad-based committees conforms to this point of view. Each subgroup — the students, teachers, parents, community members — will have the opportunity to assume and understand the roles of the others on the committee.)

Of course, there is the fear that, without the teacher exercising direct control, the group will define as "normative" behaviors the teacher (and other adults) will find abhorrent. Beane (1986, p. 28) argues to the contrary: "Proponents of this view believe that if these processes are really learned and legitimately used, young people will logically affirm fundamental values." On those occasions that the group does not "affirm fundamental values," the adult in charge has two choices. Each addresses opportunity-to-learn potential.

If the unacceptable consensus position is not likely to cause any serious personal damage to anyone, and, very importantly, if the teacher is fairly certain that future events will convincingly demonstrate that the consensus position was unwise, then the teacher should back away. If there exists little real potential for personal damage, allowing the students have the opportunity to learn the correction on their own is preferred to interfering before the "future events" are allowed to happen.

On the other hand, the teacher may fear some fundamental rights are being ignored, someone is in a position to be hurt, or there is little hope that future events will occur to clarify the situation. In this case, Beane (1986, p. 28) argues, ". . . by virtue of their societal role, adults have a right to interfere in value deliberations where there is evidence that the process has been corrupted or where fundamental values are not recognized." The adult, at such a time, should avoid adopting an authoritarian response, but rather get the discussion redirected.

This first mechanism, then, depends on the range of responses to a given situation which can be found in a group of students. Opportunity-to-learn time will be maximized if the issue is a realistic one, if the range of responses is clarified by the teacher, if all students feel free to offer their responses, and if the group continues the discussion until some consensus agreement can be reached.

Part 2. Personal examples

The first mechanism depended on student-to-student interactions; this second depends on interactions between the student and the adults in the school, and the students and the school organization itself. Aspy and associates (1986, p. 14), comment that "students expect to see in our lives the virtues that we extol; when they do not see them, they know our words lie." At issue here is the behavior of the adults (not only the teachers, but the administrators and others in the building); the other issue is the appearance of the institutional traditions.

The mechanism is that these are the elements with which the student is constantly interacting. The student sees how teachers treat one another, and treat other students; sees how decisions are made and how conflicting viewpoints are treated; sense the extent to which the organization values him/her; and is frequently faced with situations where a choice between a more-acceptable and less-acceptable mode of behavior must be made. To the extent that the school can increase opportunity time — build in a positive way on these naturally occurring events — the student can be guided to personal growth.

The exemplary types of adult models included above can also be portrayed in the content students study for their classes. Wynne and Walberg (1986) call for ". . . literature, proverbs, legend, ritual, and folk tales." Although those sound mostly like English or literature class topics, some aspect of character development could be part of any instruction — from English to foreign language, from social studies to math and science.

The mechanism of providing more opportunity minutes in character education cannot be allowed to interfere with the more direct purposes of each of these instructional areas. As mentioned earlier, character education and cognitive learning should be seen as supportive, complementary. The teacher should not replace a solid content unit in the course with a "soft" unit included only because of the intention of presenting some aspect of character development.

But it is not necessary to soften the program just because some exemplary examples of character development are included. Both mechanisms can be served at the same time. That is, the student can have the opportunity to learn content which is logically part of the instructional program, while at the same time the material provides some exposure to an issue of character development deemed important by the oversight committee of the school.

The student-observes-world examples can come through contacts with educators in the building or through the material used in all courses. They can also come through controlled contacts with agencies outside the school. Community service work in hospitals, homes for the elderly, child care centers, health agencies, or other schools can provide the desired types of experiences. These are more structured, permanent institutions. Student participation can also be organized around specific issues: for example, issues of national or international breadth (a program to feed the hungry) or might have a more local focus (pollution in a nearby lake.)

The mechanism, in both cases above, is to structure some minutes when the student is involved in activities or discussions which fit under the heading of character education. The function of the committee at each school is to encourage, select, and monitor these activities and discussions. As has been routinely true throughout all of the learning events covered, setting aside some minutes is not enough. The minutes must be opportunity-to-learn minutes; the committee must make sure that the experiences are meaningful.

**Step 5. What content, classroom organization, teacher
behavior and expected student behavior is consistent
with the mechanisms listed above?**

Character education should mostly appear as an element in the other things
happening in the school because it is a school. Direct instruction will frequently look too much like indoctrination. Direct instruction would involve
the use of slogans, concentrate on defining specific traits, see students
taking pledges, and involve memorization of creeds, patriotic poems, or
deeds of great courage.

The direct method has a lot of problems. Each school committee will
be encouraged, through the principal's leadership, to primarily be interested in behaviors. Behaviors happen in context; they are situation-specific.
The direct method is artificial. Since the material is not presented in context, it is also frequently dull. The event is preplanned; thus it frequently
will not occur at the right time. And, supposing the teacher is able to cause
the students to memorize a heroic piece, or make "desirable" responses
to situations presented, there is still no guarantee that the desired behavioral tendency has been acquired. McKown (1935, p. 135) says quite directly, "Memorizing and reciting a creed, oath, code, or similar material
may be accomplished fairly easily and may warm the heart of the teacher,
principal, parent, or visitor, but what should cool this warmth is a recognition that such memorization and repetition may be just about as useless
as saying 'blah, blah, blah,' or reciting the alphabet, the multiplication
tables, or 'Mary Had a Little Lamb.' " Finally, with the direct method,
those teachers *not* assigned units or courses in this area will feel no ownership.

A few courses, such as Family Living at the high school level, might
involve direction instruction, but this type of program should mostly be
integrated into the other activities of the school. The activities of the school
consist not only of the courses but also institutional features, specialized
programs, counseling services, clubs, athletics, and other extracurricular
activities.

Part 1

Two mechanisms were proposed in the previous section. The first involved
student-to-student learning in a cooperative atmosphere.

The content of this type of learning cannot be allowed to be entirely
serendipitous. In the first place, the issues each committee would like to
see addressed may not occur naturally. Even if they do, the instant they
occur may be a clumsy time to embark on these kinds of discussions. If

the students are going to have an experience which provides opportunity-to-learn minutes, instead of just minutes, some prior preparation is necessary.

The topic needs the preparation. The issue needs to be put on the floor. The *content*, at that point, is the *variety of responses the students in the group make to the issue*. The students are carrying the content around in their heads.

Suppose, for example, a junior high school teacher proposes to the committee a unit on the limitations of free speech. The issue can fit quite nicely into the context of a history course. It could also fit into a reading course, since many of the Supreme Court rulings on this topic are actually quite interesting reading. In either case, such a topic could be developed in a manner which does not generally lower the cognitive level of discussion just because a character education issue has been brought to the floor.

The teacher's responsibility is to bring the issue to the floor in a manner which can and will bring responses from the students, but which does not lead them. For example, the teacher might pose this situation: An American Nazi organization applies to march in the July 4th parade in a predominantly Jewish community. The community committee refuses permission. The Nazi organization sues, declaring this is an abridgement of their rights to free speech. The teacher could provide other material that traces the history of free speech rights.

The mechanism calls for drawing each student into the discussion. Each of these junior high school students will have an opinion. What they do not know, before hearing what the others say, is that not everyone feels exactly the same way about this issue. That's a key purpose; not only do they learn from each other a range of responses, but they learn that reasonable people can disagree about fundamental issues like free speech.

The teacher can hardly withdraw. Left alone, junior high school students tend toward anarchy. But, to the extent possible, the teacher should not comment on each student's response; not attempt to categorize; and particularly not attempt to judge. Each student must be somehow brought to expressing an opinion. Once this has happened, the discussion should continue until the group comes to consensus on some sort of boundaries on the issue. Which examples are clearly, by consensus, undue infringements on freedom of speech? Which examples of limitations are acceptable to them?

The content and teacher behavior, and to a certain extent expected student behavior, have been addressed. What about classroom organization?

The type of process envisioned in this mechanism might be hard to do in a whole-class environment. Many students have already been socialized into a passive mode. Such students wait to see which direction the majority, or an influential classmate, is going before they express themselves. This type of mimicking behavior is an example of a student's having class time but no opportunity-to-learn time. A classroom organization must be developed which causes each student to express a response freely, from the context of his/her own existence.

One organization would be to break the group into small groups of two or three each. Each group chooses a leader and a spokesperson (role-taking). Within a defined time period, each group must make a decision on the issue in question, and explain why it came to that decision. To the extent practically possible, the groups should not interchange ideas; each group works alone. The spokesperson then presents to the entire class each group's decision and rationale.

An alternative would be to develop a unit for a microcomputer to accomplish this task. This kind of activity would use the full range of unique capabilities of a computer. The computer can branch. The response a student makes determines what the student will see next on the screen. The computer can keep records and summarize them for immediate feedback. After the last student has interacted with the machine, the computer can group and organize the responses in a manner which would "drive" instruction immediately thereafter.

On the free speech issue, the computer program could have stored 20 or 30 short vignettes, possibly taken from Supreme Court cases, which address these issues. The vignettes would range from an extremely permissive interpretation to an extremely restrictive interpretation of free speech. The software would begin at a rather central position, and continue challenging the student until a fairly stable estimate of that student's degree of permissiveness is found. The data from all students would then be summarized on a continuum. Names, of course, would at this point be excluded.

There would be the temptation, at this point, for the teacher to attach to each vignette the actual Supreme Court decision for each case. But the students need the opportunity to internalize that it was not a bunch of gray-haired judges who made this range of responses, but was rather their classmates, in that room with them. They need to discuss the issue, to experience the concept that reasonable people can disagree on an issue like this. It is not just the content of the range of responses, but the fact of the range which is important.

Only when they have had these experiences (these opportunity-to-learn minutes) should authority be brought back in. It would be well to end the discussion with the link to reality; the actual decisions made by the Supreme Court on the vignettes presented.

Of course, there are a myriad of different ways to organize the classroom in conformity with this mechanism. Small groups and computerized adaptive software are but two examples; a paper-and-pencil worksheet might replace the computer; individual reports might replace the committees. The issue is that the relationship among content, organization, and teacher/student behavior must conform to the mechanism, which calls for the students to learn from one another. If the teacher takes control, the lesson will look like indoctrination.

Most of the extracurricular programs should be designed to conform to this mechanism. Clubs provide good opportunities for students to adopt leadership positions and adopt one another's roles. It is important for the sponsor of these activities to remember the mechanism; no opportunity-to-learn minutes will occur if the adult in charge is authoritarian and maintains too much control. Even when the consensus decisions of the students are likely to lead to less-than-satisfactory results, the sponsor should guide, not dictate. This is the time for opportunity-to-learn minutes, not perfection.

Part 2

The second mechanism involved learning from examples. The examples appeared in the behaviors of the adults in the school, through content of the courses, the organizational behavior of the school, and experience with agencies outside the school.

The way the adults in the school behave — toward students, toward each other, toward events that happen in and out of school — undoubtedly plays a role in the character development of the student. The events, however, are difficult to define, measure, or control. The content is what is happening at that moment, and this may not involve any organization. The adult behaves in some way; the student just observes. The committee at each school might want simply to heighten the awareness of all of the adults (from the janitor to the superintendent) that what they do does have an impact on the students, and add to this some general guidelines.

The second category of examples available to students has to do with the content in courses. The content discussed in step 5, part 1, where the students learned in a cooperative setting, really came from the students themselves. Their varied responses to a relevant situation become the basic content. Under this heading, the content is specifically defined. The lesson is in the content.

Every instructional area can find appropriate content for a program in character education. As mentioned earlier, the content should fit naturally into the usual flow of instruction for the course at hand. Additionally, the instruction should stay at a high intellectual level. The notion that cognitive suggests higher levels of thinking than affective is foolishness; evaluation is the highest cognitive level, and it requires values and judgment.

The committee for each school might ask each teacher to outline a few units — say, one each quarter — designed to fulfill the requirements listed above (fit in naturally to the course of study, not lower the intellectual level of the course). As it takes on the role of approving or altering these suggestions, the committee would be in position to operationalize their unique definition of what character education really is.

The way the school is organized and administered is really not a classroom issue, so the usual focus on content, classroom organization, and teacher/student behavior is inappropriate. Yet these issues are important, for they have an impact on the student's developing perceptions.

Autocratic administration is so much easier than dealing with democratic decision-making and the cumbersome processes so often associated with it. And many times the adult needs to remain clearly in charge if the educational program is to go forward efficiently. For example, in objectives-driven areas like math computation or punctuation, the mechanisms proposed previously put the teacher firmly in control.

But it is not always necessary to avoid process. The committee at each school might heighten the awareness of not only teachers but also club sponsors, class sponsors, the nurse, guidance people, and administrators that students develop awareness of these elements of character when they have the opportunity to participate and, even better, make decisions which dictate practice. These suggestions are particularly appropriate when directed at the usual control functions in the school; the systems of rewards and punishments.

A major of organizational impact is in the manner used to group and sort students, and assign grades. It seems contradictory to attempt to develop learning based on cooperation and a sharing of ideas in an environment that screams of individual competition and class rank. A perceptive young educator, part of a high school with five academic tracks in most departments, commented recently, "We have three schools here. One for the top two tracks, a second for the regular track, and third for the lower two tracks. How you perceive the school, as a teacher or student, depends on which track you teach or attend." The committee involved with decisions about character education at such a school would have to weigh the academic benefits of tracking against the picture such practices provide to the students at each level.

Step 6. Measurement

Authors do a great deal of writing about character development and character education; but they rarely hurry to say explicitly how they would measure the results of such a program. A recent curriculum journal (ASCD, 1986) used the issue of character development as its theme. Nineteen articles were devoted to the topic. Only one (Schaps et al., 1986) addressed the measurement issue at all, and the descriptions there were both brief and general.

The concept of defining character development in terms of traits, then accompanying such definitions with paper-and-pencil measures of these traits, has already been rejected by the superintendent. In chapter 10, such traits were termed acquired behavioral dispositions. The superintendent is not terribly disposed to finding out how the students are disposed to behave; he wants to know what experiences they receive and how they actually behave.

These kinds of measurements require patience. They require a long-term commitment to a comprehensive information system. If the program is worth doing it is worth monitoring; without longitudinal data, even an excellent principal needs to operate on the basis of perceptions and anecdotes. The superintendent reaffirms his commitment to the school itself being the primary unit of analysis. He authorizes that a microcomputer with substantial storage capacity will be dedicated to an information system at each building. The systems are to be compatible such that district-wide reports, as necessary, can be accumulated upward.

Although time spent is not a fully adequate measure, since certain intense two-minutes experiences can probably have more impact than less-intense day-long experiences, it is a reasonably manageable measure. The superintendent has already made the key decision that a planned character education program, under the guidance of a broad-based committee at each school, is preferable to just letting things happen as they will. The superintendent wants to measure the amount and intensity of experiences without breaking the district's budget. He decides that "number of minutes" will be the common metric used to determine the amount of experiences each student has. He also is impressed by the need for students to operate in different roles during these experiences, particularly in a leadership role. Thus he decides to keep track of the intensity of the experience at three levels: did not participate (code 0), participant (code 1), assumed some leadership position (code 2). The "leadership" designation has to do with the student's doing something beyond just participating. It does not necessarily mean the student is the club president or has the lead in a play.

It means the student is doing a little more: setting up a stage, reporting for a committee, recording the minutes for a meeting, or buying the soft drinks for a party.

The experiences will come in different settings. The measures for each are a little different. Here is listing with some thoughts about measures:

1. Planned experiences (indirect instruction) which are part of a regular courses of study. The committee determines the number of planned experiences which will occur in each classroom. Mentioned earlier was a frequency of one such activity per quarter — the frequency is one of the variables under the school committee's control. A simple information system is established to record:

a. The topical area into which the four (one per quarter) planned experiences were interwoven (the content areas are also coded for further disaggregation).

b. A one-page summary of each experience.

c. The number of class minutes devoted to each (a reasonable estimate is satisfactory).

d. A class list, with the intensity code (0, 1, or 2) for each experience filled in by the teacher.

2. Courses whose major themes are legitimately included under this topic. For each such course, a one page summary attached. The class list is structured to include the number of minutes students are participating, and the number of minutes each assumes a leadership role.

3. Extracurricular activities, including not only the usual ones like athletics, clubs, school government, and music, but also (at the lower grade levels) school plays, musical events, cookie sales, and other one-time-only events. The adult sponsor of each would provide:

a. A list of participants.

b. An estimate of the number of minutes each participated under codes 1 and 2 (participating and leadership).

c. A one-page summary of the purpose and activities of the activity.

4. Planned experiences away from school, including special community projects and volunteer work. The adult in charge of such a program should provide:

a. A list of students participating.

b. An estimate of the number of minutes of participation.

c. The number of minutes of participation under the codes 1 and 2.

d. A one-page summary of the activity.

5. Lessons learned from the institutional operating procedures, including rules for control, sorting and placement, and pupil evaluation. Measuring the number of minutes these procedures impact the students will be beyond the scope of the information system.

6. Lessons learned from the behavior of the adults in the school building.

Measuring the impact of these behaviors will also be beyond the scope of the information system.

The information system is designed to answer the question, "To what extent are the students having experiences considered to be part of a character education program?"

A second question is probably even more important: "To what extent are the experiences the students are having consistent with what the school committee wants them to have?" The information collection system is designed to help the school committee respond to this question. For areas (1) to (4) above the committee has the responsibility of reviewing and coordinating the one-page summaries for approval into the overall character education program. Two issues need to be reiterated in this regard:

First, the committee should make sure the each proposed classroom experience conforms to the two restrictions named earlier: The experience fits into the regular sequence of instruction one finds in such a course, and the intellectual level of the activity at least maintains the usual level of that class. The notion that cognitive means "hard" and affective means "baby stuff" needs to be avoided.

Second, this is the time, in reviewing the various proposals, when the committee will finally define what it means by character education. The words all seem to be cross-referenced; but when the committee sees a specific proposal from a teacher to do a certain thing in the name of character education, then they will have some basis to find out the extent to which they have a common definition for this concept.

Areas (5) and (6) cannot really be put into this information system. The committee will need to address the issue of the "face" put forward to students by the various institutional policies. On the issue of the behaviors of adults, the committee will need to establish some guidelines, and make sure they are generally disseminated.

The measures discussed above are programmatic input measures. They address information which will allow the committee to structure an overall program which conforms to their group consensus of what character education is, as well as a way to monitor the extent and intensity of the experiences. There are also some outputs which should be part of this information system. The listing of such outputs below is meant to be illustrative; the school will actually have many more.

Some negative indicators:

1. Absentee information.
2. A daily record by the principal of disciplinary actions taken.
3. A listing by the counselor(s), kept in terms of minutes of student contact, of minutes spent with students addressing problems

related to what the school committee terms "manifestations of bad character."

4. Requests from teachers to seek help with disruptive students.

Some positive measures should be included, such as:

5. Amount of contributions brought for various charity drives.
6. Number of volunteers in helping situations.
7. Count of letters or calls from community members commending the behavior of a student.

Finally, some external measures:

8. A survey addressing the punctuality, honesty, and cooperation of employers of students who work part-time (or whatever other issues are of interest to the school committee).
9. A similar survey of parents and teachers.

And some routine information which should be on a school's information system:

10. Grades.
11. Standardized test scores.

Some analyses could yield useful results after just the first year. For example:

1. Tabulate the data to see the extent to which all individuals are participating; to see if the leadership roles are being assumed by only a small proportion of students; to see if there are subgroups of students who are participating in no extracurricular or out-of-school activities.

2. If nonparticipating subgroups are identified, link other parts of the information system (grades, disciplinary action, even the part of town they come from) to them.

3. Cross-tabulate the in-course experiences by grade and content area to make sure there is a fairly even distribution. (This presumes that the school oversight committee determines that character education is everyone's job.)

These types of analyses would be run at least once each year. The rest of the information sources are best interpreted in terms of trends. Accumulations of each should be run quarterly and displayed in graphical as well as tabular form.

This chapter represents an interesting type of learning event. Character development, like the development of good citizenship, is a general goal of every school. Both terms are difficult to define; experts do not agree on what they mean. The school could just acknowledge that they believe in character education as a general goal, get all the teachers and principals to nod their collective head in assent, and stop there. Most schools do.

The evaluate-your-instruction steps provide a useful way to operationalize a broad concept like character development. Surrounding the issue and defining who will be in charge are big steps. The definition of expectations is not so easy here as with high school math or reading comprehension; but the discussions at least clarify the issue. The definition in the above example will really not come until the oversight committee chooses among teachers' proposals for in-course programs. Establishing the proposed mechanisms is important because the mechanisms suggest new ways for the teacher and students to interact. The measures are very difficult. Patience and a commitment to a thorough information system are required.

The chapter reinforces some themes in this book. The superintendent's educational philosophy called for local school control of this important issue. He chose to let the parameters of character education be defined by a broad-based community committee. These philosophies will obviously be reflected in the practices that are adopted at each of the schools in the district. The philosophies and practices will most certainly have an impact on outcomes. The information flow will reverse, probably, when certain outcomes cause differences in philosophy or practice.

Central to all is that things don't have to just happen. Even a very difficult concept like character education can be addressed directly. Perhaps the first approximation of a program will be faulty, but with some care and nurturing the issue can be defined to the consensus agreement of the important parties. Reason is preferred over randomness.

REFERENCES

Aspy, D., Aspy, C., and Roebuck, F. (1986). "Fulfilling the great tradition through interpersonal honesty: A response to Wynne." *Educational Leadership* 43(4):13–14.

Association for Supervision and Curriculum (1986). *Educational Leadership* 43(4).

Beane, J.A. (1986). "The continuing controversy over affective education." *Educational Leadership* 43(4):26–31.

Brandt, R. (1986). "Overview." *Educational Leadership* 43(4):3.

Coles, R. (1986). "The moral life of children." *Educational Leadership* 43(4):19–25.

Lockwood, A.L. (1986). "Keeping them in the courtyard: A response to Wynne." *Educational Leadership* 43(4):9–10.

McKown, H.C. (1935). *Character Education*. New York: McGraw-Hill Book Co.

Paske, G.H. (1986). "The failure of indoctrination: A response to Wynne." *Educational Leadership* 43(4):11–12.

Peshkin, G.H. (1986). "God's choice: The total world of a fundamentalist christian school." *Educational Leadership* 43(4):36–41.

Primack, R. (1986). "No substitute for critical thinking: A response to Wynne." *Educational Leadership* 43(4): 12–13.

Sugarman, B. (1973). *The School and Moral Development*. New York: Barnes and Noble.

Schaps, E., Solomon, D., and Watson, M. (1986). "A program that combines character development and academic achievement." *Educational Leadership* 43(4):32–35.

Shane, H.G. (1975). "The future mandates new moral directions." In *Emerging Moral Dimensions in Society: Implications for Schools*. Washington, D.C.: Association for Supervision and Curriculum Development.

Wynne, E.A. (1986). "The great tradition in education: Transmitting moral values." *Educational Leadership* 43(4):4–9.

Wynne, E.A., and Walberg, H.J. (1986). "The complementary goals of character development and academic excellence." *Educational Leadership* 43(4):15–18.

8 TESTING ISSUES GERMANE TO EVALUATING YOUR INSTRUCTION

8.1. The Changing Testing Environment at Three Levels of Schooling

For the purposes of this discussion, separate schooling into these three levels: preschool to the end of grade 1; end of grade 1 through junior high school; and high school.

8.1.1. Needs and Responses

Testing needs, and available responses, are quite different at these three levels.

As a kindergarten class assembles to begin the school year, the children in the class have different performance capabilities for at least three reasons:

1. Their ages vary by about 20%. The oldest is not yet six, the youngest is not yet five, a one year difference (out of five) which translates to 20% more learning time for the older children.

2. Their experiences vary widely. Some have been to preschool, others

not; some have been taught the alphabet and can form every letter; others have been taught nothing. Some have traveled extensively; others have not yet been out of the neighborhood.

3. Developmental rates vary. Even for two children with precisely the same age and background, the timing at which they demonstrate certain skills is different.

The children who could have learned, but had no opportunity to do so, should not be penalized. Testing, at this level, should focus on determining whether or not the child has the entry-level skills for a new task, and not on achievement. Testing should be done to identify those children *not* ready to learn, so they can be helped.

Here are two examples of the distinction between testing for an entry-level skill and testing for achievement:

1. For Chall's (1983) level 0 reader (a prereader), it is important that the child learn that symbols (like letters) can be used to indicate sounds (e.g., the symbol "B" stands for the sound "bee.") If the test shows four letters (ARTB) and the teacher says, "Circle the B," it is an achievement test. The only way the child could have learned that the symbol "B" goes with the sound "bee" is through someone teaching him/her that relationship. The children who were not fortunate enough to have someone teach them that relationship should not be held back or labeled "developmentally delayed."

2. It is also important that the child learn that combinations of letters, called words, can stand for things. Suppose the readiness test shows a picture of a dog, below which are the words "DOG CAT TREE APPLE" and the teacher instructs, "Circle the one that means dog." The correct answer depends not only on the child's understanding that letter combinations can stand for objects but also on the child having the prior experience (being read to, most likely) of having seen DOG in combination with pictures of dogs.

In each case, the entry-level skill falls under what Cazden (1974) calls metalinguistic awareness. To test them fairly with all children, each child should have had the opportunity to learn. If testing must be done before school starts, or within the first few weeks of school's opening, then the responses should be nonsense syllables or figures unfamiliar to all. In this way, the concepts (symbols can stand for sounds, combinations of symbols can stand for things) are tested directly, without the intrusion of prior experience. If testing can be delayed, then some direct instruction could precede, such that all children have had the opportunity to learn prior to testing.

The primary use of tests for this age group should be to avoid placing the child in a learning situation where failure is very likely. As Stroud (1964, p. 127) put it, "It is difficult to see any good in spending a year in reading without any progress. It is easy to see much harm. It is, to say the least, understandable if the pupil who puts in a year in not learning to read does not show up next year filled with enthusiasm."

These early years are not the time for percentile ranks, stanines, grade equivalents, or other normative scores. Better to screen out, for special help, those who cannot demonstrate necessary entry-level skills. Let the rest spend the two years being socialized into the schooling process.

8.1.2. Years for Achievement Testing

The years between the end of grade 1 and the completion of junior high school are the golden years for standardized achievement testing. Schools differ, textbooks differ, pacing differs; but overall, there exists a great deal of commonality in what elementary schools offer. Standardized tests sample from this commonality. It is likely that 80% of the basic skills objectives taught during these years are sampled somewhere in the test's coverage in grades 2 to 8. In the next chapter, some procedures are presented for finding the battery which best matches the instructional flow in a district.

Of course, the fact that the battery assesses areas of commonality is also a weakness. The battery will not assess uniqueness. Appendix B lists language arts objectives. Included are quite a number of grammar objectives; things like finding the subject or a noun, knowing the various types of pronouns. Many districts teach very little grammar; they concentrate entirely on usage. Because grammar instruction is not common, standardized tests concentrate almost entirely on usage.

Measurement in mathematics is a second example. At this time, much confusion exists in the area. Should metric only be taught, English only, both without conversions, or both with conversions? The variable responses to this by districts makes the test-makers cautious. They include only the most common English units. When equivalencies are needed, they are usually provided in the problem.

Nevertheless, common objectives are sampled satisfactorily. An annual administration of a good battery from grades 2 to 8 can serve three purposes:

First, it can provide longitudinal performance information by area tested. The outcomes should be displayed, preferably with a graph, for each sub-tested area across all the years that particular battery was administered.

When forms or batteries are changed, the longitudinal data are pretty much lost, since norming populations across tests are not equivalent.

Second, it can provide cross-sectional information about the comparative performance of subtested areas. From an equity viewpoint, these comparisons should go across the distribution; a look at the average performance at the first quartile (25th percentile), median (50th percentile), and third quartile (75th percentile) would be worthwhile. If the percentile rank of the average student at some level varies dramatically across subtests, that diagnostic would be worth some further investigation.

Third, it can provide some feedback to the parent/guardian of the children. Publishers have developed some good home reports. Recommended are those that show the child's scores in percentile rank units, displayed in graphical form with performance bands, and accompanied by a simply narrative report. These are understandable by and useful to parents.

8.1.3. Decline of a Battery's Efficacy

If a test is supposed to measure what is taught, then the efficacy of an achievement battery declines sharply at the high school level. At least 90% of what is tested in a typical standardized survey high school battery was taught prior to the beginning of grade 9. The high school battery primarily assesses the maintenance of previously taught skills.

This situation exists not because test publishers are trying to dupe the public. It exists because the environment changes. High schools have courses in areas like foreign language, business, vocational training, computer studies, and fine arts. The standardized high school battery will not have coverage in these because they are basically electives; since not all students elect them, test coverage would be unfair.

What about the required areas? Again, the publisher cannot presume common coverage. In mathematics, not all freshmen take algebra; even a smaller percentage take geometry. The publisher pretty much excludes these from the math test at all high school levels; the only thing left to test are the common skills, taught first prior to high school. This story can be repeated for science, social studies, and language arts.

The high school test user should fully understand that the high school battery is primarily monitoring the maintenance of previously taught skills. As a technique for monitoring the instructional program which exists in a high school, the standardized test is inadequate. If monitoring is important, as it should be, then other techniques need to be developed.

8.2. Maximum-performance tests and typical-performance measures

When an algebra teacher prepares a semester exam, the teacher's expectation is that the students will try their best to get the maximum number of questions correct. The test, like all achievement and aptitude tests, is a maximum performance test. Some psychomotor measures, like time required to run a mile or number of situps in a five-minute period, are also maximum performance measures. The tester wants the student to give his/her best.

On the other hand, suppose a program evaluator wanted to find out the attitude of taxpayers toward the education of deaf children. An attitude measure might include this item:

Expenditures for the education of deaf children are too high.

    ( ) Strongly agree
    ( ) Agree
    ( ) Disagree
    ( ) Strongly disagree

The question for the taxpayer is not, "Respond in the manner which would maximally support the education of the deaf," or "Respond in the manner which maximally not support the education of the deaf." Instead, the question seeks the typical response, "To what extent do you typically agree with the statement?"

Chapter 9 deals with issues wherein maximum performance tests are used with the evaluate-your-instruction process. Chapter 10 covers areas where typical performance measures are most frequently needed in the process. Note the distinction in terms. Typical performance measures are not tests; they are not examinations. Thus maximum performance *tests* and typical performance *measures* are used.

The distinction suggests some potentially serious interpretation problems.

1. Given a good reason to do so, most people, including children, are capable of faking responses on typical performance measures. What they do is make a maximum performance test out of a typical performance measure. A candidate for a job in an accounting firm, taking a typical performance measure, will try hard to maximize apparent interest in things like accuracy, interest in numbers, and clarity.

2. Typical performance measures are situation-specific. If a student knows how to add $451 + 384$, the student will demonstrate the same maximum performance in school, church, at home, or on the playground. With a

measure of an area like "assertiveness," however, the student's response depends on the situation. It is situation-specific. This issue is covered more completely in chapter 10.

3. Interests and attitudes change in the face of information. An honest response to the question, "Would you enjoy having a family of a different race living next door to you?" might change if the hypothetical situation actually occurred. The message is that it is not sensible to ask students questions about issues with which they have had no experience.

4. Sometimes a student argues, in a maximum performance situation, that some extraneous variable interfered with the delivery of maximum performance. Three potential threats are test bias, lack of motivation, and text anxiety.

It is important to remember that achievement tests are designed to be biased; they are designed to be biased against those who do not know the material, and in favor of those who do. One might call that "fair" bias. Tests can be unfairly biased as well. In a high school reading comprehension test, an intricate passage about football rules would be generally biased against females and in favor of males. Reading passages which deal with jet travel, suburban living, or other issues which tend to correlate with the amount of family income would be biased against those at the lower socioeconomic levels. A test which shows only pictures of males or stereotypes male-only occupational fields is biased against females. A test that reflects, in its material and illustrations, only those of one ethnicity is biased against all others.

Standardized tests now on the market go through considerable scrutiny to avoid these types of bias. Through "aggressive destereotyping," boys cook, girls play baseball, and elderly people run for airplanes. Knowing that state or local selection committees will eliminate from consideration any test with a hint of bias, publishers invest substantial effort into pre-publication efforts to insure none are present.

The test anxiety and motivation issues are complicated; they need a book of their own. However, human nature suggests that a student who perceives himself/herself as doing poorly on the test will search for ways to maintain ego. "I didn't really care" or "I was too anxious" are frequently protection devices. A student who arrives in a testing situation without adequate prior preparation has good reason to be anxious.

The issues cannot be dismissed; there undoubtedly are people who become so anxious they cannot respond, and situations where the student can see no reason to persevere so doesn't even try. But as a user, it is important to remember that when a person does poorly on the test, it is not necessarily the test's fault. The test is purposely biased against those who are inadequately prepared.

8.3. Aptitude versus achievement tests

Aptitude tests are sometimes called intelligence tests.

Measures like the College Boards or the ACT are scholastic aptitude tests administered to help colleges assess the potential for success of students applying for admission.

The usual distinction between achievement and aptitude tests is that achievement tests measure what the student *has learned* while aptitude tests measure the student's *ability to learn* in the future. This clear-sounding distinction has two problems. In the first place, tests designed as achievement tests are frequently used to predict future performance; they are used as aptitude tests. In the second place, the domains of coverage for achievement and aptitude tests are not independent. It is foolish to think that one could test for future capabilities without tapping into prior learning. That is, one cannot test for aptitude without measuring some achievement.

To address the first issue, a more operational distinction is needed between the two types of test. This definition, proposed by the author in an earlier book, is as follows (Wick, 1973):

> If the test results are used to determine the student's current performance level, it has been used as an achievement test. If the test results are used to make some sort of decision about the student's future (e.g. assign the student to a reading group or course level), it has been used as an aptitude test.

The ACT, used by colleges to help with admission decisions, is an aptitude test used as an aptitude test. A semester exam used to assign a grade of "B" to a student is an achievement test used as an achievement test.

A high school that limits enrollment in a particular math course level to those who demonstrated a percentile rank in excess of 90 on the math section of an achievement test administered in eighth grade is using an achievement test as an aptitude test. A decision about the student's future is being made; no matter what the achievement test is called, it is, in this instance, an aptitude test.

A district which evaluates its gifted program and reports that IQ, for some target group, increased by ten points is using an aptitude test as an achievement test. The ten-point-higher score is a measure of current performance, not future capability. An aptitude test was used as an achievement test.

Aptitude and achievement tests are both done with group tests using printed directions and multiple-choice items. Each has a heavy reading load. Each measures vocabulary and math problems. The aptitude test will have analogies and number sequences not usually found in an achievement test. Nonetheless, the domain of coverage between the two is not independent. In fact, the domains probably overlap considerably. For one coordinated achievement/aptitude testing battery, correlations between performance on the reading comprehension section of the achievement test and the verbal score on the aptitude test ranged from 0.80 to 0.88, which is just slightly less than the range of reliabilities. Clearly they are tapping the same domains (Beggs and Mouw, 1981).

By ignoring these two issues, that an aptitude test is any test used that way and that the domain of content for achievement and aptitude tests overlap, serious interpretation errors can occur. One such error is the pervasive belief that aptitude is fixed and unchangeable. At a lunch table in 1979, a group of teachers in a district told the author that the proposed performance improvement program for the district could not succeed, because IQ scores indicated the students were already working up to capacity. Six years later the average student was performing more than 20 percentile rank points higher. They could grow.

The point is that the IQ scores, at the time of the 1979 meeting, were at the same general level as the achievement scores. The two different-sounding tests are measuring a good deal of the same domain of content! Does it surprise anyone that generally low achievement scores are accompanied by generally low aptitude scores, and vice versa? Likewise, when a program to raise achievement scores is introduced which does raise achievement scores, it should not come as a surprise that aptitude scores are raised also. The high correlations give educators the false sense that the tests have tapped into a causal relationship, that the aptitude is causing the achievement levels.

The damage occurs when educators view the relationship as causal and therefore impermeable to change. A superintendent in a nearby school district, looking at the summary results from a testing program, commented, "Our median IQ is 103, and our median percentile rank is 52. The students are working up to their ability, and we are doing as good a job as could be expected."

No achievement improvement program can flourish in that kind of environment. Aptitude is not unchangeable; since aptitude and achievement tests sample from the same general domains of content, both can be increased by intervention programs.

A second potentially debilitating misuse of aptitude tests results when the skills tapped by the predictor test are not consistent with the skills necessary in the predicted task, course, or program. Consider these two examples:

> . . . A high school requires a grade of B or better in sophomore geometry before a student is allowed to enroll in chemistry.
>
> . . . A governmental agency requires a high school diploma before a person can apply for a position at a vehicle maintenance facility.

These two situations involve the use of achievement measures as aptitude tests. A high school diploma results if the student completes enough high school units with a passing grade; it might be called an accumulative achievement test. Many people are alert to potential misuses of IQ tests, and indeed some large cities have actually legislated them out of the schools. But in these two cases the achievement tests are used precisely as if they were IQ tests; they are used to make an estimate of a person's potential in the task at hand.

Isn't that reasonable? After all, for group data, there exists a fairly strong correlation between the grade in the geometry course and grade in the chemistry class, for those who take both. And the agency may be able to demonstrate that, in general, employees with a diploma have stayed longer than employees without a diploma.

But group data come from individual decisions, and it is at the individual level that harm can be done by these decisions. The correlations in group data are not germane; the basic educational question is this: To what extent do the skills tapped by the predictor correspond to the skills needed in the predicted task, course, or program?

One could probably find some overlap between the skills tapped in geometry and chemistry. Both require reading; both require math. But in general, it's not a good fit. It is realistic to imagine a "C" student in geometry who would be excellent in chemistry, or an "A" student in geometry who would find chemistry very difficult. In the second example, while it may be generally true that the personality factors which caused the student to quit high school may also lead to less job longevity, this general rule will not hold for all individuals.

The two examples illustrate what the British call "creaming" — literally, "take the best from the top." Creaming is a form of prejudice. In each example, group decisions are being made without an examination of the effect on each individual in the group. If screening for a chemistry class is necessary, then the screening should be done on the basis of skills necessary to succeed in chemistry, which have been called entry-level skills throughout. The governmental agency also has the responsibility to screen candidates on the basis of their entry-level skills for the job in question — a motor vehicle facility.

8.4. Some Interrelated Measurement Topics

8.4.1. Measurement Defined

A common, but as shall be seen later, flawed definition of measurement is: the assignment of numbers to objects or events according to rules.

Schools have objects (desks, people, computers, square feet of space) and events (school days, classes, assemblies, board meetings). Even apparently straightforward measures need precise rules. To measure average class size, for example, is average daily attendance or current enrollment used as the numerator? Are all certified teachers, including the nurse, guidance person, and assistant principal, used in the denominator, or does this include only those who actually teach regularly scheduled classes? The assignment of numbers must be according the specific rules otherwise different people will measure the same event in different ways. When the rules are imprecise, the measures are unreliable.

The limiting aspect of the definition above is that a substantial proportion of the things educators want to measure are neither objects nor events. An object can be seen or touched; an event is a happening. Gifted behavior, math problem-solving, reading comprehension, and a positive attitude do not fit either category well. Each is the name for a construct; people use the names to summarize a general domain of behaviors. Measurement is needed to link the name to the behaviors in a reliable manner. Here is an expanded definition:

> Measurement is the assignment of numbers to objects or events according to rules. When that being measured is a theoretical construct, the measurement rules define the behavioral indicators of the construct as well as the way the behavioral indicators are quantified or categorized.

Reading development, discussed extensively in chapter 5, is a theoretical construct. Chall (1983) has linked a set of behavioral indicators to the construct; she has defined the transition points between levels of development in terms of behavioral indicators. Math for the college bound, reading comprehension, language arts basic skills, and character development are all theoretical constructs. The meaning of each only comes to life through the assignment of behavioral indicators; the definition of the indicators is at the heart of each of the chapters.

If clear communication is the goal, then the behavioral indicators of a theoretical construct and the construct itself are inseparable. The way a construct is measured is the best indication available of how the measurer defines the construct.

8.4.2. Reliability

For a measure to be of value in an evaluation, the measurement process must assign the numbers consistently. That is, replication of the measurement process, by the same or different persons at another time, must lead to consistent results both times.

All measuring instruments, from the most sensitive electron microscope to a 15-item scale to assess motivation for schooling, include measurement error. The question is never whether or not the measuring device has error associated with it; the question is always "how much?"

Some of the error is completely random, and therefore unbiased. This is the type of error related to reliability. The more the random error in a measure, the less reliable the measure; the less the random error, the more reliable the measure. Random errors occur due to things like errors in coding, ambiguous instructions, differential backgrounds of those being tested, and the differential meanings the same word has across people.

Psychometricians estimate reliability a number of ways, including:

. . . testing a group of students once with a test, waiting for some time period, and testing them again. The test is reliable to the extent it rank orders the group the same way at both administrations. This is called test-retest reliability.

. . . developing two parallel forms of the test, and administering the two forms to the same group of people. The test is reliable to the extent the two forms rank order the group the same way both times. This is called alternate forms reliability.

. . . administering one form to a group one time, but splitting the test in half. The test is reliable to the extent the two halves rank order the group the same way both times. This is called split halves reliability

. . . repeating the above, except finding the average reliability across all possible ways to split the test in half. These are called internal consistency measures, and usually associated with the names Kuder-Richardson.

An extension of this last technique is called Cronbach's coefficient alpha (see Crocker and Algina [1986, pp. 119–121]). It is the most general approach, since it can be used with dichotomous items (i.e., items which are scored either right or wrong) as well as with scales allowing ratings (e.g., with attitude measures ranging from "strongly agree" to "strongly disagree").

The reliability of a test or measure should be determined using a sample from the population for whom the test is written. The sampled group should be randomly chosen; it should represent the full range of performance from the population at hand. For example, think of estimating the reliability of a test written to measure biology performance at the end of a high school course. The sample must be drawn from students who had completed the course. The students selected should represent the full range of capabilities; it must be drawn randomly from all possible consumers. Inappropriate to the sample would be students who had not yet completed the course, as well as students who had completed this biology course as well as an advanced one. The population sampled must conform to the population of expected use.

Not just tests, but all measures must be reliable. The reliability of an observation scale, an interview, a content analysis, or an essay test can be estimated by having two or more people replicate each process to determine if consistency is observed across replications. A research report which does not estimate the reliabilities of the measures used is inadequate.

8.4.3. Validity

If the measurement process is to be useful, the assignment of numbers must be consistent and must fulfill the purpose for which the measure was designed. The consistency issue is determined by measuring reliability; the last part, the extent to which the measure fulfills the purpose for which it was designed, is the validity question.

Validity, or the lack of it, refers to the nonrandom errors in the measures. Nonrandom errors are biased; they are directional. The validity issue goes right back to the definition of measurement; a measure is invalid to the extent the behavioral indicators defined inadequately or improperly the theoretical construct at hand.

For example, suppose the theoretical construct is reading comprehension. Four different people identify the behavioral indicators and associated measures, as follows:

Person 1: Reading success is measured by the degree of enjoyment the students manifest in the reading process. The indicators are collected by interviewing the students and evaluating the responses on the basis of reading enjoyment.

Person 2: Reading comprehension is measured by analytical skills during reading. The student will be asked to critique various passages for coherency, internal consistency, story line, logical development, interest, and so forth and, based on their performance, a level of comprehension will be assigned to each.

Person 3: Reading comprehension will be measured by giving the student reading passages, along with questions about the passages, which are designed to be normatively age-grade appropriate for the student (e.g., all fifth graders read materially conceptually at a fifth-grade level). Performances will be ranked according to number of items scored correct.

Person 4: Reading comprehension will be measured by determining the highest possible conceptually leveled reading material the student can comprehend. The students will be ranked on the basis of the level of material to which they can respond.

Assume the the reliabilities of all four measurement scales are very high and the same. Look at the first person's definition. This person defines reading success in terms of reading enjoyment. The measures (interviews) are the behavioral indicators *for this definition* of reading success. It is invalid, for this purpose, to the extent it is inappropirate and/or inadequate. The measure itself may introduce a systematic bias. Speaking (the communication mode for the interview) and reading (a decoding skill) enjoyment may actually be inversely related; the more one reads, the less that person likes to talk, and vice versa. The bias is not random; it is systematic. Additionally, the measure (the interview) is reactive; the person being measured cannot help but react to the interview. To the extent the behavioral indicators need, but do not use, nonreactive measures (measures taken without the subject knowing it, such as counting the number of library books checked out in a year), the measures are inadequate. The measure is invalid because it did not sample enough behavioral indicators.

The same series of arguments could be made for each person's measures. Invalidity occurs when measures inadequately sample the domain of behavioral indicators or include more than one construct in the indicators actually sampled. Additionally, the measurement procedure itself may be flawed; for example, a reading test whose administration time is too short (measuring speed, not power) would systematically bias results.

The four measures of reading success illustrate another very important distinction between reliability and validity. A measure designed for one group (e.g., fifth grade readers or high school students who have finished a biology course) has one reliability, estimated for the targeted group. But validity is situation specific; validity is determined for each potential use.

This can partially be seen by thinking of mixing up the four definitions and measures of reading success given above. Person 4's measure (finding the highest conceptual level of material the student can handle) seems strangely out of place with person 1's definition (reading success means reading enjoyment). Person 4's measure might actually work (the question is empirical), but on the surface it seems invalid.

Validity, then, relates to the bias in the relationship between the underlying definition of the construct and the behavioral indicators chosen. Validity is specific to a particular use; a reading comprehension test may be valid as a measure of reading comprehension, but invalid for screening students for a program to develop artistic giftedness.

Psychometricians measure validity under three general headings:

A measure is a valid to the extent the content of the measure itself adequately samples the domain of content of the construct itself. This is called content validity.

A measure is valid to the extent its outcomes rank-order people the same way a well-known, commonly accepted measure ranks them (concurrent validity) or its outcomes rank-order people the same way the outcomes actually occur in the predicted event (predictive validity).

A measure is valid to the extent it can predict outcomes which are consistent with the definition of the theoretical construct itself (construct validity).

In most instances, content validity begs the question. The behavioral indicators were selected by the measurer as the way the construct is defined. Content validity asks for a recheck. The proof of the pudding, as the saying goes, is in the tasting, not through a content validation of the recipe. Concurrent or predictive validity measures can provide some useful information. They do, however, operate under the assumption (in the concurrent case) that the other "well-known, widely accepted" measure is indeed valid, or that (in the predictive case) the event's outcome measure is valid.

The preferred technique, and, unfortunately the most difficult, is through construct validation. Construct validation involves responding to the question, "Do the results from this measure conform to what is really meant by the underlying construct in question?" Use a fifth grade math computation test as an example. A content validation would determine the extent to which the items match typical fifth grade texts; a concurrent validation would correlate results from this test with another standardized test. Neither adequately addresses the construct "math computation," including the purpose for including math as part of a school's program. Math is included because the broad construct called "mathematics" is seen as a necessary ingredient in an adult for purposes of citizenship, employment, and personal satisfaction. A construct validation addresses the question, "Does the fifth grade math test address the underlying purposes of the construct?"

Of course, that's a nontrivial question; a complete answer to the question is probably unattainable. But that doesn't mean the validation efforts should be limited to what is available and easy. Construct validation focuses on the ultimate meaning of the construct; the measurer should continually shoot as high as possible toward the ultimate validation. (For a further discussion of the construct validation of achievement tests, see Haertel [1985].)

8.4.4. The Standard Error of Measurement and the Standard Error of the Mean

All measures have random error associated with them. Decisions are made about students, teachers, and programs on the basis of measures. The decisions need to be informed by knowledge of the amount of error associated with the numbers in question. Consider these two statements made to a school board comtemplating a bond issue:

> "Of the parents chosen at random for the survey, 55% said they would favor increasing school taxes. I am 99% confident that the percentage of parents favoring the issue in the entire district is between 44% and 66%."
>
> "Of the parents chosen at random for the survey, 55% said they would favor increasing school taxes. I am 99% confident that the percentage of parents favoring the issue in the entire district is between 51% and 59%."

The percentage favoring was the same for both statements, but the random error was lower in the second (reflecting a larger sample). The second statement would seem like a clear call for the board to initiate the bond vote; the first report is equivocal.

The two statements each provide a confidence interval. The standard error of measurement and the standard error of the mean are used to provide these confidence intervals. They differ, however; the standard error of measurement is used to provide a confidence interval around the measure of one individual's performance. The standard error of the mean provides the confidence interval around the mean score recorded for a group. The distinction between the way the two are defined is quite important with respect to the appropriate use of tests in evaluation projects.

The standard error of measurement is a function of the test's reliability.

The higher the reliability, the less random error; the less random error, the less standard error of measurement. High reliability is associated with many factors; but important among these are test length and the homogeneity of what the items measure. To be sure, coefficient alpha, mentioned earlier as the preferred measure of reliability, measures internal consistency, or the extent to which all of the items measure from the same domain. If one's goal were to develop a test with very small standard error of measurement, the test should be fairly long and focus on a fairly specific target domain. College aptitude tests, like the ACT or College Boards, are designed to help colleges make decisions about individuals, which means they are designed such that the standard error of measurement is minimized. They need high reliability; they are therefore long, narrowly focused measures.

The standard error of the mean, on the other hand, is a function of the size of the group being tested. The larger the group being tested, the smaller the confidence band around the mean score. Obviously, as discussed above, a test must be at least somewhat reliable if it is to be of any value whatsoever; but the level of reliability for decisions made about the mean performance of a group, using the standard error of the mean, is not so critical as with decisions about the performance of one of the individuals, using the standard error of measurement. If the decision at hand is about a group, not an individual, then the test length and homogeneity demands required for the case of individual interpretations can be relaxed.

8.4.5. Tests written primarily for use with an individual versus tests written primarily to make decisions about groups

Most tests are used primarily to provide individual scores on some area of content or skills. The College Boards or ACT (scholastic aptitude tests) are taken by the individual. The score is used by the college as part of its entrance decision-making process. Elementary school districts give standardized achievement tests to help evaluate the progress of individuals. Of course, these individual scores can be accumulated to provide group data such as means, medians, or standard deviations. But a primary, if not the primary, reason for testing every pupil every year is to obtain a measure on each individual. It is well to remember, when group summaries are developed, that the group summaries reflect an accumulation of data from a test designed for individual use.

A few testing programs are designed to provide only group information; there is no intention in such programs to report back individual scores. The National Assessment of Educational Progress (NAEP) is an example of such an approach. The NAEP is designed as an educational parallel to the Gross National Product. The results are to provide a census-like summaries of educational attainment of 9-, 13-, and 17-year-olds in this country, as well as young adults. Areas tested include math, reading, science, literature, social studies, writing, citizenship, music, and art.

The test design is quite different. A math test for 13-year-olds, for example, in an standardized achievement battery would have about 40 to 55 items. About an hour would be set aside for math testing. In the national assessment, three or four times that number of items may be tested for the 13-year-old group. No one student could be expected to endure such a long testing experience, so the test is split into segments. As many as 15 different separate, nonparallel tests are developed. A different random sample of 13-year-olds is assigned to each of these segments.

Out of all of these independent samples of 13-year-olds working on different portions of the entire list of math items comes a statistical composite of group performance.

Each type of test has its appropriate use. The NAEP design is the more appropriate for estimating the average national performance of the group of 13-year-olds. The range of coverage of the math domain for 13-year-olds is much more extensive. If all students had been expected to take exactly the same items, then a much shallower sampling from the domain would have been necessary. Obviously, a test designed primarily for individual interpretation cannot be structured like the NAEP.

8.4.6. Interrelatedness

This section deals with the interrelated nature of the definition of measurement, reliability-validity, standard error of measurement-standard error of the mean, and tests designed for individuals versus groups. Wow!

The relationship among the definition of measurement and validity was discussed in section 8.4.3; and the relationship between reliability and the standard error of measurement was covered in section 8.4.4. How does this fit together with the issue of tests originally designed for individual interpretations, and tests originally designed for group interpretations?

Consider this two-way table:

		The way the test is used:	
		Decisions about an individual	Decisions about a group
Primary purpose of the	an individual	OK	See A
test was to test	a group	See B	OK

The two cells marked "OK" indicate situations where the test is designed and used in the same way. The NAEP, designed to be a group measure and used that way, and a standardized achievement test, designed as a measure of individual performance and used to provide a home report to parents, are examples of the two categories.

The cell marked "A" represents a situation where a test designed primarily for individual use was also used to make group comparisons. This is widely done. The standardized achievement tests in an elementary school are meant to be individual tests, but comparisons for average performance across years and within areas is pervasive. A few years back, when the average performance on the Scholastic Aptitude Test (the College Boards) went into a steep decline, this decline was used as ammunition by critics of the schools.

This evaluative use of group means of tests originally designed for individuals is not totally inappropriate. As was stated earlier, the standardized achievement battery in grades 2 to 8 samples a very substantial proportion of the skills taught during those grades. But review again section 8.4.4. The demands for small confidence intervals for group versus individual measures are quite different. The individual measure needs a small standard error of measurement; therefore it needs a very high reliability; therefore it needs to be long and internally consistent test. The group measure needs only an increased sample size (presuming it has at least some acceptable level of reliability).

The point is this: If the group comparisons are the topic of major interest, and not just an afterthought to the testing process, than the tests should be designed for groups. Group measures can have a whole series of short, different subtests; the demands for length and homogeneity can be relaxed. If it is primarily the group measure which is at issue, then the coverage of the domain should be dramatically expanded; not every person in the population needs to take every part of the test, since it is the group's performance, not the individual's performance, which is at issue.

A classic example of this type of misuse is the case of using College Board scores to evaluate performance of high school graduates. Other independent data indicated that the decline was indeed real; but that is not the issue. The College Board has excellent reliabilities. These reliabilities are high because the test is long and stays within a domain entitled "verbal and mathematical reasoning abilites that are commonly needed for successful academic performance in college." The test measures a very small slice of the instruction offered in a high school.

If decisions were to be made about the declining performance of the group completing high school in the United States, then a measure designed to assess group performance should have been developed. Such a measure could have sampled the entire domain of content in the equity sense, covering not only reasoning skills needed for college but the whole range of high school purposes. Of course, that was precisely what the NAEP was designed to do. Unfortunately, those in charge of the NAEP have never quite figured out how to invade the consciousness of the public. The NAEP results are reported item-by-item, showing percent of increase or decrease across testing times. The public, it would seem, needs a simpler, more comprehensive measure.

Cell "B," the situation where a group test is used to provide individual feedback, may sound a little absurd. But one illustration of such use comes to mind.

In section 8.1.3, it was argued that a high school survey achievement battery basically monitored only the maintenance of previously instructed skills. That is not, after all, so bad; these skills include many which are necessary for an adult to function in society. Many school boards would like to see measures of incoming performance for a group contrasted with exiting performance, to make sure the skills have been enhanced by the high school experience — or at least maintained!

This means each cohort has to be tested as freshmen and as seniors. The cost of such testing, however, is fairly high. Even the shorter batteries demand two full testing sessions, a day apart; many require three long mornings of testing. If all freshmen and seniors are included in this long program, the sophomores and juniors are impacted as well. In high school, a substantial proportion of courses are shared by students from different class levels.

The situation can be greatly improved by rethinking the issue. The school board (or superintendent or public) didn't actually ask that every student be tested with the same test. The goal was to monitor cohort performance.

One approach to this issue, used by the author, is to separate the battery by subtest. Suppose a battery has six subtests, each requiring 50 minutes of testing time (a fairly common assumption). One 50-minutes period is now set aside for testing. In each room, the first student takes the first subtest (e.g., English), the second person the second subtest (e.g., Math), until the sixth person takes the sixth subtest (e.g., Science); then the process repeats. The subtests are randomly assigned within each classroom. Accumulated, they represent a statistical picture of the class — and the data were gathered in one 50-minute period.

Now back to cell "B." Experience has shown that students are not terribly anxious to participate in testing programs which provide no feedback, and teachers have been known to view the monitoring task with something less than enthusiasm. For a variety of excellent reasons, which will not be pursued because they tend toward Machiavellianism, it is important to provide feedback to each testing room, with a score for each individual — in other words, individual feedback for a testing situation designed primarily to assess group performance.

In this section, some background issues important to the interpretation of evaluations have been presented. They have all been included in one section because they are interrelated. College programs for educators frequently have a requirement of at least one course in statistics, but background in measurement is less common. The way a construct is measured frequently provides the only realistic information available on how the measurer defines the construct. And the definition is related to validity; and the reliability is related to both validity and the standard error of measure, and is critical if the test is designed to provide individual feedback.

The user need not be able to compute coefficient alpha or the standard error of measurement. But it is important for the user to have a sense of what each of these names stands for and how they interrelate.

References

Beggs, D.L., and Mouw, J. (1981). *Developing Cognitive Abilities Tests*. Glenview, IL: Scott, Foresman and Co.

Cazden, C.B. (1974). "Play with language and metalinguistic awareness: One dimension of language experience." *Urban Review* 2:28–39.

Chall, J.S. (1983). *Stages in Reading Development*. New York: McGraw-Hill Book Co.

Crocker, L., and Algina, J. (1986). *Introduction to Classical and Modern Test Theory*. New York: Holt, Rinehart and Winston.

Haertel, E. (1985). "Construct validity and criterion-referenced testing." *Review of Educational Research* 55(1):23–46.

Stroud, J.B. (1964). *Psychology in Education*. New York: David McKay Company.

Wick, J.W. (1973). *Educational Measurement*. Columbus, OH: Merrill.

9 INSTRUCTIONAL MONITORING WITH MAXIMUM PERFORMANCE TESTS

This chapter has four sections. The first addresses information systems, the second, the use of standardized tests; the third, the use of criterion-referenced tests; and the final, an explication on the use of computerized adaptive testing to monitor instruction.

9.1. Information system to monitor instruction

Information systems for objectives-driven areas (see chapter 6) and difficulty-driven areas (see chapter 5) differ. The high school's system (see chapter 4) needs are also unique.

9.1.1. Objectives-driven areas of the elementary school

These objectives-driven areas are defined by a sequence of fairly specific learning objectives. In most cases, these objectives represent a logical sequence. In mathematics, for example, the student learns addition without renaming before addition with renaming; and both of these logically precede long division, which requires both skills as prerequisites. Objectives-driven areas of instruction include mathematics computation and concepts; grammar, grammar-usage, punctuation, and capitalization; and study-reference skills. Reading is *not* objectives-driven; reading is difficulty-driven. Once the student has "broken the code" and learned to read, the task is to sequence the child through material which is conceptually and structurally more difficult. Reading tests continue to ask the same types of questions (e.g., main idea, mood or purpose, cause and effect) throughout the growth period. Objectives-driven tests have different objectives throughout the growth period.

In the presentation of the evaluate-your-instruction process, the concept of a "finished system" was used. In response to the question, "Why are you having this learning event in the first place?," one response was, "Because this is a finished system, wherein there is a 'truth' — a specific body of known content (characterized by a specific set of objectives) which the student needs to learn." As was noted previously, because the purpose of having these learning events is to bring the students to mastery on a known body of content, about which little discussion is needed, the projected teacher and student behaviors are expected to be quite different than for learning events where discussions, interactions, and idea-sharing are central to the mechanism believed to cause student growth.

Cooley and Bickel (1986, p. 77) list five functions of an information system. These include record-keeping, report generation, record retrieval, data analysis, and tailoring practices to data. They state (p. 78) that "one principle in this work is the need to have the data become part of the operating system of the school."

It is difficult to imagine anything more important to the local school than the way the instructional program "flows" through the grades. The first step, then, in monitoring instruction in objectives-driven areas is to put in place such an information system. Specifically, for each basic skills objective, the grade of *initial instruction* and the grade at which every normal child is to exhibit *entering mastery* (i.e., mastery will be tested as the student enters that grade, hopefully as early as the first week of school) must be defined.

Such an information system obviously requires, as a first step, a list of the objectives to be included. Too many districts begin the task of assembling an objective list by appointing a teacher committee, handing them some pencils and blank tablets, and assigning them the task of generating objective lists for each grade. As they soon find out, developing an objectives list which is exhaustive, consistent, specific, and nonoverlapping is a very difficult and time-consuming task. Too often any initial teacher enthusiasm which did exist is used up. Just to give one example of how this apparently simple process gets complicated, take the objective, "Multiplication of a whole number by a 1-digit whole number." Although this sounds like a fairly precise statement, it is not, in terms of an information system designed to assign instructional responsibility by grade level. A problem like "12 × 3 = " (no renaming required) will be initially taught at least one grade, and possibly two grades, earlier than "72068 × 8" which requires more than two renamings and multiplication across an internal zero. In the objective list in Appendix A, this objective is broken into four steps — no renaming, one renaming, two renamings, and unlimited renaming.

Appendices A and B provide a starting point for mathematics and punctuation, capitalization, and grammar-usage. Gronlund (1985, p. 508–509) lists some publishers who have objective-item pools. The district may have a list in place the completeness of which has been demonstrated. The objective list accompanying the standardized test is probably *not* a good place to start; such lists are primarily developed for marketing, not educational, purposes.

Irrespective of where the objective list comes from, the task breaks down to these necessary steps:

First, for each objective on the list, the question is asked, "Is this an objective which is part of the instructional program in this district?"

There are areas of legitimate disagreement on this question. For example, some districts present place value in math by naming the digit in a place ("In the number 417, which digit is in the tens place?"); some present place value by asking for the value of a numeral in a number ("What is the value of the numeral 1 in the number 417?"); and some do both. In measurement, some districts use only English units, some only metric units, some both kept independent from one another, and some both including equivalency relationships. In grammar, some districts no longer present terms like "direct object" and "indirect object" or even "simple subject" and "simple predicate."

For each objective which is part of the school's instructional program, two additional questions must be answered:

1. At which grade is this objective initially taught?

2. At which grade will all normal children be expected to demonstrate mastery as they enter the grade?

"Initially taught" does not mean "first familiarization" or "first use in the classroom." Initially taught should be defined as the grade at which this objective is first clearly a part of the lesson plans, as was discussed in chapter 6.

Some districts have set up a mastery schedule based on exiting, not entering, mastery. These districts set up mastery objectives for each grade and monitor mastery as the children leave the grade. There are three fairly compelling reasons for preferring entering mastery to exiting mastery. The first two reasons have to do with education; the last with public relations.

1. By testing in the fall, as soon as the students are back from vacation and before any review is done, the results become diagnostic to the instructional process. Now the teacher can avoid reviewing objectives on which the students demonstrate they have attained mastery and concentrate instruction on those objectives where the students had trouble. Defining the entering mastery objectives and bringing students to mastery on them before the rest of the year's instruction begins is called by Bloom (1984) "enhancing prerequisite mastery," and he reports that this process raises student achievement by the end of the year.

2. Testing after vacation is more in line with the level of learning the schools should ultimately want from their students. The goal is long-term learning. If the only way a student can demonstrate mastery on an objective is to precede the testing with an intensive period of drill-and-practice, it is not sensible to argue that the objective has been mastered.

3. Testing in the fall also dilutes the real or imagined suspicion, on the part of the teachers, that the testing is being carried out to evaluate *them*, and not the students. As the year begins, the students in a particular classroom will probably include transfer-ins as well as students who came from varying previous classrooms. This dispersion, along with the knowledge that some forgetting does occur over the summer, seriously reduces the potential for assigning responsibility for low performance to any particular teacher. Fall testing is more likely to be viewed by the teachers as useful diagnostic testing.

In the question about entering mastery, the term ". . . all normal children . . ." was used. Some small percentage of children have such serious educational deficits, or social or emotional problems, that it would be neither fair nor realistic to have expectations of mastery. The percentage of students who would fall under the heading "all normal children" will vary from a maximum of around 95% to a minimum of around 90%, depending, to a certain extent, on how the district defines certain special education categories and the extent to which the children are mainstreamed. (This attention to "all normal children" does not presume that the monitoring of the rest will be ignored. Most districts now devise an Individualized Educational Plan (IEP) for each child enrolled in some special education category, and considerable attention is paid to the child's progress in this IEP.)

How should a district set about to make these decisions? Here are four possible ways, ordered from least to most desirable:

1. Have an outside consultant make the placements. Throughout this book the local school has been seen as education's profit center. A strength of this viewpoint is that the educators in the school are in the best position to make curriculum and instruction decisions. With an outsider, ownership is lost and so is a sensitivity to local conditions. The nicest thing one could say about having a consultant do the task is that if the results are grossly inadequate, at least no internal person is embarrassed.

2. Have the internal person with direct instructional responsibilities do the placements. This might be the principal, although in larger districts it could be an assistant superintendent for instruction or a math or English coordinator. The internal person would undoubtedly be far more familiar with the materials and past practices in the district. The major drawback to this approach is teachers' generally unenthusiastic response to edicts which come from "downtown." Teachers tend to view decision-making about the ebb and flow of objectives as within their sphere of responsibilities.

3. This suggests having a teacher committee make the decisions. A teacher committee would consist of one teacher from each grade level, beginning with kindergarten and going through (if at all possible) someone to represent the instructional area from the high school. Each teacher on the committee needs to have two primary characteristics: Experience teaching at that grade level and wide general respect as a teacher by the other teachers in the system. (My experience, working with a number of different districts, is that the committee needs about a full day per instructional area to make the placements.)

4. The technique described in (3) is perfectly satisfactory, particularly if special attention is paid to providing feedback to the entire staff. However, it is even more desirable to precede the appointment of a teacher committee with a process which involves all the teachers (described in detail in Wick, 1983). In this process, each teacher is given a copy of the list of objectives. Taking one objective at a time, each teacher, for the grade level at which s/he teaches, responds in one of the following five categories:

L This objective is taught later, after the grade level at which I now teach.
I This objective is initially taught at the grade level at which I now teach.
R This objective was introduced prior to the grade level at which I teach, and I review it during the year.
M I expect all normal children to have mastered this objective prior to entering this grade level.
N This objective is not taught in our school system.

The results from the entire teaching staff are summarized. A typical outcome usually looks something like the one shown in figure 9.1.

Figure 9.1.   A Typical Summary of Initial Teacher Placements for an Objective

Objective: Grammar-usage — Positive, comparative, and superlative form of regular adverbs.

					Grade				
	K	*1*	*2*	*3*	*4*	*5*	*6*	*7*	*8*
Later	5	9	2	1	0	0	0	0	0
Initial	0	0	7	5	3	1	0	0	0
Review	0	0	0	4	5	7	4	2	1
Ent. Mstry.	0	0	0	0	1	1	4	2	3
Not	0	0	0	0	0	0	0	0	0

The results from this data collection activity with the teachers usually document a great deal of confusion about when each objective is first taught and when entering mastery is expected. A teacher, by and large, knows quite well the textbook used *at the grade level she/he taught.* When the fourth grade teachers saw the objective, they knew it was in their grammar textbook and presumed that was the first time this objective had appeared in the series. At the other end, as long as the objective continues to appear in the series, the teachers will assume it has not been mastered.

This kind of confusion is terribly wasteful. If the objective has been initially taught once, there undoubtedly was a percentage of the children who had already mastered it after the first teaching. If the teacher at the next grade repeats "initial" instruction, not knowing it has been previously initiated, these children, who could have demonstrated mastery on a pretest, will have no opportunity to learn anything new, since they already have mastered this concept. To maximize opportunity-to-learn time, it is important to eliminate the type of confusion shown in figure 9.1.

In this fourth and most desirable approach to assigning instructional responsibilities for initial instruction and mastery for every objective, the summary data from all the teachers are now given to a teacher committee, assembled in the manner described in (3). Using this input from the entire staff, the committee now irons out differences, coming to consensus on the grades of initial instruction and entering mastery.

Two summaries of the decisions made by the teacher committee should be disseminated to all teachers. The first, and more important of the two, shows a typical grade-level list. Table 6.1, p. 131, shows a typical fourth grade listing. Shown, in an order which generally follows their introduction into the classroom, are: the objectives designated for entering mastery at grade 4; the objectives designated for review (called pretest objectives, since that is what the teacher is instructed to do for each) at grade 4; the objectives designated for initial instruction at grade 4; and the objectives designated for entering mastery when this group of students moves on to grade 5.

Table 6.2, p. 135, shows a complete matrix of language arts placements. The matrix shows the grade of initial instruction (I), the grade of review (designated P for pretest), and the grade of entering mastery (M).

These first placements cannot be viewed as fixed. The instructional placements should be viewed as dynamic; but some stability is needed. The decisions made by the teacher committee should be viewed as fixed for one school year, but should be subject to change at the end of each school year. As soon as possible after the school year ends, the same teacher committee, or a new one, should take the assembled output information for the just-completed school year (standardized test and criterion-referenced test information, plus anecdotal evidence from teachers on the committee) to adjust placements as seems appropriate. Some reasons for changes include:

1. Evidence that the students are mastering an objective before the designated grade. Since continuing teaching an objective past mastery takes time away from teaching objectives on which mastery has not yet been demonstrated, it is important to move the mastery grade down to the lowest appropriate level.

2. Evidence that at the end of the year of initial instruction, the students at that grade level have made almost no progress toward demonstrating mastery. This might suggest the grade of initial instruction was too low, or inadequate materials and/or time are available for the instructional process at the designated grade.

3. Evidence that the students are taking too long to attain mastery on an objective (are "limping up to mastery"). This might necessitate alloting extra instructional commitment to the objective shortly after the grade of initial instruction to bring the students to mastery more quickly.

The year of initial instruction will generally be fixed by the textbook series in use in a district. The year of entering mastery, on the other hand, tends to be a variable subject to local conditions. As a district systematically reduces the number of years between the grades of initial instruction and entering mastery, while simultaneously maintaining or increasing the levels of student mastery, instructional efficiency increases. Wasted opportunity time is squeezed out of the system. By teaching the basic skills more efficiently, time is saved to address higher order learning.

9.1.2. An information system for a difficulty-driven area like reading?

Word analysis skills such as initial, medial, and ending sounds; blends; and syllabication can be described by a specific set of reasonably sequential objectives and are therefore objectives-driven. Another structured set of necessary skills, frequently called language expression or study skills, in which questions like "Which is the topic sentence?," "Which second sentence is consistent with the topic sentence?," "Which sentence in this paragraph is out of order?," "Which sentence in this paragraph does not belong?," and "How could this sentence be reworded to be more clear?" are asked, is likewise not the same as, and should not be confused with, reading comprehension.

One mechanism expected to improve the student's level of reading comprehension was described in chapter 5. Reading specialists might propose other mechanisms or restate in more elegant terminology the one described in chapter 5. In this section, however, the main concern is with the requirements of an information system for reading comprehension during the elementary and junior high school years. Regardless of the mechanism for growth one believes in, it seems reasonable that the major demand on an information system would be to provide timely estimates of the child's current functioning reading level.

These estimates should be based on reading samples at the child's functioning level, and not on extrapolations up or down. A fifth grader whose current functioning reading level is at least two grades lower cannot be adequately diagnosed with a test designed for fifth graders. To do so would require an extrapolation downward beyond the conceptual level of the material in the test. In the same manner, the functioning level of a fifth grader whose functioning level is considerably higher than grade 5 cannot be adequately estimated by a test whose material is chosen because it is at a fifth grade level. Table 5.2, p. 112, and the discussion which accompanies it, addresses this issue further.

So one requirement of the information system is to estimate each child's functioning reading level with material designed for that level. A second is that these estimates be "timely." In chapter 5, "timely" was defined as six testings per year at grades 2 and 3, five per year at grades 4, 5, and 6, and four per year at the junior high level. The rationale for the decreasing frequency had to do with the slowing growth rate as readers mature.

The information should provide timely assessments of the functioning level; and these assessments should be with material developed for this functioning level. One final requirement of the information system is to maintain these records — not just during any one given school year — but over these years of growth.

Cooley and Bickel's (1986) comment, mentioned earlier, about the need to make an information system part of the school's normal operating procedures, is recalled. Accurate diagnosis and feedback are integral to the process of student growth. With these data on the information system, the possibility of a sense of ownership by the teachers would be greatly enhanced.

9.1.3. The requirements of the information system at the high school become even more complicated.

As briefly discussed in section 8.1, the instructional environment of the elementary school is fairly common for most students. In a comprehensive high school, while there is some commonality in course requirements, a good deal of specialization begins. Some subgroups enroll in a concentration of advanced math courses; some enroll in four years of a specific foreign language; some take five courses in small machine design and maintenance; some take six science courses; some are enrolled half-days for two years in an agriculture program. Sometimes these subgroups partially overlap.

One could define each high school course as an independent learning event, and use the evaluate-your-instruction process for each course. But that seems terribly disjointed. Generally speaking, high school courses are not designed to stand alone; they are meant to be part of some planned concentration of courses. It would seem most sensible to identify those various planned concentration of courses, and view the endproduct of each as formative, not summative, evaluation information.

A first requirement of an information system at the high school level, then, would be its development around planned concentrations of courses. Two obvious planned concentrations at a high school would be: Spanish I, Spanish II, Spanish III, Spanish IV; and Algebra I, Geometry, Algebra-Trig, Analytic Geometry-Calculus.

These two are not only planned concentrations; they are planned sequences, since a student would take them in the order shown. Two planned concentrations in the business department are: Introduction to Business, Office Practice, Business Communication, Business Law, Business Machines, and Business Principles and Management; and Typing I, Introduction to Computers, Computer Programming: BASIC, Computer Programming: COBOL, and Automated Office: Word Processing.

These are concentrations, not sequences, since some might be taken out of the order shown. In vocational education: Electricity, House Wiring, Electronics I and II, and Electronics with Microcomputers; and in science, Physical Science, Biology, Chemistry, Physics.

These are both planned concentrations — sometimes sequential in nature, sometimes not.

A course might be part of more than one concentration (for example, an introductory course where the concentrations branch off thereafter). It is difficult to imagine a course that stands alone, is not part of any planned concentration. A student is considered to have participated in a concentration by enrolling in some minimum number of the courses; it would not be necessary for a student to take all the courses listed.

Now the evaluate-your-instruction questions can be asked of each planned concentration. Why is this concentration part of the high school program? What is the mechanism whereby growth is expected? The answers to these two questions will imply the types of learning expected. The information system for each planned concentration should fulfill the same types roles as were filled at the elementary school level. For math computation at the elementary school level, the information system defined the coverage and the expected placements (grade of initial instruction and grade at which entering mastery expected). The information system for a planned concentration should address the same issues.

Obviously, not all planned concentrations are objectives-driven, like math computation. But that does not reduce the need for an information system to deal with coverage and placement. For each concentration, the information system could include these elements:

1. What are the necessary entry-level behaviors needed in order to be successful in the first course in this concentration? These behaviors might included knowledge (specific content or knowledge of processes), skills (even motor skills like a minimum keyboarding speed), or personal commitment (willingness to rearrange one's schedule to allow three hours of work experience each day.) "Entry-level behaviors" are not the same as prior experiences; but this issue has been addressed previously.

2. What exit-level behaviors are expected? The behaviors might deal with specific knowledge (factoring second-degree quadratics, dissecting a poem, or reconstructing the U.S. judicial system). The behaviors might require performance of some task (type faster than 15 words per minute; reassemble a small motor; run a mile in less than ten minutes) or completion of a product. They might deal with performance level in a structured set of necessary skills, like interpretation of a particular type of novel.

Linked to these defined exit-level behaviors could be some sort of statement relating level of performance to assigned grade. In some cases, schools handle this by percentage designations (above 90% is an "A" grade, 80% to 90% is a "B," and so forth). These statements might also address minimal expectations — the level of performance below which a passing grade cannot be given.

3. Finally, the information system should address the course-interface issue. The exit-level behaviors expected for the first course in a concentration should be compared to the necessary entry-level behaviors in the next (and subsequent) courses *as well as* to the exit-level expectations in the next and subsequent courses. The comparisons have obvious instructional consequences, such as the following two examples.

a. To the extent that exit-level behaviors from the first course coincide with entry-level behaviors for the next (or subsequent) courses, information about exit-level performance at the end of the first course should be made available to the teacher in the subsequent one. The teacher can skip these areas, if mastery was previously demonstrated; find a way to concentrate attention on those who need initial help, if only a small number had some level of difficulty; or reteach, if prior performance indicates this is necessary.

b. To what extent do expected exit-level behaviors from two or more courses intersect? In terms of opportunity-to-learn time, having the same objectives in subsequent courses makes little sense. At a minimum, when subsequent courses address the same expected learning outcomes, a pretest of some sort should be given, prior to instruction, in the subsequent courses to see if learning levels acquired previously have been adequately maintained.

9.2. Monitoring the Instructional Program with Standardized Tests

9.2.1. Objectives-driven areas at the elementary school and junior high school

How good a job does a standardized test do in monitoring these objectives? An illustration should be instructive.

A particular district known to the author has established the grade of initial instruction and entering mastery for mathematics. At grade 4, 65 objectives are "in the system." Of these, 17 are tested for entering mastery, 26 for initial instruction, and 22 for review (pretested).

The test chosen for analysis is the widely-used *Comprehensive Test of Basic Skills* (1981). The district uses a spring testing program (in the eighth month of school), with level D at grade 1, level E at grade 2, level F at grade 3, level G at grades 4 and 5, level H at grades 6 and 7, and level J at grade 8. These are within the stated ranges of each level, as shown on page 1 of the Examiner's Manual (1982) for levels F, G, H, J, and K.

Of the 65 math objectives at grade 4 for this district, 20 (about 30%) are not covered at any point in the standardized testing program. If this seems like a large percentage of omission, here is one explanation: given the time restraints on testing, the standardized test samples form a domain of content. No publisher would be foolish enough to claim exhaustive coverage of every objective in the domain. As an example of this domain sampling, multiplication of a 4-digit and 1-digit number with two renamings is covered (one item level G) but unlimited renaming is not covered. Reading a clock to the quarter hour is covered, but reading a digital clock and reading a regular clock to the minute are not.

Most of the "missing" objectives can be explained by sampling from a domain — but not all. Time equivalencies (second, minute, hour, day, week), a part of nearly every program, are not covered. No items demanding knowledge of metric equivalency values are included. (There are many problems of the type, "If 1 kiloliter = 1,000 liters, how many liters of water will fill a 3 kiloliter tank?" Such a question gives the equivalency; it is basically a ratio problem. If the child has been taught to set up $1/1,000 = 3/x$, and cross multiply, the answer can be found. Although metric units are used, no knowledge of metric equivalencies was demanded.) The battery contains no questions on temperature interpretations, Fahrenheit or Celsius, at any level.

The key question is, "How well does this test fit the instructional flow in this district?"

Table 9.2.   The Match Between One Standardized Test and the Instruction in One District

---

CTBS Item Distribution, D1, E2, F3, G4–5, H6–7, J8–9, End of Year

---

322.   Addition, two numbers, 2 digits, one renaming
Initial Instr. Grade 3   Entering Mastery Expected Gr. 4

GRADE	1	2	③	④	5	6	7	8	9
Items per grade	2	1	0	0	0	0	0	0	0

323.   Addition, to 4 numbers, to 4 digits, one renaming
Initial Instr. Grade 3   Entering Mastery Expected Gr. 4

GRADE	1	2	③	④	5	6	7	8	9
Items per grade	0	4	2	0	0	0	0	0	0

Table 9.2.   continued.

---

332.   Addition, to 4 numbers, to 4 digits, two renamings
Initial Instr. Grade 3   Entering Mastery Expected Gr. 4

GRADE	1	2	③	④	5	6	7	8	9
Items per grade	0	1	1	0	0	0	0	0	0

342.   Addition, to 4 numbers, to 4 digits, unlimited renaming
Initial Instr. Grade 4   Entering Mastery Expected Gr. 6

GRADE	1	2	3	④	5	⑥	7	8	9
Items per grade	0	0	3	2	2	1	1	0	0

362.   Subtraction, to four digits, one renaming
Initial Instr. Grade 3   Entering Mastery Expected Gr. 4

GRADE	1	2	③	④	5	6	7	8	9
Items per grade	1	2	4	1	1	0	0	0	0

372.   Subtraction, to four digits, two renamings
Initial Instr. Grade 3   Entering Mastery Expected Gr. 5

GRADE	1	2	③	4	⑤	6	7	8	9
Items per grade	0	0	1	0	0	0	0	0	0

382.   Subtraction, to four digits, unlimited renamings
Initial Instr. Grade 4   Entering Mastery Expected Gr. 6

GRADE	1	2	3	④	5	⑥	7	8	9
Items per grade	0	0	0	2	2	1	1	0	0

391.   Multiplication, basic facts
Initial Instr. Grade 3   Entering Mastery Expected Gr. 5

GRADE	1	2	③	4	⑤	6	7	8	9
Items per grade	0	7	3	0	0	0	0	0	0

392.   Multiplication, 3-digit times 1-digit no., no renaming
Initial Instr. Grade 3   Entering Mastery Expected Gr. 5

GRADE	1	2	③	4	⑤	6	7	8	9
Items per grade	0	3	5	0	0	0	0	0	0

394.   Multiplication, 2-digit × 2-digit number, no renaming
Initial Instr. Grade 4   Entering Mastery Expected Gr. 6

GRADE	1	2	3	④	5	⑥	7	8	9
Items per grade	0	0	0	2	2	0	0	0	0

402.   Multiplication, 3-digit × 1-digit number, one renaming
Initial Instr. Grade 3   Entering Mastery Expected Gr. 5

GRADE	1	2	③	4	⑤	6	7	8	9
Items per grade	0	0	1	1	1	0	0	0	0

Table 9.2.   continued.

---

412.   Multiplication, 4-digit × 1-digit number, two renamings
Initial Instr. Grade 4   Entering Mastery Expected Gr. 6

GRADE	1	2	3	④	5	⑥	7	8	9
Items per grade	0	0	0	1	1	0	0	0	0

422.   Multiplication, 4-digit, × 1-digit number, unlimited ren.
Initial Instr. Grade 4   Entering Mastery Expected Gr. 6
No CTBS items this objective from level D through J

431.   Division, basic facts
Initial Instr. Grade 3   Entering Mastery Expected Gr. 5

GRADE	1	2	③	4	⑤	6	7	8	9
Items per grade	0	6	4	2	2	0	0	0	0

432.   Division, whole number by 1-digit divisor, no remainder
Initial Instr. Grade 3   Entering Mastery Expected Gr. 6

GRADE	1	2	③	4	5	⑥	7	8	9
Items per grade	0	0	3	2	2	1	1	0	0

442.   Division, whole number by 1-digit divisor, remainder as R =
Initial Instr. Grade 3   Entering Mastery Expected Gr. 6

GRADE	1	2	③	4	5	⑥	7	8	9
Items per grade	0	0	2	0	0	1	1	0	0

661.   Money, determine amount or make change
Initial Instr. Grade 2   Entering Mastery Expected Gr. 4

GRADE	1	②	3	④	5	6	7	8	9
Items per grade	1	1	1	0	0	0	0	0	0

681.   Numbered scale, use when all points are numbered
Initial Instr. Grade ②   Entering Mastery Expected Gr. 4

GRADE	1	②	3	④	5	6	7	8	9
Items per grade	1	0	0	0	0	0	0	0	0

682.   Numbered scale, use when not all points numbered
Initial Instr. Grade 3   Entering Mastery Expected Gr. 5

GRADE	1	2	③	4	⑤	6	7	8	9
Items per grade	0	1	2	0	0	0	0	0	0

692.   Clock, translate digital minute readings to clock face
Initial Instr. Grade 2   Entering Mastery Expected Gr. 4
No CTBS items this objective from level D through J

695.   Clock, read standard clock face to quarter-hour, five minutes
Initial Instr. Grade 2   Entering Mastery Expected Gr. 4

GRADE	1	②	3	④	5	6	7	8	9
Items per grade	0	1	0	0	0	0	0	0	0

Table 9.2.   continued.

696.   Clock, read standard clock face to the minute
Initial Instr. Grade 3   Entering Mastery Expected Gr. 4
No CTBS items this objective from level D through J

701.   Time equivalencies, seconds, minutes, hours, days
Initial Instr. Grade 2   Entering Mastery Expected Gr. 4
No CTBS items this objective from level D through J

704.   Time equivalencies, days, weeks, months, year
Initial Instr. Grade 2   Entering Mastery Expected Gr. 5
No CTBS items this objective from level D through J

793.   Relative values, whole numbers > 999, use sequence
Initial Instr. Grade 3   Entering Mastery Expected Gr. 5
No CTBS items this objective from level D through J

796.   Relative values, fractions, like denominators, use sequence
Initial Instr. Grade 3   Entering Mastery Expected Gr. 5

GRADE	1	2	③	4	⑤	6	7	8	9
Items per grade	0	0	1	0	0	0	0	0	0

797.   Relative values, fractions, unlike denominators, use sequence
Initial Instr. Grade 4   Entering Mastery Expected Gr. 5

GRADE	1	2	3	④	⑤	6	7	8	9
Items per grade	0	0	0	1	1	1	1	0	0

801.   Relative values, round/estim. left-most place, whole nbrs to 99
Initial Instr. Grade 4   Entering Mastery Expected Gr. 6

GRADE	1	2	3	④	5	⑥	7	8	9
Items per grade	0	1	0	1	1	0	0	0	0

802.   Relative values, round/estim., left place, whole nbrs. 100–999
Initial Instr. Grade 4   Entering Mastery Expected Gr. 6
No CTBS items this objective from level D through J

803.   Relative values, round/estim., left place, whole nbrs. >999
Initial Instr. Grade 4   Entering Mastery Expected Gr. 7

GRADE	1	2	3	④	5	⑥	7	8	9
Items per grade	0	0	1	0	0	0	0	0	0

821.   Place value, whole numbers, name digit in place, to 10's
Initial Instr. Grade 2   Entering Mastery Expected Gr. 4

GRADE	1	②	3	④	5	6	7	8	9
Items per grade	0	1	0	0	0	0	0	0	0

822.   Place value, whole numbers, name digid in place, 100's, 1000's
Initial Instr. Grade 3   Entering Mastery Expected Gr. 5

GRADE	1	2	③	4	⑤	6	7	8	9
Items per grade	0	0	1	0	0	0	0	0	0

Table 9.2. continued.

---

823.   Place value, whole numbers >9999, name digit in place
Initial Instr. Grade 4   Entering Mastery Expected Gr. 6
No CTBS items this objective from level D through J

831.   Place value, whole numbers, name value of digit in place, to 10's
Initial Instr. Grade 2   Entering Mastery Expected Gr. 4

GRADE	1	②	3	④	5	6	7	8	9
Items per grade	3	0	0	0	0	0	0	0	0

832.   Place value, whole numbers, name value of digit in place, 100's, 1000's
Initial Instr. Grade 3   Entering Mastery Expected Gr. 5

GRADE	1	2	③	4	⑤	6	7	8	9
Items per grade	1	0	2	1	1	0	0	0	0

873.   Altern. representations, numeral to word, whole numbers >99
Initial Instr. Grade 3   Entering Mastery Expected Gr. 4

GRADE	1	2	③	④	5	6	7	8	9
Items per grade	2	1	2	0	0	0	0	0	0

874.   Altern. repr., numeral to word, fractions (half, third, fourth)
Initial Instr. Grade 4   Entering Mastery Expected Gr. 5
No CTBS items this objective from level D through J

879.   Altern. representations, numeral to word, currency amounts
Initial Instr. Grade 3   Entering Mastery Expected Gr. 4

GRADE	1	2	③	④	5	6	7	8	9
Items per grade	0	1	0	0	0	0	0	0	0

886.   Alternative representations, numeral to set/picture, other fractions
Initial Instr. Grade 3   Entering Mastery Expected Gr. 5

GRADE	1	2	③	4	⑤	6	7	8	9
Items per grade	0	0	1	1	1	0	0	0	0

511.   Fractions, addn. and subt., like denom., no reduce or rename
Initial Instr. Grade 4   Entering Mastery Expected Gr. 5
No CTBS items this objective from level D through J

711.   English unit equivalencies, length (inch, foot, yard)
Initial Instr. Grade 3   Entering Mastery Expected Gr. 5
No CTBS items this objective from level D through J

712.   English unit equivalencies, length (foot, yard, mile)
Initial Instr. Grade 4   Entering Mastery Expected Gr. 6

GRADE	1	2	3	④	5	⑥	7	8	9
Items per grade	0	0	1	1	1	1	1	0	0

Table 9.2. continued.

714. English unit equivalencies, pounds, ounces, ton
Initial Instr. Grade 4   Entering Mastery Expected Gr. 7

GRADE	1	2	3	④	5	6	⑦	8	9
Items per grade	0	0	0	1	1	1	1	0	0

721. Metric unit equivalencies and use, mass
Initial Instr. Grade 4   Entering Mastery Expected Gr. 6
No CTBS items this objective from level D through J

722. Metric unit equivalencies and use, volume
Initial Instr. Grade 4   Entering Mastery Expected Gr. 6
No CTBS items this objective from level D through J

723. Metric unit equivalencies and use, length
Initial Instr. Grade 4   Entering Mastery Expected Gr. 6
No CTBS items this objective from level D through J

724. Metric units, estimate an amount or identify proper unit
Initial Instr. Grade 4   Entering Mastery Expected Gr. 6

GRADE	1	2	3	④	5	⑥	7	8	9
Items per grade	0	0	1	1	1	0	0	0	0

731. Temperature (F), choose temperature for common situation
Initial Instr. Grade 3   Entering Mastery Expected Gr. 5
No CTBS items this objective from level D through J

732. Temperature (C), choose temperature for common situation
Initial Instr. Grade 3   Entering Mastery Expected Gr. 5
No CTBS items this objective from level D through J

741. Geometry, match name or use knowledge of figure (cir., sq., rect., tri.)
Initial Instr. Grade 2   Entering Mastery Expected Gr. 4

GRADE	1	②	3	④	5	6	7	8	9
Items per grade	2	2	0	0	0	0	0	0	0

757. Geometry, match name to a common solid figure (cube, cone, etc.)
Initial Instr. Grade 3   Entering Mastery Expected Gr. 7

GRADE	1	2	③	4	5	6	⑦	8	9
Items per grade	1	2	3	1	1	0	0	0	0

771. Geometry, find perimeter, area, volume where formula is provided
Initial Instr. Grade 4   Entering Mastery Expected Gr. 6

GRADE	1	2	3	④	5	⑥	7	8	9
Items per grade	0	0	1	1	1	0	0	1	1

922. Number sentences, basic mult./div. facts, supply missing number
Initial Instr. Grade 3   Entering Mastery Expected Gr. 4

GRADE	1	2	③	④	5	6	7	8	9
Items per grade	0	0	2	2	2	0	0	0	0

Table 9.2.   continued.

---

924.   Number sentences, answer requires more compu. than basic facts
Initial Instr. Grade 3   Entering Mastery Expected Gr. 6

GRADE	1	2	③	4	5	⑥	7	8	9
Items per grade	0	1	3	3	3	1	1	0	0

943.   Choose nbr. sent. described by word problem, mult./div. facts
Initial Instr. Grade 4   Entering Mastery Expected Gr. 6
No CTBS items this objective from level D through J

951.   Pre-algebra, use properties of o,1
Initial Instr. Grade 3   Entering Mastery Expected Gr. 6

GRADE	1	2	③	4	5	⑥	7	8	9
Items per grade	0	1	0	2	2	0	0	0	0

956.   Set up equation from word pbl. or tell operation needed
Initial Instr. Grade 3   Entering Mastery Expected Gr. 7

GRADE	1	2	③	4	5	6	⑦	8	9
Items per grade	3	4	1	0	0	0	0	2	2

961.   Logic problems
Initial Instr. Grade 4   Entering Mastery Expected Gr. 8

GRADE	1	2	3	④	5	6	7	⑧	9
Items per grade	0	0	0	1	1	2	2	0	0

965.   Problems using menu or price list where each compu. trivial for age
Initial Instr. Grade 3   Entering Mastery Expected Gr. 7

GRADE	1	2	③	4	5	6	⑦	8	9
Items per grade	0	0	0	0	0	3	3	0	0

971.   Terms: Add, subtract, sum, product, etc.
Initial Instr. Grade 4   Entering Mastery Expected Gr. 6
No CTBS items this objective from level D through J

973.   Terms: Even, odd, whole numbers
Initial Instr. Grade 2   Entering Mastery Expected Gr. 4

GRADE	1	②	3	④	5	6	7	8	9
Items per grade	0	1	1	0	0	0	0	0	0

985.   Terms and operations; set, subset, union, intersection
Initial Instr. Grade 4   Entering Mastery Expected Gr. 7

GRADE	1	2	3	④	5	6	⑦	8	9
Items per grade	0	0	0	0	0	1	1	1	1

986.   Terms and operations, prime factorization
Initial Instr. Grade 4   Entering Mastery Expected Gr. 6
No CTBS items this objective from level D through J

Table 9.2. continued.

---

987. Terms and oper., greatest com. factor, least com. multiple
Initial Instr. Grade 4   Entering Mastery Expected Gr. 6
No CTBS items this objective from level D through J

999. Word pbl. where math task trivial for age; a reading problem
Initial Instr. Grade 4   Entering Mastery Expected Gr. 8

GRADE	1	2	3	④	5	6	7	⑧	9
Items per grade	0	3	7	2	2	3	3	0	0

Table 9.1 shows how the items are distributed in the CTBS for the 45 math computation and concepts objectives which are still in the instructional system for this district at grade 4 *and* are covered at some point in the CTBS. For each objective, the first circle shows the grade of initial instruction and the second shows the grade of expected entering mastery.

For spring testing, these four diagnostic uses of a standardized test are possible:

1. Monitor performance on the 26 objectives designated for initial instruction in grade 4. By the eighth month of the year, it is reasonable to expect initiation to have occurred on most. Knowledge of how well this instruction "took" with the students could be useful in deciding how much review (if any) is still needed on these objectives in subsequent years.

Of the 26 objectives designated by the teachers in this district as initial instruction objectives for grade 4, table 9.1 shows only 12 are actually tested at grade 4 by level F of the CTBS. The coverage ranges from 1 to 2 items per objective.

2. Monitor mastery objectives designated for entering mastery at grade 4 (this might more appropriately called "mastery maintenance" since mastery was expected in the fall of grade 4). Of the 17 objectives designated by the teacher group for entering mastery at grade 4, only 3 are actually tested by level F of the CTBS.

3. Monitor mastery objectives for the coming fall, as the students enter grade 5. This information would make a lot of sense for, if the standardized test results could be returned early enough in May, the teacher could remediate diagnosed problems before the students leave for the summer. Unfortunately, of the 18 entering mastery objectives designated for grade 5, only 5 have items included in the fourth grade test (level F).

4. Monitor objectives initiated prior to grade 4 on which mastery is expected after grade 4. In level F, items are included on 8 of the 22 objectives that fall into this category.

It seems like a lot of items are in the test, and 45 of the 65 grade 4 objectives are covered somewhere in the battery, yet the diagnostic capabilities for the four purposes above are not too good. What *are* the items testing?

Reviewing table 9.1, it can be seen that *for the way this particular district organizes instruction*, a lot of objectives are tested before they are first taught — sometimes as much as two years before they are taught. In fewer cases, the test covers objectives for some number of grades after that district considered them mastered. From the student's viewpoint, the former is a more difficult setting (being tested on a concept prior to when it is taught); the latter should cause no problem if mastery was really attained and is maintained.

When a standardized test doesn't seem to be a good match for the way a given district organizes for instruction, it isn't necessarily the fault of the committee of teachers who laid out the objective placements for that district or of the authors who designed the test coverage. The teachers are matching instruction to the conditions, traditions, and materials which exist in that district. The authors try to match placements to some sort of a national average placement. These mythical national placements are inferred by reviewing the instructional materials available to districts across the country.

The analysis done above, showing how the coverage of one standardized test matches the instructional flow in one district, can offer some insights into how a district should select a standardized test. After watching a scoring service for one publisher of tests, the author has concluded that the largest percentage of districts test in the fall; a slightly smaller percentage test in the spring; and the lowest percentage test in the winter. For the time of testing, the following selection rules could be used.

For fall testing, a battery would be chosen which has, grade by grade, maximum monitoring of objectives which have been taught, but not mastered, in an earlier grade. If objective-by-objective feedback were provided in a timely manner, the teacher could use this information to review places where difficulty was diagnosed and avoid objectives the students had clearly mastered. Fall testing is not good for objectives which are going to be first introduced during that grade (that does seem a bit unfair to the students). Fall testing is not too valuable for testing entering mastery, since standardized test feedback usually takes four to six weeks, and entering mastery information which arrives that late has little instructional value (although it may have evaluative value).

Spring testing, on the other hand, can monitor the initial instruction objectives, since most will probably have been presented by April. If the results can be returned by mid-May, spring testing can also provide information on the entering mastery objectives for the following grade, allowing the teacher some time to bring the students to mastery on objectives where trouble is diagnosed.

Winter testing can also be used to diagnose performance on entering mastery objectives for the following year. It can also monitor objectives taught but not mastered in a previous grade. Winter seems too early to monitor initial instruction objectives for that grade, and too late to monitor entering mastery objectives.

The process described in section 9.1.1, which leads to selecting objectives and defining the grades of initial instruction and mastery, would take some time. So would the task of doing an item-by-item match between the test itself and the objectives (although a district can probably expect to get some help on this task from the publisher's representative). But districts generally use a standardized test for five to eight years. People will view the standardized test results as a major, and perhaps the major, overall measure of the efficacy of the instructional program. And, presuming the district is going to use a standardized test for this external evaluation function, it seems reasonable to get one which also provides the maximum level of diagnostics. Getting the test which best matches the instructional program, using the techniques described here and in section 9.1.1, can be time-consuming. But, from the author's viewpoint, it is a justifiable one-time effort.

While it makes sense to take the time to choose the standardized test which best matches the instructional flow in the district, doing so does not imply that the standardized test can serve all necessary testing needs. As a diagnostic tool for the instructional program, the standardized test has these four drawbacks, none of which is trivial.

1. The coverage is incomplete. Scores on subtests like Punctuation or Math Computation are derived from items sampled from these domains, and not from exhaustive coverage of these, or any, domain.

2. Diagnostic feedback needs to be more often than annually. Just how frequently feedback is needed is open to some question, but annual feedback is clearly inadequate, even if it were complete.

3. The feedback from a standardized test is delayed. Although publishers make promises of quick turnaround, the usual interval between the day the class is tested and the day the results arrive is from five to eight weeks.

4. Finally, as illustrated in table 9.1, the number of items per objective, for those tested in the standardized battery, is pretty small. Most people would demand a minimum of three items per objective (with three out of three correct necessary for mastery); many would demand more.

The above is not meant to be an attempt to dissuade a district from an annual standardized testing program. The annual testing program has a whole variety of external validity uses; sections can be used to monitor growth in quality-with-equity; it can help be used to assess places where the district's program has followed a path which differs from the "normative" school nationally; it provides a way of communicating with the home. To maximize the validity of test use in these areas, the test should match, to the extent possible, the (perhaps unique) way the instructional program is presented in a district. And, since the standardized test is necessary for these other reasons anyhow, the district might just as well get the maximum diagnostic information possible from it.

9.2.2. Using a standardized test to monitor a difficulty-driven area like reading comprehension at the elementary school and junior high school level

This topic has been covered extensively in chapter 5. In reviewing this discussion, the following points should be considered.

1. A "pure" reading comprehension score should be used. Publishers frequently include Word Analysis, Vocabulary, or Study Skills in the Reading Total score. These are important areas, but they are not reading comprehension.

2. The conceptual level of a test designed for a grade level is primarily at or slightly below that grade level. Table 5.2, p. 113, illustrates. The implication is that when a student's functioning reading level deviates from current grade placement, the conceptual level of the reading comprehension test becomes inappropriate. A test with too-hard or too-easy items provides little diagnostic feedback.

3. This suggests that the standardized reading comprehension test provides feedback in only three general levels: the student was tested with a test which was too difficult, the student is functioning at about normative grade level, or the student was tested with a test which was too easy. Of course, percentile ranks and stanines are useful for communication with parents, but the diagnostic feedback is limited.

4. Summary reports, provided longitudinally, were suggested which accentuate this issue. Table 5.3, p. 114, shows the percentages of students across a five-year period who performed below, at, or above the conceptual level of the material with which they were tested.

This is not to argue that a standardized test of reading comprehension is of no value. The standardized test is only somewhat a formative measure;

it is primarily an evaluative tool. The test provides longitudinal growth data, links the district's performance to other districts in the country, becomes the basis for home reports, and can be used in summary reports. But it is important to remember that children whose functional reading level is more than a grade ahead or behind their grade placement are not adequately assessed by such a battery.

9.2.3. Using standardized tests to monitor achievement at the high school level

Section 9.1.3, addressing the issue of information system needs for high schools, suggested that the total program be viewed from a perspective of planned concentrations of courses. The information needs included, for each such planned concentration, a list of entry-level behaviors, a listing of exit-level behaviors for each course, an indication of the extent to which exit-level behaviors for one course become entry-level requirements for the next, and the assignment of initial teaching responsibility for objectives or goals which appear in more than one course.

The measurement needs are fairly obvious. To what extent are there standardized tests available to meet these needs?

As discussed in section 8.1, the survey achievement batteries developed for high schools are more useful for monitoring performance maintenance in previously taught skills than for monitoring material presented at the high school level. The usual subtest names, Reading, Math, Science, Social Studies, Written Expression, Using Sources and Language Mechanics, are certainly not course-specific; they are not even concentration-specific.

Course-specific tests do exist. The High School Subject Tests (Gatta, 1980) consists of a series of end-of-course measures for 15 commonly taught courses. The 1985 version of CTB/McGraw Hill's CAT contains end-of-course measures for nine specific courses. In the mid-'60s, Educational Testing Service developed the Cooperative Foreign Language Tests in French, German, Spanish, Russian, and Italian. Assorted and specific tests dealing with history, American government, specific science areas, vocational education, agriculture, and fine arts can be found. The Buros Institute of Mental Measurements at the University of Nebraska-Lincoln publishes summaries of tests in print, plus reviews by test experts. Educational Testing Service (ETS), in Princeton, New Jersey, maintains a substantial test collection which is available for review. Both the Buros Institute and ETS test surveys are available to users for on-line computer review.

These kinds of instruments could serve as a good starting place for monitoring performance outcomes in a high school program. Of course, a list of objectives tested, along with a copy of the test, should be reviewed by the teachers in the appropriate department before any use is made. If a given test conforms to local needs, or even is appropriate for part of the assessment needs, then it makes sense to make it a part of the outcome-monitoring program.

However, there are many reasons, enumerated below, why one should not become too optimistic about putting together a total high school assessment system with available published tests.

1. The tests will usually be written for the high-enrollment, common courses like Algebra, Biology, World History, and American Government. Small-enrollment courses, and more specialized departments, will find little or no coverage.

2. Most course-level tests are designed for a 40- to 50-minute administration time. This obviously limits the depth with which any issue can be assessed. (This was the motivation for the earlier comment that published tests might become part — and not be viewed as the entire — monitoring program.)

3. The coverage in such a test is a consensus coverage. If the course in a particular high school is approached in a distinctly different manner, the published test will be inappropriate.

4. The norming populations across different instruments can vary greatly. For one test, a percentile rank of 50 may be outstanding; for the next, it may be quite inadequate. This makes across-test comparisons difficult and potentially misleading.

5. Finally, each is a course test; none of these was designed as an assessment device for a high school department or for a concentration of courses in a department. A series of specific tests (Physical Science, Biology, Chemistry, Physics) might be a good way to begin assessing this sequence; but the department would still need to address issues of overlapping objectives as well as themes which run consistently through the entire sequence which consist of more than the specific elements tested in the end-of-course tests.

9.3. Monitoring the Instructional Program with Criterion-referenced tests

Criterion-referenced tests fit more closely an instructional testing format than do norm-referenced tests. A criterion-referenced test will focus on a specific objective or on a fairly narrow domain of coverage. The interpretation of a student's performance is absolute, based on a predetermined mastery level. Thus a student either masters or does not master the objective.

9.3.1. Objectives-driven areas in the elementary school and junior high school

In the information system described in section 9.1.1, the grades of initial instruction and the grade of entering mastery were defined, by a teacher committee, for each objective. While a standardized achievement can provide much useful diagnostic information about objectives, section 9.2.1 attempted to show that such a battery is not a very effective stand-alone monitor of the instructional program. As was noted earlier, a standardized test is best viewed as part of the school's evaluation system (although it can provide some diagnostic information, if used properly) while the criterion-referenced test should be seen as part of the school's instructional system.

The criterion-referenced test is usually written to address a single, very specific objective. The student's performance on it is referenced to a specific performance criterion.

The way the criterion-referenced tests should be scheduled for use depends, of course, on how the classroom is organized for instruction. However, these four are useful under any instructional condition:

1. Test for entering mastery, at the beginning of the year, all of the objectives designated for entering mastery. This should be done prior to reviewing; after all, the prior teacher is presumed to have reviewed them before the students left school the previous spring. To review, then test, would undoubtedly being wasting at least *some* time, since it would involve spending time on some objectives that the students have already mastered. The entering mastery test, given very early and before review, can provide the information on what should and should not be reviewed. Of course, once the teacher finds out which of the entering mastery objectives the students have not mastered, time should be set aside to bring them to mastery.

2. Monitoring, prior to instruction, objectives which have been *initially taught* in a prior grade but which are still part of the instructional system (i.e., have not yet been scheduled for entering mastery). This type of monitoring might be called "pretesting" to signal the teacher that clearly it is to be done prior to review. Actually, making sure that the teacher is

aware that the objective was previously presented is probably about as important as testing it prior to instruction. A teacher will (or certainly should) present an objective to students differently if s/he knows it was previously presented; an initial instruction presentation would be done more slowly and more thoroughly.

The rationale for testing these previously taught objectives prior to reviewing revolves, once again, around attempting to maximize opportunity-to-learn time. If the students can demonstate mastery without a review, then no instructional time should be spent on this objective. To do so would amount to investing time wherein the students have no opportunity to learn anything new.

In the mastery learning approach usually attributed to Benjamin Bloom, this type of testing occurs after the material from a unit of instruction has been presented (Guskey, 1985.) This testing, usually called "formative testing," is the same as the "pretesting" described here, since it occurs after initial instruction and has as its primary goal the identification of those students who cannot yet demonstrate mastery.

3. Somewhere near the end of March, the next year's entering mastery objectives should be tested. If there is to be any hope that the students can demonstrate mastery on these objectives in the coming fall, mastery must be attained prior to summer dismissal, since it is unlikely students will acquire the skills while on vacation. By monitoring these objectives near the end of April, the teacher has time to devote attention to reinstruction (in mastery learning, these are called "corrective activities") before the end of the year.

4. Performance on initial instruction objectives should also be monitored. This monitoring would occur after initial instruction has occurred. The question is when should the test be given: Directly after the instruction is complete, or near the end of the year, when all initial instruction is complete? Each makes some sense, but for different reasons.

One approach would be to administer the criterion referenced test when instruction on that objective, or cluster of objectives, is complete. This timing would hold irrespective of whether the class was organized for whole group instruction or is in an individualized mode. In mastery learning, this type of monitoring is characterized as a "second formative test" and is to occur just prior to the initialization of another sequential learning unit (see Guskey, chapter 1).

A second approach would be to wait until the end of the school year (mid-May) and monitor all of the initial instruction objectives at that time. If the feedback from the testing is fast enough, some time will still be available to remediate (correct) the deficits; or, where parental cooperation can be assumed, the information on deficits could be sent home with the student along with suggestions for methods of correction.

Monitoring right after instruction, with immediate feedback, allows the teacher to adjust future instructional plans to conform to student performance on prior, possibly requisite, skills. As information, the only benefit of using end-of-year monitoring is that it provides a more realistic appraisal of long-term learning.

However, end-of-year monitoring has one other practical benefit: the logistics are easier. Since the information system described in 9.1.1 defines the initial instruction objectives at each grade level, one paper-and-pencil test could be assembled to measure all these objectives at once. By testing right after instruction for each of these individual objectives, a single test must be made available to the teacher (duplicated, with a key) when instruction is complete. The logistics of providing this type of paper-and-pencil monitoring system are nontrivial.

Before ending this section on criterion-referenced monitoring, the distinction between reporting "This student has mastered the objective," as contrasted with "This student cannot demonstrate mastery of the concept underlying this objective," needs to be addressed. The way the test is constructed should depend on which of these is to receive the reporting emphasis.

To demonstrate the distinction, consider this objective: division of a whole number by a 1-digit whole number, where the answer includes a remainder.

Here are five example problems (A through E) which fit under this objective:

Ex. A	Ex. B	Ex. C	Ex. D	Ex. E
6 R 3	13 R 4	136 R 5	1367 R 4	1010 R 3
7⟌45	7⟌95	7⟌957	7⟌9573	7⟌7073
42	7	7	7	7
3	25	25	25	0
	21	21	21	0
	4	47	47	7
		42	42	7
		5	53	3
			49	0
			4	3

Most people would argue that the examples are in order of increasing difficulty from A to E; E is placed last because it is four digits and requires the student to work across zeros, which tend to cause considerable difficulty. How does the way the reporting will be structured impact the way the items in the criterion-referenced test are to be structured?

To report, "This student has mastered this objective," strongly implies that the student has demonstrated mastery on each type of item, including tricky ones like those resulting in zeroes in the quotient. Teachers know that students (like adults) can know how to do a problem and still make occasional computational errors; still they expect "mastery" to mean just that — mastery of all problem types under this heading.

Actually, the teacher might be more interested in knowing if the student can demonstrate mastery on the concept underlying the objective, and not so much in knowing if the student can cross all the t's and dot all the i's within it. Example A does not quite test the concept underlying the objective in question, but example B does. In example B the student writes the first number ("1") in the quotient, multiplies the divisor (the "7") by the "1," and brings this product below the dividend. Now example B goes beyond A by demanding that the student bring the next digit down from the dividend (the "5") and determining the maximum number of times 7 goes into 25, bringing this amount ("3") up to the quotient. The remaining amount (4) is then brought up to the quotient, yielding the answer shown (13 R 4).

Example B tests the concept. If a student can do B, s/he should also be able to do C, D, and E. Example A doesn't go far enough; essential elements are still missing at this point. Examples C, D, and E simply require that the student repeat this essential series of steps more times; one more time in C, and two more times in D and E. Example E tests a specific application — the setting where a zero appears as one of the entries in the quotient.

The distinction is important. A student who has mastered the concept but simply makes too many routine errors or has trouble with one idiosyncratic application should have a different corrective approach than a student who has not yet even mastered the underlying concept. From a diagnostic viewpoint, it does seem that testing to determine if the student has not yet mastered the concept is the more important task. Once the concept is in place, the finer points can be developed with practice; sometimes this type of practice activity is logically part of the next instructional unit.

In any event, the test designed to support a statement like "This student has demonstrated mastery on this objective," will not be the same as a test designed to support a statement like "This student cannot demonstrate mastery of the concept underlying this objective." The teacher needs to know which approach the test writer used. To mix the two up provides confusing diagnostic information to the teacher.

9.3.2. Monitoring reading comprehension in the elementary school and junior high school

Such a system should provide timely (i.e., much more frequently than annual) diagnoses of each child's current functioning reading level. The content in the reading comprehension section of standardized tests properly assesses the functioning level for a fairly narrow range. Scores for students whose functioning level is above grade level or substantially below grade level are extrapolations. These points were raised in chapter 5, as well as sections 9.1.2 and 9.2.2.

A criterion-referenced monitoring system for reading comprehension should have these two characteristics. First, based on some sort of estimate of each child's current functioning level, the material in the test should approximate that level. Second, this process needs to be repeated over the course of the school year to keep track of the child's growth which, at some grade levels, can be rapid. Earlier, estimates of six testing periods per year for the lower grades and four for the upper grades were projected. (A third element, an information system to keep track of all these results for the teacher and principal, will be discussed in section 9.4.)

Chapter 5, which covers the evaluate-your-instruction process for reading comprehension in an elementary school, addresses ways that a school can put such a monitoring system in place. A computerized-adaptive approach is possible; but so is a paper-and-pencil approach using small optical scanners as suggested by Cooley and Bickel (1986, p. 75).

9.3.3. Criterion-referenced test requirements at the high school

Section 9.1.3 developed the idea of monitoring high school instruction based on course concentrations. For each such concentration of courses, a list of the entry-level prerequisite behaviors, as well as the exit-level expectations, needed to be part of the information system. Where certain objectives (or experiences) were common to more than one course in the sequence, the course of initial instruction would be designated in the information system.

Standardized batteries of tests designed for high schools are more useful for monitoring the maintenance of previously learned skills than for assessing performance on concepts/skills taught at the high school level. There do exist, however, an substantial array of specific end-of-course tests for high schools. However, even these will cover only the more common courses; the coverage in the test may not be a good match for the program at a given high school; and independently evaluating each course with an end-of-course test is a fragmented approach, ignoring the point that courses are almost always part of a sequence or concentration of courses. These points were all developed more fully in section 9.2.2.

For each concentration or sequence of courses, the assessment needs could be defined by going through the evaluate-your-instruction process developed earlier in this book. This process will define the pretesting needs of the sequence (necessary entry-level behaviors if the student is successfully to survive the first few weeks of the first course), formative needs, and the needs for assessing the degree to which the student outcomes are in line with expected outcomes. Where a published, standardized end-of-course test conforms to the needs delineated by the evaluate-your-instruction process, such a test could be integrated into the monitoring process. It is unreasonable to expect, however, that a large proportion of the monitoring needs can be provided by published measures.

"Criterion-referenced tests" is too narrow a term for the rest of the needed measures. Many measures of expected outcomes, such as follow-up studies of employment status or college status, or measures of attitude, are not really tests at all. The common theme for measurement needs which cannot be addressed with published tests is more like "locally developed measures" than "criterion-referenced tests."

The author is aware of the time commitment which would be necessary to implement the above recommendation. However, as is so often true in this area of instructional monitoring, it is the start-up effort, not the maintenance effort, that is substantial. Once a monitoring system was developed for each logical concentration of courses, maintaining it in the face of changing programs would be quite easy.

9.4. Using microcomputers to administer and score tests, and maintain building and district records

9.4.1. Why computers?

Monitoring students and keeping records are not contingent on using computers. People monitored and accumulated long before computers were invented. With computers, however, the kind of information systems and monitoring outlined in this chapter would be a lot less tedious.

Rather than have tests printed on paper, duplicated and distributed, in a computerized system the test would be part of the software, stored on a disk. The student sits at a terminal; the items appear on the screen; and the student responds by using the terminal's keyboard.

The beauty of this approach is in what optical scanner people call "source data capture." The responses the student makes can be scored by the computer, included in a class-level summary for the teacher, accumulated for a building-level summary for the principal, and be part of a year-long summary for the curriculum director *without anyone ever touching them again*.

The primary benefit of a computer monitoring and record-keeping system would be higher student performance. Opportunity-to-learn time, as has been noted previously, is lost when the teacher teaches things the students already know, stays with a concept long after the class has mastered it, presents as new material which has been taught before, or goes onto new material before the necessary requisites for it have been mastered. To avoid these, testing is necessary. The feedback must be immediate; it does no good to test Monday and not have the results back until Wednesday because by Wednesday the damage, in terms of wasted time, will already be done.

Paper-and-pencil systems can theoretically accomplish the same purpose. Contrast the task for the teacher. With computers, the test is on disks which are inserted in the disk drives; the "answers" are accumulated on one data disk as the students complete the testing; and the class summary, including diagnostics, is printed out within five minutes of the time the last student was tested. The teacher can begin using the information that very day. With a paper-and-pencil system, the teacher must find the test in the test file, have it copied and collated, monitor its administration, score it, and summarize the information to provide the needed diagnostics. This must be done every time a diagnostic test is given. Even if an optical scanner takes over the scoring task, the task is still substantial for each criterion-referenced test.

A computer monitoring the record-keeping system will cause student performance to improve because it will allow a level of diagnosis and feedback which is very difficult to achieve with paper-and-pencil systems. The author's experience is that paper-and-pencil criterion-referenced testing systems are unwieldy to maintain and intrusive on the teacher's time. With a computer monitoring system, the amount of diagnoses carried out will increase substantially, the feedback will be immediate, the opportunity-to-learn time will increase, and student performance will go up.

A second reason for using computers for this task has to do with the teacher. With some exceptions, teachers presumably become teachers because they like to teach. A literature search could find no call from the

major national teacher organizations for electronic teaching systems. As
the poor quality of current software is lamented and the difficulty of developing good software is discussed (see Becker, 1985), one wonders if a
lot of effort is not being spent on fixing something which is not broken.

So while teachers do like to teach, and aren't necessarily looking for
orderly semiconductors to replace this task, teachers generally do not like
to write tests, assemble them from item banks, seek them from test libraries, administer them, score them, or keep records from them. This is
not to say teachers are disinterested in information or that they would not
use diagnostic information if it were readily available.

Finally, when data are captured at the source, building- and district-
level information systems become feasible. Information, not tradition or
textbook design, can be used to plan and run the instructional system.
Student performance information will be based on information gathered
routinely as part of the instructional program and not on an annual standardized testing program.

9.4.2. A few details

Obviously, some number of computer positions would have to be in a
room. The best approach would be to have one position for each student;
however, if this were not feasible at the outset, the room should at least
be equipped so the regular classroom teacher could monitor the students
being tested as well as those waiting. In this manner additional staff would
not be needed.

In reading, the software system (the computer program which causes
the test items to come onto the screen) is adaptive to the student's responses. That is, a student would begin with a passage and questions which
are fairly easy for his/her grade. After each passage, the software system
uses the information collected from the student to predict his/her functioning reading level. If the student does very well on the first passage,
the next passage will be more difficult; if the student does poorly, the next
passage will be easier. These predictions and selections are made within
seconds; very quickly the computer has found the student's functioning
level, and the remainder of the test is at that level.

In the objectives-driven areas (math computation and concepts, punctuation, capitalization, grammar-usage, reference skills, and some areas of
science) the teacher would preselect the objectives to be tested. This would
be done to conform to the way instruction is carried out in that district.
Referring back to section 9.3.1, entering mastery objectives would be se-

lected as the year begins, followed by sessions, possibly more than one, monitoring pretest objectives (objectives which were introduced at an earlier grade and are still part of the instructional system). Later the teacher could select objectives on which prior performance was not satisfactory and remediation has been provided. In the spring, entering mastery expectations for the next fall could be chosen so that plenty of remediation time is available prior to summer dismissal. In May, all of the initial instruction objectives for that grade could be monitored to determine how much instructional time needs to be set aside for these already-taught objectives in the following year.

Frequency of testing would be a local decision. Earlier, it was estimated that reading might be monitored every six weeks in the early grades, when the growth rate is faster, and every nine weeks in the later elementary school grades. Math basic skills are pretty extensive, and some performance on some (e.g., multiplication of two two-digit numbers, long division) take a while. A 40-minute test session might be needed every month or six weeks to keep up. In language arts, the coverage, in terms of number of objectives to be tested, is about as broad, but the average response time per item is less. Six sessions a year, as an estimate, might be enough.

How many computers would be needed to deliver this level of service? If one assumes 20 testing sessions per student, that each session requires 45 minutes, and that seven such 45-minute sessions could be run in a typical school day, and that the school year consists of 160 days, table 9.3 provides estimates.

A building with three classrooms per grade level, grades 1 to 8, would have about 600 students. Eleven machines, dedicated totally to testing, could test each of the 600 students 20 different times across the school year. A logistically more comfortable approach would be to equip a lab

Table 9.3. Computer Requirements by Enrollment in a Building

Enrollment	Computers Needed If They Were 100% Dedicated to Testing	If a Lab with 30 Computers were Available, Percent of Time Would Be Needed to Service the Testing Pgm.
1,000	18	59%
800	14	48%
600	11	36%
400	7	24%
200	4	12%

with 30 machines. To maintain the testing program, those machines would be needed for testing only 36% of the time; the other 64% could be dedicated to other uses.

9.4.3. Computer monitoring in difficulty-driven and objectives-driven areas

There is good reason to keep these two — reading and objectives-driven areas — separate as one discusses computerization of the testing and information systems. Although this field is just developing, some literature has appeared over the past ten (or so) years. For example, McBride (1985), in an article announcing that "assessment, diagnosis, and placement by computer may soon replace paper-and-pencil testing," does not distinguish between reading testing and testing in objectives-driven areas. This is unfortunate for two reasons.

First, for objectives-driven areas, the flow of instruction in a classroom is preplanned. Generally speaking, this flow conforms to what occurs in the textbook, although many districts provide supplementary materials and some individualize. A computerized adaptive test in mathematics will behave like a computerized adaptive system in reading. That is, as the student does well, the computer finds harder tasks; as the student does poorly, the computer software identifies easier tasks. The approach is just fine in reading. Compare these outputs from computer testing sessions with John Jones in reading and math:

> John Jones is currently functioning at a mid-seventh grade level in reading comprehension.
> John Jones is currently functioning at a mid-seventh grade level in mathematics.

The first is a useful diagnostic. The teacher, possibly with the help of the librarian, can now attempt to find material for John which is at the mid-seventh grade level. The second is no better than a standardized test report that his Math Total grade equivalent is 7.5. Does this mean he has mastered every objective first introduced prior to grade 7? The teacher knows what topics will be introduced in that classroom in the next few math units. The teacher should be able to select the objectives to be measured. In objectives-driven areas, the "adaptive" in "computer adaptive" should refer to adapting to the teacher's needs, and not to the needs of some psychometric model. The computer report, based on computerized adaptive testing, is actually *less* valuable than the 7.5 grade equivalent in

Math Total. At least with the standardized test, all of the students took the same items, and some, albeit limited, diagnostic information can be provided. An adaptive system will search for items throughout the domain. It is possible that no single specific objective will be tested on all students.

Second, there is a fundamental difference between an item associated with a difficulty-driven test (like reading) and one which is from an objectives-driven area. Consider these two items:

A reading passage, designed for fifth graders, is presented. The item is, "What is the main idea of this passage?" The student must choose from among four responses.

A sentence is given: *Mother said, "please go to the kitchen."* The student is asked to determine if any error in capitalization has been made.

If a student has not yet been taught that the first word in a direct quotation is always capitalized, the student will always get the item wrong (except for occasionally making a lucky guess). On the other hand, once the student has been introduced to this fact, the student will almost always get it right after that (unless the student works too quickly or is temporarily distracted). In other words, the probability that the student will get this item correct is near zero if no effective instruction has occurred or near one if prior instruction has occurred. The average performance for a class, of course, will take all the values from 0% to 100%, but that is an accumulation of scores from individuals who either know it or do not.

The reading item is different. If a student can read at all, the probability of a correct answer can range across the entire scale. Obviously, excellent readers have a higher probability of a correct answer than poor readers, but it would make sense to estimate that a student has "a 60% chance of getting this item correct." (Of course, the student is actually going to either get it right or wrong.)

This "probability of a correct answer ranging across the entire scale" is an assumption of the psychometric theories underlying computerized adaptive testing. It is a sensible assumption in reading; it is not so sensible at the individual student level in mathematics or other objectives-driven areas. Only an extremely careless student would have a 60% chance of getting items about capitalization of the first word in a direct quotation correct. For a specific objective like this, the student either knows or doesn't know. The primary use of this information at the classroom level should be in the diagnosis of current deficits of the individual student. The theory is appropriate for groups (it does make sense to say the probability of the average fifth grade getting the capitalization item correct is 60%) but not sensible for an individual in an objectives-driven area. The theory is sensible for both groups and individuals in difficulty-driven areas.

Much of the work described by McBride (1985) was done with the support of the U.S. Department of Defense. Most of applications of the psychometric models have been in state or national assessment programs, or with survey measures like college aptitude tests. These uses are more appropriate, even in objectives-driven areas. The Defense Department is probably satisfied to know that applicants' current functioning math level is "mid-seventh grade." That is probably sufficient information to allow an appropriate placement. A state report which says the average math level of 11-year-olds is "mid-seventh grade" is adequately communicating with the audience. An estimate from the domain called "mathematics" is satisfactory for the college to help with an admission decision. It is only when these methods are used in objectives-driven areas to make individual diagnostic statements that the author quarrels with the method. In the first place a statement like "John Jones is functioning at a mid-seventh grade level in math," is not diagnostic; in the second place, an important assumption in the theory is inappropriate at the individual student level.

References

Becker, H.J. (1985). "Computers in schools today: Some basic considerations." *American Journal of Education* 93(1):22–39.

Bloom, B.S. (1984). "The search for methods of group instruction as effective as one-to-one tutoring." *Educational Leadership* 41(8):4–18.

Bloom, B.S. (1984). "The 2 Sigma problem: A search for methods of group instruction as effective as one-to-one tutoring." *Educational Researcher* 13(5), 4–16.

Comprehensive Tests of Basic Skills (1981). Monterey, CA: CTB/McGraw-Hill.

Comprehensive Tests of Basic Skills (1983). *Examiner's Manual, Forms U and V, Levels F, G, H, J, K*. Monterey, CA: CTB/McGraw-Hill, 1982.

Cooley, W.W., and Bickel, W.E. (1986). *Decision-Oriented Educational Research*. Boston: Kluwer-Nijhoff Publishing.

Gatta, L. (1980). "High School Subject Tests." In J.W. Wick and J.K.Smith (eds.), *Comprehensive Assessment Program*. Iowa City, IA: American Testronics, Inc.

Gronlund, N.E. (1985). *Measurement and Evaluation in Teaching*. New York: Macmillan Publishing Co.

Guskey, T.R. (1985). *Implementing Mastery Learning*. Belmont, CA: Wadsworth Publishing Co.

McBride, J.R. (1985). "Computerized adaptive testing." *Educational Leadership* 43(2):25–28.

Wick, J.W. (1983). *Planning For Improvement*. Glenview, IL: Scott, Foresman and Co.

10 SELF-REPORT AND TYPICAL PERFORMANCE MEASURES

Many real and very important goals of a school cannot be measured by maximum performance tests of the types described in the preceding chapter. Some commonly asked questions in the evaluate-your-instruction programs derive from a need to know what people outside the school, including former students, are doing or thinking. Some common questions are:

> To what extent do taxpayers understand and approve of our advanced placement programs (or vocational education programs; or fine arts performances; or expenditures for intramural sports; or . . .)?
>
> What experiences are our graduates having after leaving this school?
>
> To what extent are our former students' behaviors consistent with the school's goals?

Questions like these would most likely be answered by some type of self-report instrument. A questionnaire through the mail or an interview, over the telephone or done personally, are the most common techniques for gathering these kinds of data. These measures are very personal to the local district; the questions tend to be idiosyncratic to local needs. With this in mind, the first part of this chapter will be addressed to a fairly complete and specific set of guidelines for developing self-report instruments, and to instruction on how to gather and report the data.

So much for the easy part of this chapter. The chapter also deals with affective measures, those dealing with emotions, feelings (including affection or lack thereof). Just about everyone agrees that there is a noncognitive component in learning. Carroll's (1963) influential model for school learning included perseverence as one of its five elements. Perseverence is a trait internal to the student. Bloom's (1976) explication of mastery learning, built on the foundation of Carroll's model, was more specific in the definition of characteristics included under perseverence. General attitude toward school and specific attitude toward the subject matter in questions are included by Bloom. The North Central Association's outcomes accreditation program calls for the inclusion of at least two affective measures in its program (North Central Association, 1985). Bloom (1977) states that success positively influences the student's feelings and attitudes toward learning that which follows. Success breeds good attitudes; and good attitudes breed more success. That seems like a pretty defensible viewpoint.

The importance of these noncognitive elements is pretty well established. The tough part is obtaining valid measures that don't cost an unacceptably large portion of the district's budget. There are some serious pitfalls in developing, using, and interpreting measures of this kind.

Following Bloom's strategy, the easier part (self-report measures) will be covered first. Maybe if the reader can see some relevance of these techiques for local needs some positive feelings will be established. These positive feelings might make the second part more palatable.

10.1. Self-report measurements

The most common forms of gathering these kinds of data are mailed questionnaires and telephone interviews.

Personal interviews might be used, but they raise the cost tenfold without much improvement in the validity of the results. In fact, many people will be far more candid to a stranger over the telephone than they will in a face-to-face interview.

Each of these asks questions. Before moving into specific details of mailed questionnaires and telephone interviews, some specifics about question-writing will be covered. This trivial-sounding topic is not trivial at all; there are some things to do and not do if the results from a survey are to have maximum usefulness.

Before actually writing a single question, consider these issues:

1. The respondent needs to know immediately why this intrusion into his/her life is being made. The cover letter for a questionnaire or the first words out of the mouth of the telephone interviewer should cover this.

For example, "The elected school board for your local school has asked that I find out your views about . . ." or "Eisenhower High School is thinking about making major changes in its vocational programs and needs help from you, a graduate, to. . . ."

Think of those first words in terms of a headline on a newspaper article. Catch the person's attention; make the respondent curious, at least. If the questionnaire hits the circular file, or the respondent slams the receiver down before saying a word, it's bad enough that the information is lost. It's even worse that the randomness of the sample, and therefore the credibility of the data collected, is injured. This is a critical point. Amazingly enough, there are people out there who are not as interested in your school district as you are!

2. Stay on the topic; don't give into the tendency to want to piggyback a few extraneous questions into the survey. Any kind of a survey takes time and costs money. Often, particularly when the questions are being developed by a committee, someone will say, "Since we're going to all of this effort, why don't we ask about . . . also?" to which another will reply, "Yes, and our other committee is studying . . . so let's get a question about that, too."

Don't give in. Keep the survey on the topic for which it was originally undertaken. In the first place, the other questions make the survey longer; and shorter is better than longer. More importantly, these other issues can interact with the issue at hand. If the survey was designed to assess current activities and attitudes of the graduates of a high school's vocational program, an innocent-sounding question about the athletic program or school closings or bus routes can bring to the respondent a strong emotional reaction which will interfere with feelings about vocational education, which was the major issue at hand.

3. The respondent must be able and competent to respond. The corollary is that you cannot use the survey as an instructional device first, then ask for an opinion. Consider this interchange in a telephone survey:

> "What is your attitude toward the mainstreaming program at your school?"
> "What's mainstreaming?"
> "That has to do with the least restrictive placement of children with special problems. Mainstreaming means to put them back into regular classrooms as much as is possible."
> "What special problems? You mean blind or deaf?"

And on and on. Like any profession, educators use some codes which are not fully understood by those outside the field. The respondent must not only understand the terms used but must have enough understanding of the program in question to be able to provide useful information. An honest tryout, outlined below, should identify these kinds of problems. From the interchange above, about the only potentially useful information to be obtained is that a citizen was contacted who did not know the meaning of "mainstreaming."

So much for the general rules. Now some suggestions for the questions themselves.

1. Avoid double-barreled questions. Take issues one at a time. "Should Eisenhower High School expand its vocational education programs and eliminate Latin and Russian from the foreign language program?" "Do you think the intramural sports program was fair to women and minorities?" are double-barreled questions. The respondent might want to answer "no-yes" or "possibly-absolutely not" or some other combination.

2. Short questions are better than long ones. Long questions demand two characteristics which are not always found in respondents. First, if the item is in printed form, the respondent for a long question needs to be a pretty good reader, and second the respondent must be willing to persevere through the question. Don't overestimate the capability of the respondents. Many people can, and do, survive quite nicely in our society with a sixth or seventh grade reading level. Keep the questions short. Make little ones out of your big ones.

3. Avoid negative items. Ask the question directly. "Should the school board approve funds to begin a computer repair program at Eisenhower High School?" is better than "Should the school board disapprove . . . ?"

4. Don't try to be clever or cute. "Oh, hi there it's me again just trying to. . . ." There is a tendency for an inexperienced item writer to try to make items which are different and entertaining. The purpose of the survey is neither to entertain nor to demonstrate the writer's cleverness. Inclusion of what the writer feels is clever might actually get in the way of gathering the data. A survey is a two-way street. As you try to get information from the respondents, they are judging you by what is heard in the question. The questions should be straight, to the point, and as emotion-free as possible.

5. Be specific. "As you were growing up . . ." ("Hold on; I'm not done growing up yet!"). "During the war, did your feelings about curriculum control change?" ("Which war? I've seen three so far in my lifetime.") "Do you believe teachers are generally competent to serve the needs of the students?" ("You mean here at Eisenhower High? Or in big cities? Or in the country?") These kinds of ambiguities, too, can be identified in a tryout prior to use.

6. Don't lead the respondent. "Wouldn't you agree that not enough

effort is being directed toward preparing students toward the world of work?" "To help the school psychologist serve suicide prone students, do you think. . . ?" Most questions don't need any preamble, no matter how strongly the writer feels about the issue.

7. If you have a series of questions which are repetitive, it is best to put them in a matrix than ask them one by one. (I know this sounds like it contradicts with (2), which asked for shortness, but you also don't want the respondent to think you're stupid.) Here are some repetitive questions:

If you had to assign a letter grade (A to F) which expresses your opinion about the courses you took in the English Department at Eisenhower High School, which grade would it be?

(A)   (B)   (C)   (D)   (F)

If you had to assign a letter grade (A to F) which expresses your opinion about the courses you took in the Math Department at Eisenhower High School, which grade would it be?

(A)   (B)   (C)   (D)   (F)

and onto social studies, foreign language, and so forth. Better to put this into a matrix:

Assign a letter grade (A to F) which expresses your opinion about the courses you took from each department listed. Check "No courses" if you did not take any courses in that department.

Department	GRADE					
1. English	(A)	(B)	(C)	(D)	(F)	( ) No courses
2. Math	(A)	(B)	(C)	(D)	(F)	( ) No courses
3. Science	(A)	(B)	(C)	(D)	(F)	( ) No courses
4. Foreign Lang.	(A)	(B)	(C)	(D)	(F)	( ) No courses
5.						
6.						

Not only will the respondent find this easier but s/he will be forced to do some relative comparisons of grades assigned as s/he responds.

8. Questions for which every person has one and only one response position are called closed-end questions. The "has one" part of that statement means the categories must be exhaustive; the "and only one" means the categories must also be mutually exclusive. "Check which you are: ( ) Male ( ) Female" is pretty obvious. (I've quit wording this question, "Check your sex," because it draws too many responses like "Yes" or "As often as possible.")

Sometimes the categories appear to be exhaustive but are not. A good final category is simply:

( ) Other (please list) _____________________________

which is good for questions like "Which degree are you working toward?" (in case the school has at least one obscure one) or "Which elementary school did you attend?."

Here's a question-type frequently seen which, for some respondents, is neither mutually exclusive nor exhaustive.

Check highest educational level:
( ) Less than eighth grade graduation.
( ) Eighth grade graduation.
( ) High school graduation.
( ) Degree from four-year college received.
( ) Masters degree received.
( ) Ph.D. received.

A medical doctor will not have a place to respond. A medical doctor with a Ph.D. might resent calling the Ph.D. the highest educational level. Since the frequency of degrees beyond a college degree is not high, ambiguity could be eliminated by dropping the last two categories and adding this catch-all:

( ) Other (please list) _____________________________.

9. Keeping more categories in the survey question than will be used in the report on the results makes no sense at all. If your survey calls for ages of respondents, or number of credits taken, or years the family has lived in the community, set up in advance the final reporting categories and make the survey questions have the same categories.

10. When contingency questions are used, make sure the respondents understand the directions by using arrows and margin changes. A contingency question has parts or stages. Only at the first stage is a response expected from everyone; thereafter, the response determines if the person goes to the next item or continues to another stage. Consider this item:

Item 5. While at Eisenhower High School, did you enroll in more than two years of one foreign language?

( ) No.   (Go onto item 6)
( ) Yes.   If yes ______

Which language was it?
( ) French   (Go onto item 6)
( ) German   (Go onto item 6)
( ) Greek   (Go onto item 6)
( ) Spanish.   If Spanish ______

How many years of Spanish did you complete?
( ) 2
( ) 3
( ) 4
( ) 5.

The margin change and the arrows guide the respondent along, even if s/he is moving quickly through the questionnaire and not reading directions carefully. Note that the response that triggers continuation in the item is placed last in the list of categories.

11. If you must ask threatening questions, at least word them in the most unoffensive method possible. A question like

Did you ever cheat on a final exam at Eisenhower High School?
( ) No
( ) Yes. If Yes ______

If Yes, about how many times?
( ) 1
( ) 2 to 5
( ) 6 to 20
( ) more than 20.

would be less threatening if worded

How many times did you cheat on an exam at Eisenhower High?
( ) 0
( ) 1
( ) 2 to 5
( ) 6 to 20
( ) more than 20.

The first format demands a confession. After the confession, the penance is filling in the second part of the question. The second question essentially assumes that the respondent has probably engaged in this socially unacceptable behavior. The respondent who has indeed cheated in high school can still mark the "0" but at least the second format doesn't conjure up an image of a stern, black-robed judge peering over his half-glasses, shouting, "Did you cheat?"

A second way to soften this is to give the idea that the behavior is relatively common. Here, breaking the rule about "no preambles," the question might be worded

> Most people acknowledge that some cheating on final exams occurred at Eisenhower High. While in high school, how many times did you cheat on a final exam?

The same categories would be used.

If these kinds of threatening questions are not central to the purpose of an evaluate-your-instruction process, it would be worthwhile to avoid them. On a telephone survey, these are the types of items that make the respondent hang up. With mail surveys, they might cause the respondent to quit. Additionally, with mail surveys, privacy and anonymity become more important with questions like these. A coding system such that follow-up letters or calls can be made becomes a real threat.

Keep these suggestions in mind as a first draft is made of the questions needed. Then, irrespective of whether the survey will be conducted by telephone or through the mail, consider these steps:

1. Give some thought to question order. First look for any question to which, in your opinion, the respondent will be delighted to respond. A nonthreatening, burning issue on which everyone has an opinion or an opportunity to let the respondent brag are good items to place first in the survey. The goal is to get the respondent interested enough to start. Usually, if they will start, they will finish.

After those, put the easy questions next. The questions, however, should be in a logical order; don't jump around through a person's history just to get the easy questions first. People are generally logical, taking events in serial order. Don't confuse them.

Save the more controversial, difficult-to-answer items for last. This is particularly true with a mailed survey; with a telephone survey, these might be more toward the middle, to make sure the respondent doesn't terminate the call before the key questions are asked.

2. Find a friend or colleague known to be detail-oriented. Have this person respond to the questions presented orally (if the survey is to be by

telephone) or in writing if a mail survey is to be used. Listen carefully to this person as s/he responds. Any question or point of confusion, no matter how trivial, needs to be corrected, for others will have the same problems. Keep your mouth shut during this trial (except, in the telephone format, to ask the questions); don't take it upon yourself to explain, defend, or justify an item. If the person has a substantial number of misunderstandings about your wording, correct the questions and repeat this one-on-one trial again.

3. Next, try the survey out with a very limited sample from the population in question. Five telephone calls will probably be enough to provide an honest estimate of how long the calls will take, questions the respondents do not understand, or categories that have been designed wrong. To make sure enough mailed questionnaires are returned to make a judgment, about 20 should be sent out for this tryout purpose.

10.2. Acquired Behavioral Dispositions

Now *that* sounds like educationese! The term in this section's title is due to Campbell (1963). The term may sound like educationese, but, as a sports announcer was known to say, the term "says it all."

In the term "acquired behavioral disposition," the "disposition" keeps the user aware that the behavior in question is not being directly addressed. Paper-and-pencil measures of attitude, interest, personality, and valuing do *not* directly monitor behaviors; instead, they monitor the person's self-reported *disposition* to behave in a certain manner. The "acquired" reminds us that these behavioral dispositions come from someplace; specifically, they are mostly learned. (I'm backing off on saying they are entirely learned. Observing my own five children, I do believe some behavioral dispositions are hard-wired.)

School people have developed a sense of confidence in maximum performance tests of achievement. Measures of reading comprehension or math computation for the elementary school years have demonstrated high levels of reliability, and an apparent face validity. They correlate closely with what actually occurs in the classroom. Given this generally satisfactory history with measures of achievement, the teacher or school administrator quite logically begins looking for published measures of character development, moral development, attitude toward mathematics, or whatever affective objective is in question at a particular moment. There exist some very fundamental differences between these achievement tests (maximum performance measures of cognition) and the measures of acquired behavioral dispositions (typical performance measures of affective areas). The goal of the following set of disclaimers is not meant to discourage people entirely from using paper-and-pencil measures of acquired behavioral dispositions. The goal is to try to improve the validity of interpretations through suggestions for selection or development of such measures.

10.2.1. Start with issues of development

A test of math computation or punctuation needs very little additional description. Depending on the grade level for which it is developed, someone experienced with education will have a pretty good sense of what will be included in the test. Additionally, there will be no quarrel about which answer is correct, or at least most correct. Neither of these conditions — common understanding of the concept being measured and common agreement on which answer is correct — are as clear for measures of self-confidence, thoroughness, initiative, fair-mindedness, persistence, responsibility, respect for the law, cooperation, tactfulness, amiability, punctuality, or courtesy.

The too-long list of traits ending the above sentence was meant to point out another issue: there are thousands of terms or phrases which can be used to describe affective characteristics in people. The terms differ subtly. These subtle difference are different across people. Math computation means math computation; parents would agree that they would rather have their children be able to do math computation than not. Is "respect for the law" always viewed so positively? When the law is unjust or unfair, should children be taught blindly to respect it? Not all people agree about what is "right" within the confines of the trait "respect for the law." That can also be argued for each of the traits listed at the end of the last paragraph.

The meaning issue intrudes as the student takes the measure; the interpretation issue intrudes as the responses are scored. Consider this item: a person should respect the law. Is the "law" the police, the judge, a religious leader, a set of printed rules, something else, or some combination thereof? The questions recalls the "acquired" in "acquired behavioral disposition." Each student has a unique set of prior experiences; the interpretation each brings to "the law" will naturally differ. The item has another difficult word: respect. The author generally challenges the students for which he has the most respect. Does "respect" mean "avoid violation of"? Or does it mean to "honor" or "hold in high esteem" or "treat with deference?" Many will find each of these descriptors subtly different.

For measures of affect, the "correct" answer is determined logically or empirically. Logical keying defines itself. If the scale has to do with "attitude toward conservation of resources," then logic would suggest that the "correct" answer to "I go out of my way to turn off unnecessary lights" is "agree." If the scale is "attitude toward the study of science," logic would suggest a reply of "always" or "almost always" to the statement, "I am curious about the way things work."

A second approach is empirical keying. Here an "attitude toward science" scale would be constructed by first identifying a known group of people who are believed to have a preferred attitude toward science; probably a group of people actively involved in this field. A long list of questions, not necessarily having anything to do with science, would be administered to this "scientist" group as well as another randomly chosen group of individuals. Any item that discriminates between the two groups (i.e., on which members of the two groups give sharply different responses) is retained in the scale to identify "attitude toward science." Thereafter, any person who responds close to the way the scientist group responded is viewed as having a "good" attitude toward science; those whose responses differ are viewed as having a less positive attitude toward science.

The point of all the above is that when students who have been introduced to the concept of addition of numbers greater than one digit see a question like "$412 + 33 = $," the question has exactly the same meaning to each student. In addition, the answer of 445 will be counted as correct. But when the students see

A person should respect the law.
( ) Always agree
( ) Usually agree
( ) Usually disagree
( ) Always disagree

they are each essentially answering a different question. Which answer is "correct"? Should the "correct" answer be found empirically, by norming on a random sample of typical respondents and "correctness" defined by the largest response frequency? Should "correctness" be defined logically by the American Bar Association, the Fraternal Order of Police, the National Parent Teacher Association, the school board, the classroom teacher, or. . . ?

10.2.2. Now move to the issue of responding

Two issues need attention here: inaccurate responses, purposeful or not, and the intricate and varying interaction between how one is disposed to behave and the environment (situation) at the moment. More simply, this last issue has to do with the notion that the way one is disposed to behave is situation-specific.

The most obvious reason for inaccurate responses is outright dishonesty. The respondent wants to present a picture that is positive, at least not insulting. Or the respondent might perceive that in this situation it would be best to appear questioning and curious, or not. The respondent might perceive that in this situation it would be best to appear quiet, withdrawn, and studious, or not.

If the respondent feels there is a reason to distort the responses (to give untypical answers when typical ones were requested) the respondent can certainly do so. If the school cannot create a situation where the respondent feels free of these needs to distort, the school might as well not trouble itself with paper-and-pencil measures of acquired behavioral dispositions.

But there is at least one other reason for inaccurate responses which has nothing to do with purposely distorting answers; namely, the respondent is asked a question about which s/he has no knowledge. Many years ago, before anyone had any real experience with behavioral objectives, an administrator might have responded to the question, "How often should behavioral objectives be the basis for instruction in the school?" with the answer "always." After supervising a few summer writing sessions, the duplication of volumes of pedantic statements of objectives, and observing the staff responses ranging from anger to apathy, the administrator is ready to change the response from "always" to "in certain settings" or some such thing. The original answer was inaccurate in that it was not based on enough knowledge and experience. When an eighth grader is asked, in a vocational preference measure, "Which would you rather spend two hours doing: go fishing alone on a remote lake, engage in a discussion with friends, or repair a broken toy?," it is possible the student has never had any experience in at least two of those activities. An accurate response is hardly possible without some prior background.

The other issue, termed earlier the situation-specific issue, has to do with the interaction between the trait and the environment. Take "Shows initiative," a common item on the affective side of report cards. In the home situation, a student may show no initiative, constantly needing reminding for the simplest of tasks; in math class doing the minimum, and only when told specifically what to do; in art, constantly seeking out new and different mediums of expression; with a small group of close friends, actively searching for new experiences; while in a large group only following. At school, in each class, the situation changes. Even when the situation doesn't really change that much, the student may feel that the situation is different and the responses will conform to those perceptions or feelings.

The issue is not just for the clinicians; it has real meaning for educators. Learning theorists, cited earlier, address the relationship between learning in an area and attitude toward that area. As one attempts to tap, with a paper-and-pencil measures, the student's attitude toward reading, the student, probably sitting in a classroom at a desk, reponds in terms of some prior situation or experience. As the student's attitude toward reading is assessed, is the student thinking about the embarrassment of reading aloud in social studies class, the joy of reading *The Hardy Boys* in third grade, the total lack of any comprehension of the way the English teacher interprets poems, or the thrill gotten from the erotic sections of a just-completed paperback novel? The student probably will not give a composite answer; the student will answer with respect to the situation which comes to mind at the time the question is asked, even though the student is sitting at a desk in the classroom. The responses are situation-specific.

10.2.3. So what can be done?

As stated earlier, the goal of the above was not to convince everyone to back away from paper-and-pencil measures of acquired behavioral dispositions. The goal was to better inform potential users. If measures like this are to be used, then

. . . the terms in the questions must be specifically defined, probably with a series of examples before the student starts responding;

. . . the user must study the way the items are "keyed" and be in full agreement with the decisions made;

. . . the respondent must be willing to cooperate and provide a truly typical representation of his/her behavioral disposition in the stated situation; and

. . . the stated situation must be made very explicit and not allowed to be whatever the student's prior experiences bring into consciousness at that moment.

The easiest approach for the school would be to find a published instrument about the topic at hand and see if it conforms to the four statements given above. The best place to start is *Tests in Print III* (Mitchell, 1983). Many unpublished measures, used for doctoral research or other research projects but whose appeal is not generally enough to interest a commercial publisher, can be found by undertaking an ERIC search. Many university libraries are sources for these searches. Usually that same library can provide a complete text of the measure on microfiche for viewing or duplicating.

There are some legitimate times for making up your own questions as part of an evaluate-your-instruction process. Section 10.1 gave a series of suggestions for writing survey questions; many of these are germane for writing items addressing affect. Here are some more specific suggestions for the development of items to assess acquired behavioral dispositions:

1. Write the item. At that moment, circle the answer which, in your opinion, is the "correct" one.

2. Make sure this "correct" answer is obviously at one of the extreme response positions. For example, it is difficult to justify the extreme position "Always agree" as the correct answer to the question,

> Reading is the most important part of schooling.
> ( ) Always agree
> ( ) Usually agree
> ( ) Usually disagree
> ( ) Always disagree.

3. Have a few colleagues read the items and see if they agree that the correct answer is the one you chose, and that the correct answer is one of the extreme positions.

4. Set the context specifically for the respondent: "Suppose you are in the library and have an hour free, with no homework. Under this condition: . . . ." Try to get all respondents to perceive themselves as being in about the same situation.

5. As stated earlier, try to avoid asking questions that threaten. Even if you promise anonymity, many students will suspect some sort of a trick and thereby given inaccurate responses.

6. Try to be somewhat numerical in the response categories. Instead of wording a question,

> Laws are made to punish people.
> ( ) Strongly agree
> ( ) Agree
> ( ) Disagree
> ( ) Strongly disagree

state the item as

> What proportion of laws are made to punish people?
> ( ) All of them
> ( ) About half of them
> ( ) A few, but less than 5%
> ( ) None of them.

The response categories have been put into a more common metric. Of course, you can presume no one is cynical enough to respond to "All of them" and change the scale to

( ) About half of them
( ) About 10% of them
( ) About 5% of them
( ) None of them

or some other distribution, set to conform the range of real expected responses.

7. Orally present each item drafted to a small group sampled from those with whom the final measure will be used. This kind of informal tryout should pick up clumsy or misleading statements, unfamiliar terminology, and unsatisfactory response categories. The tryout doesn't take long; shouldn't be viewed as a threat; and will generally identify a whole list of "Why didn't I think of that?" responses. It's well worth the effort.

Now, if the issue at hand is very important, and results obtained from this measure may lead to a final and irreversible decision, then some more formal tryouts should also be scheduled. At a minimum, a small, random sample from the target population (maybe as many as 50 to 75) should identified and given the instrument. A reliability coefficient, preferably coefficient alpha (see p. 121, Crocker and Algina, 1986), should be computed and should be minimally 0.70 or above. Independent confirmation of the results from the paper-and-pencil measure should be sought.

10.3. Some other ways to obtain measures of affect

The prior section on paper-and-pencil measures of acquired behavioral dispositions fell somewhere between informed pessimism and cautious optimism. Despite all of the problems, people do seem to find valid uses for these difficult measures. But what if some of the difficulties cannot be overcome?

There are some other ways to proceed. As shall be seen, they are frequently more difficult, require a longer time span, and are less obviously direct.

10.3.1. Behavioral assessment

Obviously, if there were a choice between finding out how a person is disposed to behave in a given situation, and how the person actually does behave when faced with the situation, the latter technique would be chosen.

Behavioral assessment focuses on an act (or acts) which occur in a defined situation. They avoid the measurement of traits as such. Suppose a teacher complains that a student seems capable enough but does poorly because of bad work habits. A trait approach would attempt to define descriptors of "good work habits" and probably come up items like purposefulness, punctuality, organized effort, tenacity, and responsibility. An attempt would be made to measure each, followed by some sort of intervention designed for those who show the greatest deficits.

The behavioral approach would address the issue quite differently. The behaviorist would want to identify the situation where the observation of poor work habits was made. The measures would be the student's actual behaviors in the specified "poor work habits" situation. At this point the difference between what was observed, and what is apparently expected, can be made. The change program focuses on the differences between expectation and actual.

The distinction, then, between a behaviorist approach and one that focuses on acquired behavior disposition is the directness of the measure. The behaviorist does not first define the concept in terms of traits, then measure the propensity to manifest the traits; the behaviorist defines the concept in terms of situations and responses to those situations.

Of course, if it were all that easy there wouldn't be paper-and-pencil measures. But behavioral measures are difficult to obtain.

In the first place, realistic "situations" appear when they appear; when a situation is staged, it is no longer real. If that were not bad enough, there is a second major problem: These types of measures generally must be done separately for each individual. Consider the difference in time and effort needed to have 30 students complete a paper-and-pencil measure of some trait, and contrast that with getting individual measures of the 30 in a given situation — but only as that situation occurs.

However, because the behavior assessment approach is more difficult does not mean it is impossible. A teacher can identify certain behaviors and systematically watch for them, and, if one wanted to be formal about these measures, keep records.

For example, behaviors falling under the general heading of "desired social behavior" could be observed and recorded within the confines of a classroom or any organized group activity. As situations occur which provide an opportunity to display (or not display) respect for authority, cooperation with others, courtesy, tact, and/or openness to new ideas, records could be kept of these. These records could be used as a basis for helping those students who do not display the desired behavior in the situation, or to monitor progress in a program designed to help students develop acceptable social behavior.

This distinction — is the evaluation used to monitor and thereby help the development of individual students, or is it to monitor general performance (and hopefully improvement) in the entire group? — is an important one to make. If the monitoring system is to monitor the development in each student, then obviously data have to be collected about each student. These individually collected data can be accumulated by classroom, grade level, building level, or district level to provide overall improvement information.

If the monitoring is to be of the overall development of a group, where the results are not viewed as being particularly useful in a diagnostic sense, then the monitoring can be done by a sample. General goals like "good citizenship" or "character development" are quite amorphous. A committee, most likely consisting of teachers, parents, and students, could identify the situations and behaviors which, to them, would demonstrate each concept. It would not be necessary to observe every student in every situation if the goal is overall group monitoring. A sample, or series of samples spaced some time apart, would suffice.

Once the decision has been made to use sampling, another simplification can be built into the evaluation system. Instead of identifying a given situation and the type of behavior which would be determined "desirable" in it, the situation could be staged. Randomly selected students, acting as individuals or in groups (depending on the goal of the measure at hand) could be put into this staged situation to see how they respond. With randomly selected small groups of students, elements like cooperation, courtesy, fair-mindedness, and responsibility could be assessed.

Of course, staging the event is not like having waited until it "just happens." Those who are selected might display atypical behavior.

Some might suggest that these situational settings don't actually have to be staged at all. Instead, the student could simply be interviewed about what the response would be to a given situation. This, however, seems only like a very complicated way to obtain information on acquired behavioral tendencies. Paper-and-pencil measures would get about the same information at a fraction of the cost.

Interviews, classroom observations, staged situations, and paper-and-pencil measures of acquired behavioral tendency dispositions have one common feature: they are all reactive. That is, the measurement process itself can interfere with the behavior of the respondent. The respondent knows a measure is being taken and has the opportunity to adjust behavior accordingly. The respondent may not adjust any behavior; but the very threat of atypical behavior provides an uncertain impact on the validity of the measures taken.

This is why the behavioral assessments made in naturally occurring situations have much to recommend them. The person doing the observing here (a teacher, hall monitor, club sponsor, coach), by definition, is part of the naturally occurring situation.

Another way to gather nonreactive measures is through what has been termed unobtrusive measures. Webb and associates (1966) describe a series of thoughtful approaches to obtaining these types of measures. In non-school settings, some interesting unobtrusive measures have been used. One museum measured the variation in visitor interest by measuring the thickness of the asphalt tiles in front of different presentations, reasoning that the more people observed, the more the tile would be worn. To check unobtrusively the relative volume of business in two liquor stores, one could count the number of trash cans full of bottles behind each store for a week.

In school settings, the availability of useful unobtrusive measures will depend quite heavily on the availability of easy access to a wide range of longitudinal measures. The impact of programs designed to improve attitude toward school could be partially assessed through attendance data, which all schools keep. These data could be broken out by definable subgroups (like those in the lowest quartile) if this group were the primary target. A program designed to heighten teacher awareness of the needs of special students might be monitored by counting referrals from teachers for help with certain students. Number of suspensions, dollars spent to correct results of vandalism, pressure on counselors for personal help — each of these is a measure, as long as the data are retained in a manner such that they can be easily accessed over a long enough period of time.

The measures described in the paragraph above are generally kept by schools. For these, the only trick to is maintain them over time and make them accessible. Schools have the capability, with very little additional effort, to expand their information systems to include records of a whole host of other things that occur each year, but which are not generally part of a routine, easily accessed information system. The names and characteristics of students who voluntarily participate as part of a sports team, musical group, or specific club can become important evaluation data if it were accumulated over time. The number of entries in science fair, speech, music, or art competitions is important — not only for the numbers, but for the characteristics of the students who participate in these activities. Complete records from counselors, separating their interactions with students into categories like "help with college choice," "help with course selection in this school," "help with a personal problem at home," or "help with problem involving interaction with teacher," could help monitor changes in students as a function of school programs.

10.4. The need for longitudinal data

Most measures of the kind described in this chapter can be most sensibly interpreted in terms of trends. That isn't fully true; if 81% of students asked indicate their highest need is to burn the school down, one might not want to wait for a trend to develop. But the responses are not generally anchored the way "percent correct" anchors maximum performance tests. The measure of Gross National Product, so extensively used by economists and legislatures, is an example of a measure whose actual value means little. Instead, it is the trend in quarterly figures that is eagerly interpreted. In a like manner, these measures of affect should be monitored continuously to detect trends.

Experienced school people might legitimately "barumph" about the call for using trend information to monitor programs. Cooley and Bickel (1986, p. 73) note, ". . . as questions emerge they must be dealt with at the time they are 'hot.' For example, school boards will not delay their deliberations until a study is done." Not only does the school board not want to wait four years; they don't even want to wait until the next board meeting.

But the data can be available as needed if some prior planning is done. Chapter 7 concerned itself with a learning event called "character development." Who can disagree that the school has a role in this important issue? This community took the position that character development should not be allowed to "just happen"; they set about the difficult and frequently contentious task of defining the behaviors, and behavioral change trends, which should take place if a program designed to improve character development were introduced.

A statement of educational philosophy from a nearby high school contains these goal statements (Glenbard High School, 1984):

> . . . To assist students in developing problem-solving attitudes and skills through the process of discovering and organizing knowledge and critically evaluating information.
>
> . . . To provide an environment which stimulates critical, creative, and evaluative thinking skills and which promotes the desire for acquiring further knowledge.
>
> . . . To help students understand, effect, and adjust to changes in science and technology.

. . . To offer students opportunities through which they may experience rights and responsibilities of our democratic society.

Each, like character development, is a noble goal. Like character development, total assessment is an unlikely possibility. But if a school establishes any one of these as a goal, the school must think it is doing something to facilitate attainment of the goal. "What are we doing here," the school should ask, "which helps students 'understand, effect, and adjust to changes in science and technology'?" Just as in the case of the character development learning event, are there not some behaviors or events which could be routinely monitored to see if the noble goal is being implemented?

In a certain sense, with these measures of affect, the actual results, and even the observed trends, are less important than the process undertaken to identify the behaviors which would be monitored. The process, noted above as sometimes contentious, involves arriving at some sort of consensus definition of what these noble-sounding goals actually mean in practice. One believes in patriotism; but does that excuse John Dean? One believes in honoring the father and mother, but does that mean child abuse is ignored? At what price are neatness, orderliness, and punctuality extracted?

As this books begins to set slowly in the western sky, this issue seems like a good place to reiterate an issue raised in the first chapter. Short-term measures of cognition (course grades, standardized tests, unit tests) are easier to obtain than are measures of citizenship, character, self-actualization, or vocational interest. And yet it is these latter areas which are central to the purpose of schooling.

What a school says it believes (its philosophy), what it actually does (its instructional and other programs), and what it gets (its outcomes) are not independent issues. The programs should be directly and explicitly linked to the philosophy; the outcomes measured should be those expected from the link between beliefs and practices.

Things don't just happen; outcomes don't just occur. Outcomes occur because of the events and experiences which preceded them. To the extent possible, schools should explicitly state their beliefs, link the beliefs to programs, define expectations, and measure the outcomes against these expectations. All of these should be done out in the open, so the public is aware of what is happening in the school.

And that, after all, has been the theme of this book.

References

Bloom, B.S. (1976). *Human Characteristics and School Learning*. New York: McGraw-Hill.

Bloom, B.S. (1977). "Affective outcomes of school learning." *Phi Delta Kappan* 59:193–198.

Campbell, D.T. (1963). *"Social attitudes and other acquired behavioral dispositions."* In S. Koch (ed.), *Psychology: A Study of Science*, vol. 6. New York: McGraw-Hill.

Carroll, J.B. (1963). "A model for school learning." *Teachers College Record* 64:723–733.

Cooley, W.W., and Bickel, W.E. (1986). *Decision-Oriented Educational Research*. Boston: Kluwer-Nijhoff Publishing.

Crocker, L., and Algina, J. (1986). *Introduction to Classical and Modern Test Theory*. New York: Holt, Rinehart and Winston.

Glenbard High School District 87, Du Page County, Illinois (1984). "Educational philosophy." In document prepared for North Central Evaluation, April 1985.

Mitchell, J.V. (1983). *Tests in Print III*. Lincoln: University of Nebraska Press.

North Central Association (1985). *Handbook for Outcomes Accreditation*. Boulder, CO: North Central Association.

Webb, E.J., Campbell, D.T., Schwartz, R.D., and Sechrest, L. (1966). *Unobtrusive Measures: Nonreactive Research in the Social Sciences*. Chicago: Rand McNally.

References

Arlin, A. (1984). "Time, equality, and mastery learning." *Review of Educational Research* 54(1):65–86.

Andrig, G.R. (1985). "Educational standards, testing, and equity." *Kappan* 66(9):623–625.

ASCD Update (1986). "Who should say what all should know?" 28(1):1,6.

Aspy, D., Aspy, C., and Roebuck, F. (1986). "Fulfilling the great tradition through interpersonal honesty: A response to Wynne." *Educational Leadership* 43(4):13–14.

Association for Supervision and Curriculum (1986). *Educational Leadership* 43(4).

Ausubel, D.P., Novak, J.D., and Hanesian, H. (1978). *Educational Psychology*. New York: Holt, Rinehart and Winston.

Barnett, W.S. (1985). "Benefit-cost analysis of the Perry preschool program and its policy implications." *Educational Evaluation and Policy Analysis* 7(4):333–342.

Beane, J.A. (1986). "The continuing controversy over affective education." *Educational Leadership* 43(4):26–31.

Becker, H.J. (1985). "Computers in schools today: Some basic considerations." *American Journal of Education* 93(1):22–39.

Beggs, D.L., and Mouw, J. (1981). *Developing Cognitive Abilities Tests*. Glenview, IL: Scott, Foresman and Co.

Bloom, A.M. (1973). "Differential instructional productivity indices." *Research in High Education* 18(2):179–183.

Bloom, B.S. (1974). "An introduction to mastery learning." In J.H. Block (ed.), *Schools, Society and Mastery Learning*. New York: Holt, Rinehart, and Winston.

Bloom, B.S. (1976). *Human Characteristics and School Learning*. New York: McGraw-Hill.

Bloom, B.S. (1977). "Affective outcomes of school learning." *Phi Delta Kappan* 59:193–198.

Bloom, B.S. (1984). "The search for methods of group instruction as effective as one-to-one tutoring." *Educational Leadership* 41(8):4–18.

Bloom, B.S. (1984). "The 2 Sigma problem: A search for methods of group instruction as effective as one-to-one tutoring." *Educational Researcher* 13(5), 4–16.

Brandt, R. (1986). "Overview." *Educational Leadership* 43(4):3.

Campbell, D.T. (1963). "Social attitudes and other acquired behavioral dispositions." In S. Koch (ed.), *Psychology: A Study of Science*, vol. 6. New York: McGraw-Hill.

Carroll, J.B. (1963). "A model for school learning." *Teachers College Record* 64:723–733.

Cawley, J.F., Cawley, L.J., Cherkes, M., and Fitzmaurice, A.M. (1980). "Beginning Educational Assessment." In J.W. Wick and J.K. Smith (eds.), *Comprehensive Assessment Program*. Iowa City, IA: American Testronics, Inc.

Cazden, C.B. (1974). "Play with language and metalinguistic awareness: One dimension of language experience." *Urban Review* 2:28–39.

Chall, J.S. (1967). *Learning to Read: The Great Debate*. New York:McGraw-Hill.

Chall, J.S. (1983). *Stages in Readiing Development*. New York: McGraw-Hill.

Clay, M. (1979). *Reading: The Patterning of Complex Behavior*. Exeter, N.H.: Heinemann Educational Books.

Coleman, J. (1966). *Equality of Educational Opportunity*. Washington, D.C.: U.S. Government Printing Office.

Coles, R. (1986). "The moral life of children." *Educational Leadership* 43(4):19–25.

Commission on Schools (1985). *An Introduction to Outcomes Accreditation* and *A Handbook for the Outcomes Accreditation of Schools*. Boulder, CO: North Central Association of Schools and Colleges, the Commission on Schools.

Comprehensive Tests of Basic Skills (1981). Monterey, Calif.: CTB/McGraw-Hill.

Comprehensive Tests of Basic Skills (1983). *Examiner's Manual, Forms U and V, Levels F, G, H, J, K*. Monterey, CA: CTB/McGraw-Hill, 1982.

Cooley, W.W., and Bickel, W.E. (1986). *Decision-Oriented Educational Research*. Boston: Kluwer-Nijhoff Publishing.

Crocker, L., and Algina, J. (1986). *Introduction to Classical and Modern Test Theory*. New York: Holt, Rinehart and Winston.

Denton, J.J., and Smith, N.L. (1985). "Alternative teacher preparation programs: A cost-effectiveness comparison." *Educational Evaluation and Policy Analysis* 7(3):197–205.

Eckland, B.K. (1980). "Education in the meritocracy." *American Journal of Education* 89: 76–85.

Gatta, L. (1980). "High School Subject Tests." In J.W. Wick and J.K. Smith (eds.), *Comprehensive Assessment Program*. Iowa City, IA: American Testronics, Inc.

Glenbard High School District 87, Du Page County, Illinois (1984). "Educational philosophy." In document prepared for North Central Evaluation, April 1985.

Greenberg, L. (1973). *A Practical Guide to Productivity Measurement*. Washington, D.C.: Bureau of National Affairs, Inc.

Gronlund, N.E. (1985). *Measurement and Evaluation in Teaching*. New York: Macmillan Publishing Co.

Guskey, T.R. (1985). *Implementing Mastery Learning*. Belmont, CA: Wadsworth Publishing Co.

Haertel, E. (1985). "Construct validity and criterion-referenced testing." *Review of Educational Research* 55(1):23–46.

Harste, J.C., Woodward, V.A., and Burke, C.L. (1984). *Language Stories and Literacy Lessons*. Portsmouth, N.H.: Heinemann Educational Books.

Levin, H.M. (1975). "Cost-effectiveness analysis in evaluation research." In E. Struening, and M. Guttentag (eds.), *Handbook of Evaluation Research* vol. 2. Beverly Hills, CA: Sage.

Levin, H.M. (1981). "Cost analysis." In N.L. Smith (ed.), *New Techniques for Evaluation*. Beverly Hills, CA: Sage.

Levin, H.M. (1984). "About time for educational reform." *Educational Evaluation and Policy Analysis* 6(2): 151–163.

Linn, R.L., Madaus, G.F., and Pedulla, J.J. (1982). "Minimum competency testing: Cautions on the state of the art." *American Journal of Education* 97(1):1–35.

Lockwood, A.L. (1986). "Keeping them in the courtyard: A response to Wynne." *Educational Leadership* 43(4):9–10.

Mager, R.F. (1962). *Preparing Instructional Objectives*. Palo Alto, CA: Fearon.

McBride, J.R. (1985). "Computerized adaptive testing." *Educational Leadership* 43(2):25–28.

McKown, H.C. (1935). *Character Education*. New York: McGraw-Hill Book Co.

Mitchell, J.V. (1983). *Tests in Print III*. Lincoln: University of Nebraska Press.

National Commission on Excellence in Education (1983). *A Nation At Risk: The Imperative For Educational Reform*. Washington, D.C.: U.S. Government Printing Office.

Nevo, D. (1983). "The conceptualization of educational evaluation." *Review of Educational Research* 53(1):117–128.

North Central Association (1985). *Handbook For Outcomes Accreditation*. Boulder, CO: North Central Association.

Paske, G.H. (1986). "The failure of indoctrination: A response to Wynne." *Educational Leadership* 43(4):11–12.

Paul, C.F. and Gross, A.C. (1983). "Increasing productivity and morale in a municipality." *Journal of Applied Behavioral Psychology* 17:59–78.

Peshkin, G.H. (1986). "God's choice: The total world of a fundamentalist Christian school." *Educational Leadership* 43(4):36–41.

Petty, W.T., Petty, D.C., and Becking, M.F. (1973). *Experiences in Language*. Boston: Allyn and Bacon, Inc.

Popham, W.J., Cruse, K.L., Rankin, S.C., Sandifer, P.D., and Williams, P.L. (1985). "Measurement-driven instruction: It's on the road." *Phi Delta Kappan* 66(9):628–634.

Primack, R. (1986). "No substitute for critical thinking: A response to Wynne." *Educational Leadership* 43(4):12–13.

Rossi, P.H., Freeman, H.E., and Wright, S.R. (1979). *Evaluation: A Systematic Approach*. Beverly Hills, CA: Sage.

Schaps, E., Solomon, D., and Watson, M. (1986). "A program that combines character development and academic achievement." *Educational Leadership* 43(4):32–35.

Sergiovani, T.J. and Carver, F.D. (1980). *The New School Executive*. New York: Harper and Row.

Shane, H.G. (1975). "The future mandates new moral directions." In *Emerging Moral Dimensions in Society: Implications for Schools*. Washington, D.C.: Association for Supervision and Curriculum Development.

Shepherd, G.D., and Ragan, W.B. (1982). *Modern Elementary Curriculum*. New York: Holt, Rinehart and Winston.

Sirotkin, K. (1983). "What you see is what you get — consistency, persistency, and mediocrity in classrooms." *Harvard Educational Review* 53(1):16–31.

Smith, F. (1983). *Essays into Literacy — Selected Papers and Some Afterthoughts*. Exeter, N.H.: Heinemann Educational Books.

Stewig, J.W. (1983). *Exploring Language Arts in the Elementary Classroom*. New York: Holt, Rinehart and Winston.

Strike, K.A. (1985). "Is there a conflict between equity and excellence?" *Educational Evaluation and Policy Analysis* 7(4):409–416.

Stroud, J.B. (1964). *Psychology in Education*. New York: David McKay Company.

Sugarman, B. (1973). *The School and Moral Development*. New York: Barnes and Noble.

Tyler, R.W. (1974). "Introduction: A perspective on the issues." In R.W. Tyler and R.M. Wolf (eds.), *Crucial Issues in Testing*. Berkeley, CA: McCutchan Publishing Co.

Walberg, H.J. (1971). "Models for optimizing and individualizing school learning." *Interchange* 2(3):15–27.

Walberg, H.J. (1982). "Educational productivity: Theory, evidence, and prospects." *Australian Journal of Education* 26,115–122.

Walberg, H. J., and Shiow-ling Tsai (1983). "Reading achievement and attitude productivity among 17-year-olds." *Journal of Reading Behavior* 15(3): 41–53.

Webb, E.J., Campbell, D.T., Schwartz, R.D., and Sechrest, L. (1966). *Unobtrusive Measures: Nonreactive Research in the Social Sciences*. Chicago: Rand McNally.

Wick, J.W. (1973). *Educational Measurement*. Columbus, OH: Merrill.

Wick, J.W. (1983). *Planning for Improvement*. Glenview, IL: Scott, Foresman and Co.

Wick, J.W. (1983). "Reducing the proportion of chance scores in Inner-city standardized test results: Impact on average scores." *American Educational Research Journal* 20:461–463.

Wick, J.W. (1985). "Including assessment of student outcomes in the school accreditation and evaluation process." *The North Central Association Quarterly* 20:363–369.

Wolf, R.M. (1979). "Achievement in the United States." In H.J. Walberg (ed.), *Educational Environments and Effects*. Berkeley, CA: McCutchan Publishing Co.

Wynne, E.A. (1986). "The great tradition in education: Transmitting moral values." *Educational Leadership* 43(4):4–9.

Wynne, E.A., and Walberg, H.J. (1986). "The complementary goals of character development and academic excellence." *Educational Leadership* 43(4):15–18.

Whole Number Computations

311. Addition, basic facts, sums < 18
312. Addition, two numbers, 2 digits, no renaming
313. Addition, to 4 numbers, to 4 digits, no renaming
322. Addition, two numbers, 2 digits, one renaming
323. Addition, to 4 numbers, to 4 digits, one renaming
332. Addition, to 4 numbers, to 4 digits, two renamings
342. Addition, to 4 numbers, to 4 digits, unlimited renaming
351. Subtraction, basic facts
352. Subtraction, to four digits, no renaming
362. Subtraction, to four digits, one renaming
372. Subtraction, to four digits, two renamings
382. Subtraction, to four digits, unlimited renamings
391. Multiplication, basic facts
392. Multiplication, 3-digit times 1-digit no., no renaming
394. Multiplication, 2-digit $\times$ 2-digit number, no renaming
402. Multiplication, 3-digit $\times$ 1-digit number, one renaming
412. Multiplication, 4-digit $\times$ 1 digit number, two renamings
422. Multiplication, 4-digit, $\times$ 1-digit number, unlimited ren.
424. Multiplication, any two numbers
431. Division, basic facts
432. Division, whole number by 1-digit divisor, no remainder
434. Division, whole number by divisor $>$ 1-digit, no remainder
442. Division, whole number by 1-digit divisor, remainder as R$=$
444. Division, whole number by divisor $>$ 1-digit, remainder as R$=$
452. Division, whole number by 1-digit divisor, remainder as fraction
453. Division, whole nbr. by 1-dig., remainder continued as decimal

Decimals

461. Decimal Addn. and Subt., tenths place or small $ amounts, no renaming
462. Decimal Addn. and Subt., beyond tenths place, no renaming
463. Decimal Addn. and Subt., unequal numbers of dec. places, no renaming
471. Decimal Addn. and Subt., tenths place or small $ amounts, renaming
472. Decimal Addn. or Subt., beyond tenths place, renaming

473.   Decimal Addn. or Subt., unequal numbers of dec. places, renaming
481.   Decimal multiplication, 1-digit whole number times decimal
482.   Decimal multiplication, > 1-digit whole number times decimal
483.   Decimal multiplication, any two decimals
491.   Decimal division, decimal divided by 1-digit whole number
492.   Decimal division, decimal divided by > 1-digit whole number
493.   Decimal division, decimal or whole number divided by a decimal

Fractions

502.   Fractions, just reduce to lowest form
503.   Fractions, rename improper fraction to mixed number, or vice versa
511.   Fractions, addn. and subt., like denom., no reduce or rename
512.   Fractions, addn. and subt., like denom., reduce answer
513.   Fractions, addn. and subt., like denom., rename answer
521.   Fractions, addn. and subt., unlike denom., no reduce or rename
523.   Fractions, addn. and subt., unlike denom., rename answer
524.   Fractions, unlike denom., tested w/ variables, not nbrs.
531.   Mixed numbers, addn and subt., like denom., no reduce or rename
532.   Mixed numbers, addn. and subt., like denom., reduce answer
533.   Mixed numbers, addn. and subt., like denom., rename answer
541.   Mixed numbers, addn. and subt., unlike denom., no reduce or
       rename
543.   Mixed numbers, addn. and subt., unlike denom., rename answer
551.   Fraction multiplication, no renaming or reducing
552.   Fraction division, no renaming or reducing
553.   Fraction multiplication or division, renaming and/or reducing

Percent; and Fraction-Decimal-Percent Conversions

571.   Fraction-percent, make conversions
572.   Fraction-decimal, make conversions
573.   Percent-decimal, make conversions
574.   Percent problems of type 'Find X% of a number'
575.   Percent problems of type '40 is X% of 60'
576.   Percent problems, based on definition of percent
577.   Percent problems of type X% of 60 is 3

Integers

561. Integers, add and subtract
562. Integers, multiply and divide
563. Integers, use a number line to determine
564. Integers, applications in story problems
566. Integers, relative values

Exponents and Roots

101. Exponents, evaluate or use in problem
102. Exponents, evaluate value of negative exponents
103. Exponents, evaluate fraction as exponent
105. Exponents, multiply and divide with
106. Exponents, use scientific notation in arithmetic operations
107. Square root
108. Roots, other than square roots

Measurement

651. Money, know value of penny through quarter (print name)
661. Money, determine amount or make change
671. Calendar, use to find days or dates
681. Numbered scale, use when all points are numbered
682. Numbered scale, use when not all points numbered
683. Graph or diagram w/ one nmbrd. scale, use value to compute answer
684. Graph or diagram, ans. uses straight (literal) interp. of legend
691. Clock, to quarter-hour, translate digital to words
692. Clock, translate digital minute readings to clock face
693. Clock, determine time intervals, to minutes
694. Clock, read standard clock face to half-hour, hour
695. Clock, read standard clock face to quarter-hour, five minutes
696. Clock, read standard clock face to the minute
701. Time equivalencies, seconds, minutes, hours, days
704. Time equivalencies, days, weeks, months, year
711. English unit equivalencies, length (inch, foot, yard)
712. English unit equivalencies, length (foot, yard, mile)
714. English unit equivalencies, pounds, ounces, ton
715. English unit equivalencies, cup, pint, quart, gallon

716.   English-metric match: given English unit, choose metric unit
717.   English units, estimate a value in a common situation
721.   Metric unit equivalencies and use, mass
722.   Metric unit equivalencies and use, volume
723.   Metric unit equivalencies and use, length
724.   Metric units, estimate an amount or identify proper unit
731.   Temperature (F), choose temperature for common situation
732.   Temperature (C), choose temperature for common situation
733.   Temperature, convert Fahrenheit and Celsius scales

Geometry

741.   Geometry, match name or use knowledge of figure (cir.,sq,rect,tri.)
751.   Triangle, match name to fig. or use knowledge about common types
753.   Geometry, match description to name, plane figures > 3 sides
755.   Geometry, angle names, to no. of degrees or with protractor
756.   Geometry, match lines types to figures
757.   Geometry, match name to a common solid figure (cube, cone, etc.)
761.   Geometry, use first quadrant graph with (x,y) coordinates
762.   Geometry, use four-quadrant graph with (x,y) coordinates
763.   Geometry, apply Theorem of Pythagoras
764.   Geometry, use similarity and congruence of angles, triangles
765.   Geometry, find and apply slope and intercept of a line
771.   Geometry, find perimeter, area, volume where formula is provided
781.   Geometry, find area and perimeter, triangle, rectangle, square
782.   Geometry, find circumference and area of circle
783.   Geometry, find area and volume of solid figures

Relative Values

791.   Relative values, whole number 1–99, use sequence
792.   Relative values, whole number 100--199, use sequence
793.   Relative values, whole numbers > 999, use sequence
794.   Relative values, decimals, 10ths and 100ths, use sequence
795.   Relative values, decimals smaller than 100th, use sequence
796.   Relative values, fractions, like denominators, use sequence
797.   Relative values, fractions, unlike denominators, use sequence
801.   Relative values, round/estim. left-most place, whole nbrs to 99
802.   Relative values, round/estim., left place, whole nbrs. 100–999

803. Relative values, round/estim., left place, whole nbrs. >999
804. Relative values, round/estimate, decimals, left-most place
812. Relative values, round/estim., whole nbrs., internal place to 999
813. Relative values, round/estim., whole nbrs. > 999, internal place
814. Relative values, round/estim., decimals to 100ths, internal place
815. Relative values, round/estim., decimals <100ths, internal place

Place Values

821. Place value, whole numbers, name digit in place, to 10's
822. Place value, whole numbers, name digit in place, 100's, 1000's
823. Place value, whole number >9999, name digit in place
824. Place value, decimals, 10th, 100ths, name digit in place
825. Place value, decimals beyond 100ths place, name digit in place
831. Place value, whole numbers, name value of digit in place, to 10's
832. Place value, whole numbers, name value of digit in place, 100's, 1000's
833. Place value, whole numbers > 999, name value of digit in place
834. Place value, decimals 10ths and 100ths, value of digit in place
835. Place value, decimals < 100ths, name value of digit in place
851. Place value, define place values using powers of ten
852. Place value, give value of a number expressed as power of ten
853. Place value, value of nmbr. expressed w/ negative power of 10

Alternative Representations

871. Alternative representations, numeral to word, whole numbers 1–12
872. Altern. representations, numeral to word, whole numbers 13–100
873. Altern. representations, numeral to word, whole numbers >99
874. Altern. repr., numeral to word, fractions (half,third,fourth)
875. Altern. representations, numeral to word, other fractions
877. Alternative representations, numeral to word, decimals
878. Altern. representations, numeral to word, ordinals (e.g. first)
879. Altern. representations, numeral to word, currency amounts
881. Alt. representations, numeral to set/picture, whole numbers 1–12
882. Alt. representations, numeral to set/picture, whole nbrs. >12
887. Alt. representations, numeral to set/picture, decimals
885. Alt. rep., numeral to set/picture, fractions (half,third,fourth)

886. Alternative representations, numeral to set/picture, other fractions
901. Altern. representations, set to printed name, whole numbers 1–12

Number Sentences, Pre-algebra, and Algebra

921. Number sentences, basic addn./subt. facts, supply missing number
922. Number sentences, basic mult./div. facts, supply missing number
923. Number sentences, basic facts, use $<$, $>$, or $=$ signs
924. Number sentences, answer requires more compu. than basic facts
941. Choose nbr. sent. described by word problem, addn./subt. facts
943. Choose nbr. sent. described by word problem, mult./div. facts
951. Pre-algebra, use properties of 0,1
952. Pre-algebra, use distributive property and parentheses for grouping
953. Pre-algebra, combine like terms
954. Pre-algebra, simple equations of type $x + 4 = 9$ or $6x = 18$
955. Pre-algebra, convert verbal stmt. into mathe. expression, or v.v.
956. Set up equation from word pbl. or tell operation needed
957. Pre-algebra, evaluate number sentences, values given
959. Pre-algebra, demonstrate knowledge of order of operations
111. Algebra equations of type $(2x + 9 = 11)$
112. Algebra equations of type $(2x + 9 = 12 - x)$
113. Algebra equations of type $(x/2 + 9 = 11)$
114. Algebra equations of type $(x/2 + 2 = 2/3)$
115. Algebra equations, solve simultaneous first degree
116. Algebra equations, set up and solve first degree from stories
117. Algebra equations, solve equations with inequalities
118. Algebra equations, factor a quadratic

Specific Terms and Problem Types

961. Logic problems
962. Ratios: Use ratios to solve word problems
963. Probability problems
964. Problem type involves costs in installment buying
965. Problems using menu or price list where each compu. trivial for age
971. Terms: Add, subtract, sum, product, etc.
972. Terms: Inside, outside, on, between, over, under, beside
973. Terms: Even, odd, whole numbers
981. Terms and operations, absolute value

982. Terms and operations, average
983. Terms and operations, prime numbers
984. Terms and operations, multiple, factor, least common den.
985. Terms and operations; set, subset, union, intersection
986. Terms and operations, prime factorization
987. Terms and oper., greatest com. factor, least com. multiple
988. Terms and operations, reciprocal
999. Word pbl. where math task trivial for age; a reading problem

Appendix B:
Objectives for Capitalization, Punctuation, Grammar Terms, and Grammar Usage

Capitalization of Names

101   Capit.-Names: The pronoun 'I'
102   Capit.-Names: Proper names.
103   Capit.-Names: Family relationships.
104   Capit.-Names: Bldgs., organiza., . . .
105   Capit.-Names: Deity, Bible, books of Bible.

Capitalization of Titles

111   Capit.-Titles: Ordinary (Mr., Mrs., Dr., . . .)
112   Capit.-Titles: Common (King, President, Captain, . . .)
113   Capit.-Titles: Unfamiliar (Section Leader, Gen. Mgr., . . .)

Capitalization, Calendar Related

121   Capit.-Calendar related: Days of week.
122   Capit.-Calendar related: Months of year.
123   Capit.-Calendar related: Common holidays.
124   Capit.-Calendar related: Important historical periods.

Capitalization, Geographic Locations

131   Capit.-Geog. location: Streets, avenues, . . .
132   Capit.-Geog. location: Cities, states, countries.

133   Capit.-Geog. location: Nationalities, ethnic groups, . . .
134   Capit.-Geog. location: Rivers, lakes, mountains, . . .
135   Capit.-Geog. location: Continents, oceans, planets.
136   Capit.-Geog. location: Regions of the country or world.

Capitalization, Specific Rules

141   Capit.-Specific rules: First word in sentence.
142   Capit.-Specific rules: Salutation, closing of letters.
143   Capit.-Specific rules: Titles of works.
144   Capit.-Specific rules: First word in direct quotation.

Overcapitalization

151   Overcapit.: Relationship preceded by possessive (My father . . .)
152   Overcapitalization: Generic product or institution.
153   Overcapitalization: Second word in closing of letter.
154   Overcapit.: Seasons, geographic location.
155   Overcapit.: First word, continued section, interrupted quote.
156   Overcapitalization of nouns

Punctuation, Comma for Separation

201   Punctuation-Comma: Separate city and state.
202   Punctuation-Comma: To separate month and year (May 2, 1985.)
203   Punctuation-Comma: Separate words in a series.
204   Punctuation-Comma: Separate phrase modifiers in series.

Punctuation in Letters

211   Punctuation-Comma: Friendly letter, after salutation and closing.
212   Punctuation-colon: Business letter, after salutation.

Punctuation, More Comma for Separation

221   Punc.-Comma: Set off nominative of address (Dad, can I . . . ?)
222   Punctuation-comma: To set off quotation from rest of sentence.

223 Punctuation-comma: Separate inde. clauses of cmpd. sentences.
224 Punc.-comma: Set off appositives (but not restrictive ones).
226 Punc.-comma: Set of nonrestrictive phrases and clauses.

Overpunctuation

231 Overpunctuation: Comma separates subject and verb.
232 Overpunctuation: Comma separates compound subject, pred., . . .)
233 Extra commas: Restrictive phrases
234 Extra commas: Restrictive appositives
235 Extra commas: Inserted in phrases
236 Extra commas: Other cases

End Punctuation

241 Punctuation: Period at end of sentence.
242 Punctuation: Period in initials and after titles like Mr., . . .
243 Punctuation: Period with abbreviations (except Mr., . . .)
244 Punctuation: Use question mark.
245 Punctuation: Use exclamation point.

Punctuation — Quotation Marks

251 Punctuation: Quotation marks direct quote, continuing quote.
252 Punctuation: Quote. mark, short works (stories, book chapter, . . .)
253 Overpunctuation: Overuse quotation marks (indirect quotes, . . .)
254 Punctuation: Quote marks, relative plmt. to other punctuation.
255 Punctuation: Quotes within quotes.

Punctuation — Colon and Semicolon

261 Punctuation: Colon in standard time notation.
262 Punctuation: Colon to introduce summary or list in apposition.
263 Punct.: Semicolon between clauses of sentences without conjunction.
264 Punct.: Semicolon in compound sentence with however, more-
     over, . . .

Punctuation — Apostrophe

271   Punctuation: Apostrophe in common contractions.
273   Overpunctuation: Apostrophe inserted in words ending with 's'
275   Punctuation: Apostrophe to pluralize letters, numbers, signs.

Punctuation — Hyphens

291   Punctuation: Hyphen to divide words at end of line.
292   Punctuation: Hyphen to form compound numbers and fractions.
293   Punctuation: Hyphen to form compound words.

Punctuation — Ellipses, Underlining (Italics)

301   Punctuation: Ellipsis to show omitted material.
311   Punctuation: Underline, italics of whole works (plays, books, . . .)
312   Punctuation: Underline, italics for magazines, newspapers.
313   Punctuation: Underline, italics for movies, radio/TV programs.
314   Punctuation: Underline, italics for trains, ships, airplanes.
315   Punctuation: Underline, italics words or numbers used as words.
316   Punctuation — underline (italics): Foreign words not naturalized.

Identify Parts of Speech

401   In context, identify nouns.
402   In context, identify verbs.
403   In context, identify pronouns.
404   In context, identify adjectives.
405   In context, identify adverbs.
406   In context, identify prepositions.
407   In context, identify conjunctions.

Identify Sentence Parts

411   Select simple subject of a sentence.
412   Select simple predicate of a sentence.
413   Select complete subject of a sentence.
414   Select complete predicate of a sentence.
415   In context, identify prepositional phrases.

Identify Sentence Parts

431   Distinguish between sentences and non-sentences.
432   Differentiate between simple and compound sentences.
433   Differentiate between simple and compound sentences.
434   Distinguish among declarative, interrogative & imperative sentences.
435   Identify run-on sentences.
436   Choose a word or phrase to make a sentence complete.

Clauses in Sentences

441   Differentiate between main (inde.) and subordinate (dep.) clauses.
442   Identify subordinate (dep.) clauses as noun, adjective, or adverbial.
443   Ident. sentence function of noun clauses, gerunds and infinitives.

Modifiers

451   Grammar Usage: Correctly use articles 'a,' 'an,' 'the.'
452   Identify sentence element modified by an adjective.
453   Identify sentence element modified by an adverb.
454   Grammar Usage: Correctly choose between adjectives, adverbs.
455   For prepositional and participial phrases, distinguish adv./adj. use.
456   For prepositional and participial phrases, identify element modified.
457   Grammar Usage: Properly use *good, well.*
461   Grammar Usage: Use posi., compara., superla. w/ reg. adjectives.
462   Grammar Usage: Use posi., compara., superla. w/ reg. adverbs.
463   Grammar Usage: Use posi., compara., superla. w/ irreg. adjctves.
464   Grammar Usage: Use posi., compara., superla. w/ irreg. adverbs.
465   Grammar Usage: Select singular or plural form of modifier.
466   Gram. Usage: Select connecting adverb (then, where, when, after, although.)

Subject-Verb Agreement in Number

471   Grammar Usage: Subj.-verb agreement, simple structure.
472   Grammar Usage: Subj.-verb agreement, inverted sentence.
473   Grammar Usage: Number in subject differs from pred. nominative.
474   Grammar Usage: Singular verb to match each, every, one, . . .
475   Gram. Usage: Subj-verb agmt. with modifiers after subject.
476   Gram. Usage: Correct form must be inferred from context.

477   Gram. Usage: Subj.-verb agmt., compd. subj. w/ plural meaning.
478   Gram. Usage: Subj.-verb agmt., compd. subj. w/ singular meaning.
479   Gram. Usage: Suj.-verb agmt., 'or,' 'nor' joins singu. subjects.
480   Gram. Usage: Subj.-verb agmt. plural form, singu. mning. in subj.

Regular Verbs (See 591 — for Irregular Verbs)

491   Gram. Usage: Regular verbs, present-past tenses.
492   Gram. Usage: Regular verbs, perfect and past perfect tenses.
493   Gram. Usage: Regular verbs, future and future perfect tenses.

Verb Terms

501   Differentiate between active and passive voice in verbs.
502   Differentiate among Action, Linking, and Helping verbs.
503   Differentiate among Indicative, Imperative, and Subjunctive mood.
504   Differentiate between transitive and intransitive verbs.
505   Differentiate among verbals.

Grammar Usage — Pronoun Case

531   Grammar Usage: Pronoun use, nominative case for subject.
532   Grammar Usage: Nom. case (who,whoever) for subject of clause.
533   Gram. Usage: Pronoun objve. case (dir./indir. obj., prepositns).
534   Gram. Usage: Pronoun objective case as subject of infinitive.
535   Grammar Usage: Pronoun with linking verbs.
536   Grammar Usage: Use personal pronouns.
537   Grammar Usage: Use possessive pronouns.

Pronoun Agreement

541   Gram. Usage: Pronoun agreement in gender with antecedent.
543   Gram. Usage: Pronoun agreement in number with antecedent.
544   Gram. Usage: Singular pronoun with *each, every, neither,* . . .
545   Gram. Usage: Plural pronoun when *and* joins singular antecedents.
546   Gram. Usage: Singu. pronoun when *or,nor* join singu. antecedents.

Grammar Usage — Miscellaneous

551   Gram. Usage: Misuse of compound personal pronouns as subject.
552   Gram. Usage: Use correct forms of compound personal pronouns.
553   Gram. Usage: Correctly use *who, that,* or *which.*
554   Gram. Usage: Place 'I' last in compound sentences.
555   Gram. Usage: Misuse of 'them' to modify a noun.
561   Gram. Usage: Do not use double negative.
562   Gram. Usage: Properly use gerunds and infinitives.

Pronoun Terminology

571   In context, identify the noun for which a pronoun stands.
572   In context, identify pronoun use as nominative or objective.
573   In context, identify personal pronouns.
574   In context, identify interrogative pronouns.
575   In context, identify demonstrative pronouns.
576   In context, identify indefinite pronouns.
577   In context, identify relative pronouns.
578   In context, identify intensive pronouns.
579   In context, identify numerical pronouns.
580   In context, identify reflexive pronouns.

Forming Plurals and Possessives with Nouns

581   Grammar Usage: Form plurals of regular nouns.
582   Form plurals of irregular nouns.
583   Grammar Usage: Apostrophe to form regular possessives.
584   Grammar Usage: Apostrophe to form irregular possessives.

Grammar Usage — Difficult Irregular Verbs

591   Grammar Usage: Correctly use *lie* and *lay.*
591   Grammar Usage: Correctly use *can* and *may.*
593   Grammar Usage: Correctly use *shall* and *will.*
594   Grammar Usage: Correctly use *sit* and *set.*
595   Grammar Usage: Correctly use *teach* and *learn.*

596   Grammar Usage: Correctly use *leave* and *let*.
497   Grammar Usage: Correctly use *rise* and *raise*.

Grammar Usage — Other Irregular Verbs

601   Gram. Usage: Correct form irregular verb *be*.
602   Gram. Usage: Correct form irregular verb *beat*.
603   Gram. Usage: Correct form irregular verb *become*.
604   Gram. Usage: Correct form irregular verb *become*.
605   Gram. Usage: Correct form irregular verb *begin*.
606   Gram. Usage: Correct form irregular verb *bite*.
607   Gram. Usage: Correct form irregular verb *blow*.
608   Gram. Usage: Correct form irregular verb *break*.
609   Gram. Usage: Correct form irregular verb *bring*.
610   Gram. Usage: Correct form irregular verb *burst*.
611   Gram. Usage: Correct form irregular verb *buy*.
612   Gram. Usage: Correct form irregular verb *catch*.
613   Gram. Usage: Correct form irregular verb *choose*.
614   Gram. Usage: Correct form irregular verb *creep*.
615   Gram. Usage: Correct form irregular verb *come*.
616   Gram. Usage: Correct form irregular verb *do*.
617   Gram. Usage: Correct form irregular verb *draw*.
618   Gram. Usage: Correct form irregular verb *drink*.
619   Gram. Usage: Correct form irregular verb *drive*.
620   Gram. Usage: Correct form irregular verb *eat*.
621   Gram. Usage: Correct form irregular verb *fall*.
622   Gram. Usage: Correct form irregular verb *fight*.
623   Gram. Usage: Correct form irregular verb *find*.
624   Gram. Usage: Correct form irregular verb *fly*.
625   Gram. Usage: Correct form irregular verb *forget*.
626   Gram. Usage: Correct form irregular verb *freeze*.
627   Gram. Usage: Correct form irregular verb *get*.
628   Gram. Usage: Correct form irregular verb *give*.
629   Gram. Usage: Correct form irregular verb *go*.
630   Gram. Usage: Correct form irregular verb *grow*.
631   Gram. Usage: Correct form irregular verb *hang*.
632   Gram. Usage: Correct form irregular verb *hide*.
633   Gram. Usage: Correct form irregular verb *hit*.
634   Gram. Usage: Correct form irregular verb *hurt*.
635   Gram. Usage: Correct form irregular verb *know*.

636   Gram. Usage: Correct form irregular verb *lead*.
637   Gram. Usage: Correct form irregular verb *lose*.
638   Gram. Usage: Correct form irregular verb *meet*.
639   Gram. Usage: Correct form irregular verb *pay*.
640   Gram. Usage: Correct form irregular verb *put*.
641   Gram. Usage: Correct form irregular verb *ride*.
642   Gram. Usage: Correct form irregular verb *ring*.
643   Gram. Usage: Correct form irregular verb *run*.
644   Gram. Usage: Correct form irregular verb *say*.
645   Gram. Usage: Correct form irregular verb *see*.
646   Gram. Usage: Correct form irregular verb *shake*.
647   Gram. Usage: Correct form irregular verb *shed*.
648   Gram. Usage: Correct form irregular verb *shrink*.
649   Gram. Usage: Correct form irregular verb *sing*.
650   Gram. Usage: Correct form irregular verb *sink*.
651   Gram. Usage: Correct form irregular verb *sleep*.
652   Gram. Usage: Correct form irregular verb *speak*.
653   Gram. Usage: Correct form irregular verb *spring*.
654   Gram. Usage: Correct form irregular verb *stick*.
655   Gram. Usage: Correct form irregular verb *strive*.
656   Gram. Usage: Correct form irregular verb *steal*.
657   Gram. Usage: Correct form irregular verb *swear*.
658   Gram. Usage: Correct form irregular verb *swim*.
659   Gram. Usage: Correct form irregular verb *swing*.
660   Gram. Usage: Correct form irregular verb *take*.
661   Gram. Usage: Correct form irregular verb *tear*.
662   Gram. Usage: Correct form irregular verb *tell*.
663   Gram. Usage: Correct form irregular verb *throw*.
664   Gram. Usage: Correct form irregular verb *wear*.
665   Gram. Usage: Correct form irregular verb *win*.
666   Gram. Usage: Correct form irregular verb *write*.

Index